Structure in Architecture

The Building of Buildings

Mario Salvadori with Robert Heller

Library of Congress Cataloging-in-Publication Data

Salvadori, Mario
  Structure in architecture.

  Includes index.
  1. Structures, Theory of. 2. Architecture.
I. Heller, Robert   II. Title.
TH845.S328   1986   624.1'7   85-9582
ISBN 0-13-854118-3

TH
845
.S328
1986

Editorial/production: Nicholas Romanelli
Page layout: Steve Frim
Manufacturing buyer: John Hall

Printed in the United States of America

10 9 8 7 6 5 4 3 2 1

PRENTICE-HALL INTERNATIONAL (UK) LIMITED, *London*
PRENTICE-HALL OF AUSTRALIA PTY. LIMITED, *Sydney*
PRENTICE-HALL CANADA INC., *Toronto*
PRENTICE-HALL HISPANOAMERICANA, S.A., *Mexico*
PRENTICE-HALL OF INDIA PRIVATE LIMITED, *New Delhi*
PRENTICE-HALL OF JAPAN, INC., *Tokyo*
PRENTICE-HALL OF SOUTHEAST ASIA PTE. LTD., *Singapore*
EDITORA PRENTICE-HALL DO BRASIL, LTDA., *Rio de Janeiro*
WHITEHALL BOOKS LIMITED, *Wellington, New Zealand*

"London Bridge is falling dow$_n$ . . ."

This book is joyfully dedicated
to my architectural students
who
for thirty years
taught me
how to teach structures.

Contents

Foreword

In this thoughtfully written book, Professor Salvadori endeavors to eliminate one of the most serious gaps between theory and practice in the field of structures. His aim is to build a bridge between the more or less conscious intuition about structure, which is common to all mankind, and the scientific knowledge of structure, which gives a fair representation of physical reality on the basis of mathematical postulates.

No one doubts that the bridging of this gap is possible and that, if achieved, it would be extremely useful.

In order to invent a structure and to give it exact proportions, one must follow both the intuitive and the mathematical paths.

The great works of the distant past, built at a time when scientific theories were nonexistent, bear witness to the efficiency and power of intuition.

Modern theories are incessantly and progressively developed, and their refinement is illustrated by the construction of ever greater and more daring structures.

If structural invention is to allow the efficient solution of the new problems offered daily by the ever-growing activity in the field of construction, it must become a harmonious combination of our personal intuition and of an impersonal, objective, realistic and rigorous structural science.

In other words, theory must find in intuition a force capable of making formulas alive, more human and understanding, and of lessening their impersonal technical brittleness. On the other hand, formulas must give us the exact results necessary to obtain "the most with the least," since this is the ultimate goal of all human activities.

Through always clear and, at times, most elementary examples, Professor Salvadori's book tends to unify these two viewpoints (I was almost going to say, these two mentalities), which must be cast into a unique synthesis if they are to give birth to the essential unity of all great structures.

Future architects will find it particularly useful to study this book in depth and to meditate upon it, since even if they can entrust the final calculation of a structure to a specialist, they themselves must first be able to invent it and to give it correct proportions. Only then will a structure be born healthy, vital and, possibly, beautiful.

I feel that we must be particularly grateful to Professor Salvadori for undertaking this anything but easy task.

Pier Luigi Nervi

Preface to the Third Edition

As stated in the preface to the first edition, this book has been written for those

who love beautiful buildings and would like to know why they stand up;

who dream of designing beautiful buildings and would like them to stand up;

who have designed beautiful buildings and would like to better know why they stand up.

The principles of structure are eternal, but new developments in structural materials, methods of design, and construction techniques constantly change the application of such principles to the building of buildings, and require frequent reassessment of the field of construction.

As one starts revising a book such as this it becomes obvious that virtually every page requires clarifications, additions, and updating. Besides innumerable changes of this nature this edition contains:

A new chapter on **structural failures,** a topic of increasing concern in our society.

A new chapter on **structural aesthetics,** a subject of growing awareness to architects and engineers, that has interested me for many years.

A new treatment of **space-frames** for large roofs that have become, because of their economy and beauty, the most popular structures of our time, the world over.

The first presentation of new techniques for the erection of **membrane roofs** unsupported by air pressure.

A new treatment of **earthquakes** and methods of earthquake attenuation.

An updating of **structural material** properties and construction methods.

A record of **new limits** reached in the field of architectural structures.

Over eighty new or modified figures by the original illustrator, Felix Cooper.

The intuitive and descriptive presentation is unchanged from that used in previous editions: irrespective of background, the book can be understood by anyone interested in why buildings stand up.

The structural concepts presented here were formerly introduced mathematically to graduate students of the School of Architecture at Princeton University and, later, to students of the graduate School of Architecture at Columbia University. The same concepts have been presented **without mathematics** to freshmen in architecture at Columbia, with the help of the models and motion pictures of my friend Robert Heller. Professor Heller did not participate in the preparation of this edition, and the changes and new material are solely my responsibility.

I hope that my latest efforts will meet with the same favor accorded previous editions throughout the world.

My deep gratitude goes
    to my former collaborator, Dr. Robert Heller, for his help in conceiving the original illustrations and for his constructive suggestions;
    to my teachers at the Faculty of Pure Mathematics of the University of Rome, who made mathematics part of my mental makeup and allowed me to move beyond it;
    to Charles R. Colbert, the former dean of the School of Architecture at Columbia, for encouraging me to try this intuitive approach to structures;
    to Felix Cooper for drawing the illustrations;
    to Tim McEwen of Prentice-Hall for suggesting that I prepare this revised edition;
    to all my friends for their interest and support during the relatively brief but intense period when the thoughts accumulated in years of study became this book;
    to my wife, Carol, who stood by me from the time this book was first conceived to the day I corrected the proofs of this present edition.

New York
    Mario Salvadori

With the financial support of the National Science Foundation a series of six 16 mm color films (average duration of 25 minutes), titled **Mechanics of Structures and Materials**, was produced by Professor Robert Heller of the Department of Engineering Mechanics, Virginia Polytechnic Institute and State University, in collaboration with Professor Mario Salvadori, to illustrate through models and experiments all the structural actions described in this book. The series consists of the following titles:

I.   Loads on Structures
II. Behavior of Structural Materials
III. Tensile and Compressive Structures
IV. Beams and Frames
V.   Grids and Plates
VI. Membranes and Shells

A series of independent video tapes (of 10 to 15 minutes duration), based on the original film series and titled **Mechanics and Structures T.V. Tape Series** by Heller and Pap, covers all the major topics taught in Statics, Dynamics, and Strength of Materials courses as well as additional topics in Structural Mechanics and Architecture. The tapes are accompanied by a **Study Guide** indicating uses and contents, and includes questions for students on the topics of each tape.

The complete film series, or single titles, and the tape series may be obtained from:

McGraw-Hill Book Company
Princeton Road
Hightstown, N.J. 08520

Chapter One

Structure in Architecture

1.1 Historical Development

Structure is an essential component of architecture, and has always been. No matter whether man built a simple shelter for himself and his family or enclosed large spaces where hundreds could worship, trade, discuss politics, or be entertained, he had to shape certain materials and use them in certain quantities to make his architecture stand up against the pull of the earth and other dangerous forces. Wind, lightning, earthquakes, and fires had to be resisted, if possible with expenditures of labor and materials that were not unreasonable in relation to their availability. And because from earliest times a sense of beauty has been innate in man, all construction was also conceived according to certain aesthetic tenets, which would often impose on the structure far more stringent requirements than those of strength and economy.

It may be thought, therefore, that structure was always considered important, and, in a sense, dictated architecture. This is simply not so. Magnificent buildings have been created in the past, and are created even today, with a notable disregard for the correctness of structure. The Parthenon, divinely beautiful as it is, translates into marble structural forms typical of wood construction and is, structurally speaking, "wrong." Since wood is a material capable of withstanding tension and compression, and horizontal elements require both tensile and compressive resistance, they are well built out of wood.

4

Stone withstands only compression, and horizontal elements can be built in stone only by reducing their length and supporting them on heavy vertical elements, such as columns or pillars. Hence horizontal elements of stone are "incorrect." On the other hand, Gothic cathedrals could span up to one hundred feet and cover hundreds of square yards crowded with worshippers by making use of the arch, a curved structural element in which tension is not developed. Thus stone is the correct material for a vaulted type of structure, and the beauty of the Gothic cathedrals satisfies both our aesthetic sense and our feeling for structural strength.

It has been argued by some architectural historians, as well as by some structural engineers, that a deep concern for structure will unavoidably lead to beauty. It is undeniable that a "correct" structure satisfies the eye of even the most unknowledgeable layman, and that a "wrong" structure is often offensively ugly. But it would be hard to prove that aesthetics is essentially dependent on structure. It is easy to show, instead, that some "incorrect" structures are lovely, while some "correct" ones are aesthetically unsatisfying. It may perhaps be wiser to say that correctness of structure is, most of the time, a necessary condition of beauty, but is not sufficient to guarantee beauty. Some contemporary architects and engineers, such as Felix Candela and Pier Luigi

Nervi, are so imbued with artistic sense that their structures are beautiful. But some grandiose buildings, recently erected by the use of daring engineering techniques, undeniably lack beauty.

We may thus conclude that a knowledge of structures on the part of the architect is, to say the least, highly desirable, and that correctness of structure cannot but add to the beauty of architecture.

1.2 The Present Interest in Architecture

In the recent as well as the ancient past the figure of the architect was unique: he was an artist and a technologist, a designer and a builder. Michelangelo could be a painter, a sculptor, an architect, and a master builder: the Vatican in Rome bears his imprint in all four fields. During the last half-century, instead, specialization of knowledge has taken over the field of architecture, and the various functions, once entrusted to the same man, are now exercised by different men. At least two men are essential in the construction team of any important building: the architect and the structural engineer. Today, no architect would dare design a building of even modest size without consulting a structural engineer. The roots of this dependence are to be found in the increasing importance of economic factors, in the technological direction of our culture, and, above all, in our mass civilization's need for an increasing number of all types of structures.

As the number of human beings multiplied at an increasing rate during the last few centuries, so as to create a "population explosion," civilized societies have also given each human more services, sharply increasing the "psychological density" of the population. Each one of us requires and is given more schooling, more travel, more medical care, more entertainment. Large numbers of people gather under the same roof for all the gregarious activities so typical of our era. Large stations, large stadia, large theaters, large churches, large arenas appear in increasing numbers. Urban agglomerations require the sprouting of taller buildings. The large structure has become a symbol of our culture and a monument to governments, churches, or corporations. On the other hand, housing the millions and supplying them with schools and hospitals are among the basic goals of civilized societies.

The architect is challenged by these tremendous tasks; the layman becomes aware of the importance of architecture in his own life. Thus, the specialists meet to solve new, difficult problems in a climate of public interest. The general public whose moneys are often used for these large projects takes a personal interest in their construction. This interaction between the specialists and the public may lead to better, and more correct, architecture, provided the layman understands the basic problems of the specialist, and the specialists themselves have a common bond of mutual understanding. This is the central theme of contemporary architectural education, including both the education of the architect and the popularization of architecture.

1.3 The Architect and the Engineer

Today, every architect and every architectural student is more or less convinced of the importance of structural knowledge, but finds the acquisition of such knowledge more difficult than expected. The rapid development of construction techniques based on the use of new materials (such as reinforced and prestressed concrete or plastics), as well as the mathematical difficulties inherent in the design of new structural forms (such as large roofs of all shapes), make it almost impossible for a man with an essentially nontechnical background to even grasp the potentialities of the new methods of design and construction. The contemporary architect, perhaps the last humanist of our time, should be conversant with aesthetics, engineering, sociology, economics, ecology, and, generally, with planning. Instead, under the influence of tradition, he is often trained primarily as an artist. His familiarity with the basic tools needed to understand modern technology is, most of the time, limited: mathematics, physics, and chemistry are not essential subjects in his curriculum.

On the other hand, the knowledge of the engineer in the fields of sociology, aesthetics, and planning is as limited as that of the architect in technology. A dialogue between the architect and the engineer becomes practically impossible: they lack a common vocabulary.

Since this dialogue is necessary, one may wonder, at first, whether the engineer should become more of an architect or the architect more of an engineer. But little thought is required to realize why it is mainly up to the architect to bridge the gap. The architect is the leader of the construction team; the engineer is just one of its members. The architect has the responsibility and the glory, the engineer but a service to render, creative as it may be.

In view of the increasing interest in architecture shown by the public at large, is it possible to give both the architect and the public an understanding of the structural facet of the architectural problem? Is this possible without a thorough indoctrination in higher mathematics, physics, and economics? In other words, can the essentials of structural action be understood by an intelligent person untrained in the mathematical and physical sciences?

The answers to these questions are all in the affirmative if a clear distinction is made between an understanding of basic structural concepts and a thorough knowledge of structural analysis.

1.4 Structures and Intuition

It is obvious that only the most serious training in mathematics and the physical sciences will allow a designer to analyze a complex structure to the degree of refinement required by modern technology. Today's structural engineer is a specialist among specialists, a subgroup among civil engineers. As new technologies develop, even structuralists specialize: at present some structural engineers specialize in reinforced concrete, others in reinforced concrete roofs only, and some in roofs of only one particular shape. One goes to these specialists for advice on a particular type of structure as one would go to a medical specialist for advice on a rare type of disease.

But it is just as obvious that, once the basic principles of structural analysis have been established, it does not take a specialist to understand them on a purely physical basis. We all have some familiarity with structures in our daily lives: we know at what angle to set a ladder so that it will carry our weight without sliding on the floor, and whether the plank over the brook will give in as we walk on it. We know whether our rope is strong enough to lift a pail of water from the bottom of the well, and how to pitch a tent at camp so that it will not be blown away by the wind. It is but a fairly easy step to capitalize on these experiences, to systematize such knowledge, and to reach an understanding of how and why a modern structure works.

The layman may find this inquiry fascinating. The architect should find it mandatory: without it he will soon be out of the field of contemporary architecture. For the interested public it may be one more hobby; for the architectural student and the practicing architect it is one of the basic requirements of the profession.

Once he has grasped the fundamentals, the architect must become conversant with the more refined points of the theory of structures. This will allow him to apply intelligently a wealth of new ideas and methods unavailable until a few years ago even to the greatest architects.

There is an obvious danger in this new availability and freedom. Art is enhanced by limitations, and freedom may easily lead to anarchy. Since today almost any structure can be built, the important question is: "Should it be built?", instead of: "Can it be built?" The architect is less hampered by technological difficulties and may be led astray into the world of the most unjustifiable structures. It is true that the average contemporary architect can aspire to greater achievements in the field of structures than even those of the exceptional practitioner of only a hundred years ago, but such achievements, the fruit of technology, are also obtained through blood, sweat, and tears.

What follows is an attempt to introduce the reader to the field of structures without appealing to a formal knowledge of mathematics or physics. This does not imply that structures will be treated in an elementary, incomplete, or simplified manner. On the contrary, some of the structural concepts presented in the last chapters of this book are refined and complex; nonetheless, they can be grasped by the reader and recognized in general architectural situations on a purely intuitive basis. It is hoped that this better knowledge of structural action may lead the interested student to a readier understanding of the finer points of structural design.

Chapter Two

Loads on Structures

2.1 The Purpose of Structure

Structures are always built for a definite purpose. This utilitarian element is one of the essential differences between structure and sculpture: there is no structure for structure's sake.

Structure's main purpose is to enclose and define a space, although, at times, a structure is only built to connect two points, as in the case of bridges and elevators, or to withstand the action of natural forces, as in the case of dams or retaining walls.

Architectural structures, in particular, enclose and define a space in order to make it useful for a particular function. Their usefulness stems, generally, from the total or partial separation of the defined space from the weather and may not require its complete enclosure: the cantilevered roof of a stadium stand protects the spectators from the weather without enclosing them in a space (Fig. 2.1).

The enclosed space may serve many different purposes: the protection of the family, the manufacture of industrial products, the worship of deity, the entertainment of citizens, the gathering of lawmakers. Different purposes, served by different spaces, require different structures, but all structures, by the simple fact of their existence, are submitted to and must resist a variety of loads. Only in rare cases is resistance to loads the primary purpose of a structure: loads are, usually, a necessary and unavoidable evil.

2.1 Partial protection from weather.

2.2 Loads

The determination of the loads acting on a structure is a complex problem. The nature of the loads varies essentially with the architectural design, the materials, and the location of the structure. Loading conditions on the same structure may change from time to time, or may change rapidly with time.

The most important loads carried by an architectural structure do not change rapidly with time: they are called **static,** and are the basis for the design of the structure.

In order to simplify the checking of structural strength, the loads most commonly encountered in practice are not evaluated case by case, but are suggested, and even dictated, to the designer by rules and regulations contained in **building codes.** The load to be carried by the floor of a building varies so much, depending on the occupant of the floor, the distribution of furniture, the weight of machines, or the storage of goods, that codes substitute for it an **equivalent load.** This equivalent load is derived, on the basis of statistical evidence, for each type of building, and is modified from time to time as new conditions or knowledge arise.

The equivalent load must be such that under the **worst** circumstances the floor will not fail, nor deflect so much as to become unusable. The **code design load** must, therefore, be a **multiple** of the load that could produce the failure or an unacceptable deflection: the greater the uncertainty about the actual load, the greater the multiple, or **factor of safety,** adopted in the codes.

Code loads are **conventional loads:** a floor load may be assumed to be a constant number of pounds on each square foot of floor, even though, in practice, no floor is ever loaded uniformly. Similarly, the pressure exerted on a building by the wind may be assumed to be constant in time and distributed uniformly over its surface. The wind, instead, blows in gusts, and wind pressure varies from point to point of a building. Here again, the code simplifies the design procedure by taking the wind variations into account statistically and suggesting "safe" conventional wind pressures.

Whenever the loads on a building are not considered by codes, and when they present characteristics that may endanger a structure's life, they must be accurately determined through experiments or by mathematical calculations. The effect of hurricane winds on a skyscraper may have to be found by means of aerodynamic tests on a model, conducted in a wind tunnel.

It is not always sufficient for the designer to consider only code loads, since the responsibility for the strength of the design rests with him and not with the code authorities; this is particularly true in circumstances where code regulations do not apply. It is therefore essential for the architect to acquire an awareness of loads.

2.3 Dead Load

The unavoidable weight of the structure itself and the weight of all loads permanently on it constitute its **dead load** (Fig. 2.2). It is one of the paradoxes of structural design that one must know the dead load beforehand in order to design the structure, while it cannot be determined until the structure is designed. The dimensions of a structural element depend essentially on the loads acting on it, and one of these loads is the dead load, which in turn depends on the dimensions of the element. The designer is compelled to start the calculation of a structure by **guessing** its dimensions and, hence, its dead load. He then adds to it all the other loads, checks its strength, and finds out at the very end of the calculation whether his guess was correct. Long practice alone will prevent innumerable wrong guesses in structural design. The checking of the strength of a given structural element for given loads, called **structural analysis,** is a fairly routine operation. The initial educated guess, called **structural design,** must come from experience and is often the result of an almost artistic intuition rather than of scientific calculations.

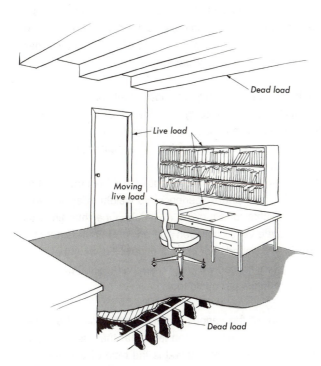

2.2 Dead and live loads.

The dead load is, in many cases, the most important load on a structure. It may outweigh all other loads by large factors, particularly in large structures and those built of heavy materials. In bridges, in roofs over wide unencumbered areas (halls, churches, theaters), in stone and masonry structures of a massive type (columns, buttresses), the dead load often dictates the dimensions of the resisting elements. In certain cases the dead load is not only important, but useful or even essential—as, for example, in a gravity dam, where it is used to resist the horizontal pressure of water.

Modern structural materials, such as high-strength steel, prestressed concrete, or aluminum, in some cases reduce the importance of the dead load in relation to the other loads, but in no case can the dead load be ignored. Its main characteristic is its continuous presence: it is a **permanent load.**

The dead load is easily computed. Once the dimensions of the structure have been determined on the basis of prior experience, its weight is evaluated by consulting tables of unit weights for structural materials. One thus finds that the average weight of concrete varies between 100 and 150 pounds per cubic foot, the weight of steel is 490 pounds per cubic foot, and the weight of aluminum one-third that of steel, while wood weighs, on an average, 30 pounds per cubic foot, and bricks 120 pounds per cubic foot.

The difference in unit weight of the various materials influences the dimensions of structural elements, but it will be seen later that the essential factor in deciding the efficiency of a structural material is the ratio of unit weight to strength. Thus, for a given purpose, steel members are not necessarily heavier than reinforced-concrete members, even though the unit weights of the materials may so indicate to the inexperienced.

Although there are few uncertainties about the dead load, its calculation is a painstaking and tedious job. It is also a fundamental job, since the amount of materials used in a structure is, together with labor, one of the major components of its cost.

2.4 Live loads

All loads other than the dead load of the structure are called **live loads** (Fig. 2.2). They include all the **movable weights** to be carried: humans and animals; machines and fixtures; partitions and other nonstructural elements; rain, snow, and ice. The pressure or suction of wind, the pressure of water, and the push of retained earth are also included among the live loads.

It was noticed that many of these loads are of such an uncertain nature as to require safe "averages" to be established by code writers. Thus, according to the New York Building Code, the live load on the floor of an apartment building is to be assumed equal to an even or uniform load of 40 pounds per square foot, while the live load on the floor of a storage house is to be taken as 120 pounds per square foot. Unless their position is known and fixed, even partitions, which act on a small floor area, are to be distributed over the entire floor in view of the uncertainty of their locations: they are considered as a uniform load of 10 to 50 pounds per square foot, depending on their type and number.

The live loads suggested by the codes are usually so conservative that, in order to avoid unrealistically high live loads, the codes allow **live load reductions** depending on the number of floors of a building and the area supported by a single structural element, e.g., a column. Live load reductions take into account the negligible chance that every floor in a building, or the entire large area supported by a single structural element, carry **simultaneously** the full live load.

The weight of snow depends on the climate of the region where the building is to be erected: according to codes, it is equivalent to 60 pounds per square foot in northern Canada, and to 40 pounds per square foot in New York City.

The wind load on a building is difficult to ascertain with any degree of accuracy, because it depends on the wind velocity **and** on the shape and surface of the building (Fig. 2.3). Average wind velocities are known with some degree of certainty, but it is difficult to measure the highest instantaneous velocity of a hurricane wind, or to forecast the largest velocity the wind will have in a certain locality. The influence of the building itself presents even greater uncertainties: its shape may produce pressures and/or suctions, and the roughness of its surface may change the value of the local pressures. In any case, codes prescribe safe, static pressures or suctions due to wind, varying with height; these are revised from time to time in order to take into account the knowledge continuously accumulated in the field of aerodynamics. The dynamic action of wind loads is considered in Section 2.6.

The dead load and the other "gravity" loads due to the pull of the earth are resisted by suitable structural systems. Resistance to wind pressures and suctions and other horizontal loads require, at times, separate structural systems. Horizontal wind-bracing systems may be seen on the underside of bridges (Fig. 2.4), while vertical wind-bracing systems are hidden within the inner walls or **core** of most buildings (Fig. 2.5).

2.3 Wind Load.

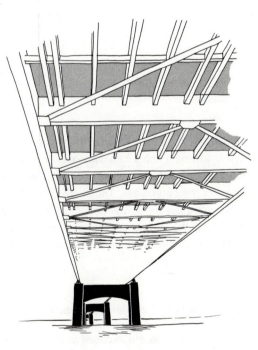

2.4 Horizontal wind-bracing systems.

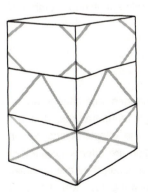

2.5 Vertical wind-bracing systems.

Framed buildings (see Chapter 8) may be wind-braced by stiffening alternate bays at alternate floors with diagonals or panels [Fig. 2.6(a)]. In the Fiat Tower in Paris, engineered by Weidlinger Associates, stiffening panels are set in the frames of the outer walls. These are pierced by window openings decreasing in area from the top to the bottom of the building, thus increasing the shear strength of the panels as the wind shear increases [Fig. 2.6(b)]. In some buildings the outer walls are wind-braced by diagonals spanning a number of floors (see Fig. 8.20).

2.5 Thermal and Settlement Loads

All structures are exposed to temperature changes, and change shape and dimensions during the cycle of day and night temperatures, and the longer cycle of summer and winter temperatures. The effects of changes in dimensions due to thermal expansion and contraction are often equivalent to large loads, which may be particularly dangerous because they are invisible. A simple example of this type of loading condition will suffice to indicate its nature and importance.

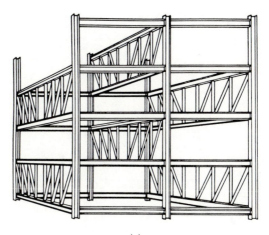

(a)

(b)

2.6 Wind bracings: (a) panel bracing of interior frames; (b) the Fiat Tower in Paris.

A steel bridge spans 300 feet over a river (Fig. 2.7); it was built in winter, when the average temperature was 35 degrees Fahrenheit. On a hot summer day the air temperature reaches 95 degrees Fahrenheit, and the bridge expands, because it acquires the temperature of the surrounding air. The increase in length of the bridge, which may be calculated to be only 1.3 inches, is small compared to its original length. But, if the bridge piers make it impossible for this elongation to take place, they develop in the bridge a horizontal compressive load capable of reducing the length to its winter value (Fig. 2.7). Since steel is very stiff in compression, it takes a large compressive load to reduce the length of the bridge by 1.3 inches: this load is so high that it would use up half the **strength of the steel,** leaving only 50 percent of its original strength to carry the loads for which the bridge was designed. The obvious way of eliminating such an overload is to **allow** the bridge to change its length with varying temperatures. This is usually done by supporting one of the bridge ends on a "rocker" (Fig. 2.8).

Due to thermal conditions, framed structures of high-rise, air-conditioned buildings may also develop stresses (see Section 7.4).

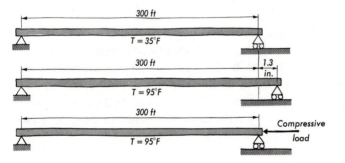

2.7 Thermal load.

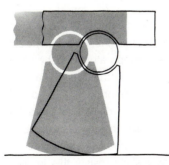

2.8 Rocker support.

25

A similar condition of thermal movements, with different but equally dangerous consequences, is encountered in large domes. When the external temperature increases or decreases, the dome tends to expand or contract. Since it is usually prevented from so doing by its underground foundations, which remain at a constant temperature, it will move mostly up or down: the dome "breathes" (Fig. 2.9). The top of a dome, covering a hall with glass walls and spanning 200 feet, may breathe up and down as much as 3 inches due to air temperature changes, and if the walls follow this movement the glass panes break. A special type of sliding support eliminates this danger.

More complicated thermal loads are developed in a dome during the daily thermal cycle, when one of its sides is heated more than the other. The dome changes shape in an unsymmetrical fashion and becomes distorted (Fig. 2.10). The stresses due to this distortion may be complex and high.

These simple examples show that a structure is particularly sensitive to thermal changes if by the nature of its shape, support conditions, and materials it tends to **restrain** the changes in dimensions due to temperature. On the other hand, acceptable deformations under loads require a structure to be stiff. Hence, the requirements for stiffness and for thermal deformations are opposite. Whenever a structure is to withstand heavy loads and small temperature changes, it may be made quite stiff. Whenever it must withstand large temperature changes and relatively small loads, it must be made flexible in order to accommodate such changes: the structure successfully resists this loading condition by giving in rather than by fighting it.

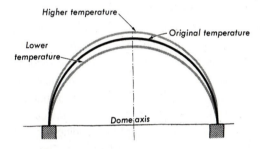

2.9 Thermal movements of dome.

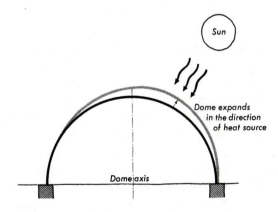

2.10 Unsymmetrical thermal distortion of dome.

Another condition, producing effects equivalent to those of high loads, may stem from the uneven settlements of the foundations of a building. A soil of uneven resistance, loaded by the weight of a building, may subside more in a specific portion of the foundation than in others. The soil deflections reduce the support of the foundation in certain areas, and the portion of the building above them either shears off the rest of the building [Fig. 2.11(a)] or hangs partially from it [Fig. 2.11(b)]. No additional load has been applied to the building by the uneven settlement, but the supported portion of the building carries more load, and of a different type, than the load it was designed for. The unsupported section of the building is also under strain, as can be seen from the deflection of its beams [Fig. 2.11(b)].

Thermal and settlement stresses are examples of a category of stresses due to deflections rather than loads. An example of a stressed but unloaded structure may be built by cutting a piece out of a steel ring and welding the ring again so that it looks untampered with. If cut, this ring snaps open, demonstrating the stresses "locked" in it. A similar condition may be found in some rolled steel beams. If one of these beams is cut down the middle with a saw, its two halves open up and curve in opposite directions, indicating a certain amount of stress locked in by the rolling process (Fig. 2.12). One of these beams might fail under load because the stresses produced by the loads are superimposed on the "locked-in" stresses and exceed safe values. Locked-in stresses are put to good use in **prestressed** and **post-tensioned** reinforced-concrete structures (see Section 3.3) and other prestressed structures (see Sections 11.3 and 12.14).

28

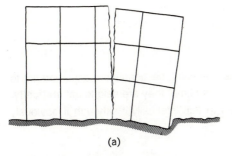

(a)

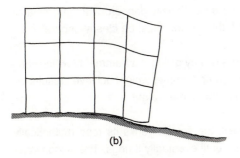

(b)

2.11 Uneven settlements of foundation.

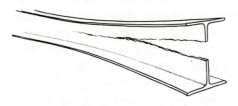

2.12 Locked-in stresses.

2.6 Dynamic Loads

All the loads considered in the preceding sections were assumed not to change, or, at least, to change slowly with time: they are said to act **statically.** In codes even the wind is assumed to act "statically," although it obviously does not.

Loads that change value or location rapidly, or are applied suddenly, are called **dynamic loads.** They can be exceptionally dangerous if their dynamic character is ignored; consequently, their action must be clearly understood.

The common experience of driving a nail by giving it a hammer blow indicates that the sudden application of the moving hammer weight achieves results unobtainable by the slow application of the same weight.

In order to ring a heavy church bell, the sexton yanks its rope rhythmically; the bell swings progressively further until eventually it rings. The sexton could not achieve this result by exerting a sudden hard pull on the rope: he must, instead, "yank in step" with the bell oscillations for a while (Fig. 2.13).

The force exerted by a hammer blow is called an **impact load;** the rhythmic pull of the sexton is a particular case of a periodic force called a **resonant load.** In the first instance, the higher the velocity of the hammer or the shorter the time for the load to reach its peak value, the greater the effect: an instantaneous blow produces an extremely high force with possibly shattering results. In the second, a relatively small force applied "in step" for a long time produces increasing effects: a small "in-step" force of a few pounds may eventually turn over a bell weighing several tons.

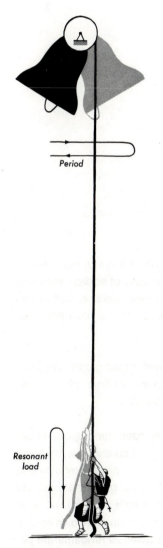

2.13 Resonant load.

Dynamic loads are exerted on structures in a variety of ways. A high velocity wind gust may be similar to a hammer blow. A company of soldiers marching "in step" exerts a resonant load on a bridge when their step is in rhythm with the oscillations of the bridge. Some small bridges are said to have collapsed under such resonant loads.

An impact load is characterized by a very short time of load growth; resonant loads by their rhythmic variations. But when is an impact time "short"? And when is a varying load "in resonance" with a structure?

All structures are, to a certain extent, elastic. They have the property of deflecting under loads, and of returning to their initial position once the loads are lifted. As a consequence of their "elasticity," structures have a tendency to oscillate: a skyscraper swings after the passing of a wind gust, and a railroad bridge oscillates up and down after the passage of a train. The time required for a structure to go freely through a complete swing, or up-and-down oscillation, depends on its stiffness and its weight, and is called its **fundamental period.** In order to go through a complete swing a modern building will take anywhere from one-tenth of a second to 10 or more seconds. A stiff structure oscillates rapidly: a low, rigid building has a short period. A flexible structure oscillates slowly: a tall steel skyscraper may take over 10 seconds for a complete swing. The fundamental period of a structure is, in fact, a good measure of its stiffness.

The time of application of a load is measured **against** the fundamental period of the structure: if this time is short in comparison with the fundamental period, the load has **dynamic** effects; if **long,** the load has only static effects. It is thus seen that the same varying load may be static for a given structure and dynamic for another. A low-velocity long wind gust on a stiff building of short period will have the same effect as a constant static pressure. A high-velocity short wind gust on a flexible building of long period may strain the structure to a much greater extent than its static pressure would lead one to predict. The blast of a nuclear bomb reaches its peak pressure so rapidly that its effects are always dynamic. Its destructive capacity, due to both its high peak pressure and its sudden application, is a dramatic example of what dynamic loads can do to a structure.

In a variety of practical cases the dynamic effects of a load are 100 percent larger than its static effects. If a one-pound load is put slowly on the plate of a spring scale, the scale hand will stop at the one-pound mark on the dial. If the same load is released on the plate suddenly, the hand will move to the two-pound mark and then oscillate, stopping eventually at the one-pound mark (Fig. 2.14).

Most of the loads applied to architectural structures do not have impact characteristics, except those due to earthquakes. An earthquake is a sudden motion of the ground. This series of randomly variable jerks, transmitted to a building through its foundtions, produces much larger oscillatory motions of the higher building floors (Fig. 2.15). An earthquake occurs whenever the locked-in stresses in the earth crust, generated by the molten core of the earth, become high enough to shift suddenly a portion of the crust with respect to an adjoining portion, opening up, at times, gaps one or more feet wide and hundreds of miles long, over underground fractures called **faults.** In the United States faults exist all over the country but are particularly numerous and active in California, where strong earthquakes occur frequently.

The prediction of earthquakes, at present in its infancy, is rapidly becoming a science. Just as circularly expanding waves are generated by a stone dropped in a lake, the explosion of a small charge embedded in the earth crust generates outward-moving stress waves, whose speed depends on the value of the stresses locked in the crust. An increase in the speed of these waves indicates an increase in the value of the crust stresses and, hence, the danger of an impending earthquake.

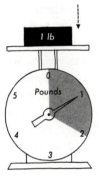

2.14 Dynamic load.

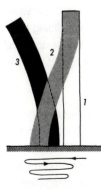

2.15 Earthquake motions.

Since the dynamic forces due to the jerky motion of the earth crust are mostly horizontal, they can be resisted by the same kind of bracing systems used against wind. Various devices have also been invented to "isolate" buildings from earthquake vibrations: one of them consists of foundation piers, made out of alternate layers of plastic and steel, which act as horizontal springs and allow the soil to move **under** the building. Other devices called **dynamic dampers** reduce the building motions by means of a large mass of concrete, attached to the building's walls by means of springs, which is free to slide on a thin layer of oil on the roof of the building [Fig. 2.16(a)]. Whenever the building moves under the impact of an earthquake, or of a wind gust, an electro-mechanical feedback system pushes the mass in the opposite direction, extending the springs on one side and compressing those on the other side, and these respectively pull and push back the building toward its original position [Fig. 2.16(b)].

In as much as the earthquake action on a building depends on the nature of the soil and the structural characteristics of the building itself, earthquake design is a complex chapter of structural theory. It is only in the last few years that enough information on earthquake motions and on dynamic building characteristics has been gathered to allow safe dynamic earthquake design. Tall buildings thus correctly designed have survived earthquakes that destroyed smaller, inadequate buildings.

Resonant loads occur at times in architectural structures. A piece of heavy machinery may vibrate because of the motion of its parts. If this vibration has a period equal to that of the supporting structure, the vibrations of the machine will be transmitted to the structure, which will swing with increasing oscillations. Floors, foundations, and entire buildings may thus be endangered by rather modest loads with a resonant period.

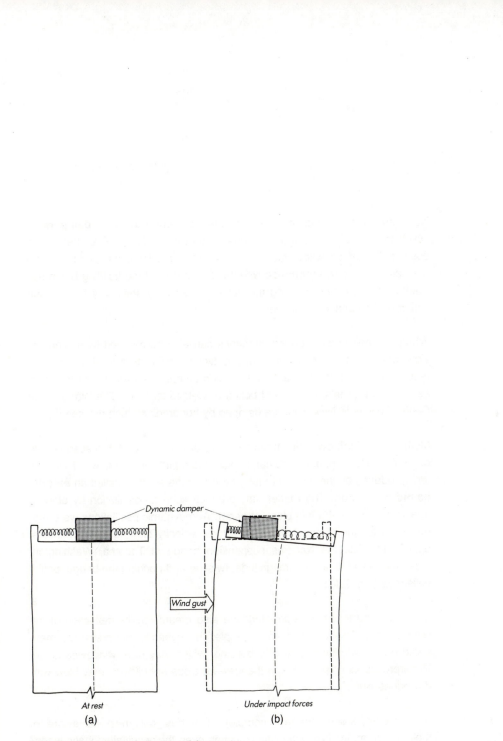

2.16 Feedback dynamic damper: (a) at rest;
(b) under impact forces.

Resonant vibrations may also be attenuated by **tuned dynamic dampers,** in which the period of the mass-springs system is made equal to that of the building. The mass, whose motion relative to the building is damped by friction devices, vibrates **in resonance** with the oscillations of the building but in **opposite** direction, thus keeping the building practically stationary through the action of the connecting springs.

Whatever their origin, building vibrations can also be damped by friction devices applied at the intersection of any two members free to slide one with respect to the other. In steel frames friction dampers are located at the intersection of diagonals that are not bolted or welded together. The World Trade Center Towers in New York are damped by hundreds of such devices.

More complicated dynamic phenomena are due to the wind. If a scarf is held out of the window of a moving car, it oscillates rapidly up and down. This "flutter," produced by the constant rush of wind on the scarf, is called an **aerodynamic oscillation.** The reader may produce such an oscillation by blowing against the edge of a thin piece of paper. Aerodynamic oscillations were produced by a wind of constant and fairly low velocity blowing for 45 minutes, against the Tacoma Narrows suspension bridge at Tacoma, Washington; these increased steadily in magnitude, twisting and bending the bridge, until it collapsed (Fig. 2.17).

Dynamic wind loads on a structure are also created by its deflection of the wind stream. This explains, for example, the dynamic overpressures measured on the windward side of a building, which may blow windowpanes in. Underpressures or suctions, on the leeward sides of buildings may blow windowpanes **out.**

All dynamic phenomena are complex. The designer must be aware of their action, and utilize with circumspection even the "equivalent static loads" suggested by codes.

2.17 Aerodynamic oscillations.

Chapter Three

Structural Materials

3.1 The Essential Properties of Structural Materials

A large variety of materials is used in architectural structures: stone and masonry, wood, steal, aluminum, reinforced and prestressed concrete, plastics. They all have in common certain essential properties that suit them to withstand loads.

Whether the loads act on a structure permanently, intermittently, or only briefly, the deformation of the structure (a) must not increase indefinitely, and (b) must disappear after the action of the loads ends.

A material whose deformation vanishes rapidly with the disappearance of the loads is said to behave **elastically** (Fig. 3.1). All structural materials are elastic to a certain extent. If they were not, and a residual deformation were present in the structure after unloading, new loadings would gradually increase the residual deformation, and the structure would eventually become useless. On the other hand, no structural material is perfectly elastic: depending on the type of structure and the magnitude of the loads, permanent deformations are unavoidable whenever the loads exceed certain values. Hence, the loads must be limited to values that will not produce appreciable permanent deformations: structural materials are usually stressed within their so-called **elastic range**.

Most structural materials are not only elastic but, within limits, **linearly elastic:** their deformation is proportional to the load. Thus, if a linearly elastic beam deflects one-tenth of an inch under a vertical load of 10 tons, it will deflect two-tenths of an inch under a 20-ton load (Fig. 3.2). Most structural materials are used, almost exclusively, in their linearly elastic range.

Materials presenting permanent deformations after the disappearance of the loads are said to behave **plastically** (Fig. 3.3). All structural materials behave plastically above their elastic range: the load at which a material starts behaving in a clearly plastic fahion is called its **yield load** or **yield point**.

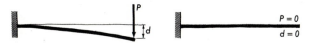

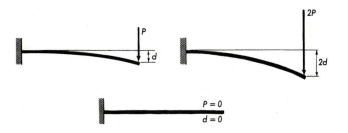

3.1 Elastic behavior.

3.2 Linearly elastic behavior.

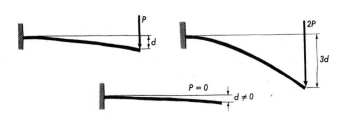

3.3 Plastic behavior.

Although large permanent deformations are to be avoided, it must not be thought that plastic behavior above the elastic range makes a material unsuitable for structural purposes: in fact, the opposite is true. For example, while the material is in the linearly elastic range, its deformations increase at the same rate as the loads. Above the yield point, deformations increase more rapidly than the loads (see Fig. 3.3) and eventually keep increasing even if the loads are not increased. This **flow** or **yield** under constant loads is thus the clearest sign, and a good warning, that failure is imminent. Other structural advantages of plastic behavior are considered in Section 9.3.

Materials to be used for structural purposes are chosen so as to behave elastically in the environmental conditions and under the type of loads to be expected during the life of the structure. The importance of this requirement can be illustrated by a simple example. If a wax candle is improperly inserted in a candlestick, the seemingly stiff candle will slowly bend out of shape at room temperature, and after a few weeks may be completely bent over (Fig. 3.4.).

This deformation would occur much more rapidly in an oven, while in a refrigerator it might be indefinitely limited. Under arctic conditions wax is "more structural" than in the tropics.

Given a sufficiently long time, a candle deforms under its own weight, but if one tries to bend it quickly, it breaks; it becomes **brittle**. All structural materials exhibit a similar behavior: at low temperatures and under fast load applications they are elastic and brittle; at high temperatures and under long-time loads they "flow." The temperature and time required for flow differ for different materials.

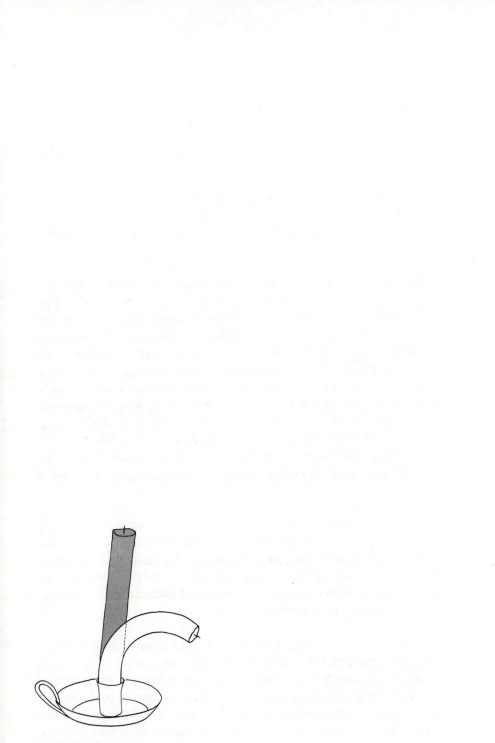

3.4 Material flow.

Materials that are linearly elastic up to failure (Fig. 3.5), such as glass, and some plastics (note the misnomer), are highly unsuitable for structural purposes. They cannot give warning of approaching failure and often shatter under impact (Fig. 3.6).

Steel at normal temperatures has a useful linearly elastic range followed by a plastic range, but becomes suddenly brittle at a temperature of minus 30 degrees Fahrenheit. Some unexpected failures of steel bridges in Canada have been traced to this sudden transition from elastic-plastic to brittle behavior at low temperature. At high temperature even steel, one of the strongest structural materials, loses most of its strength: it keeps deforming more and more, even under constant loads, and at 1200 degrees Fahrenheit it "flows" continuously. Hence, if steel is to be used safely in a building it must be protected, **fire-retarded,** so that it will not reach high temperatures at least for a few hours and the building can be evacuated. When a material is fire-retarded for an indefinite time, it is said to be **fireproof:** reinforced concrete is practically fireproof, provided the reinforcing steel is sufficiently protected by a cover of concrete.

Some materials have a relatively limited elastic range and behave plastically under low loads. Some plastics (thus correctly named) flow under almost any load. The yielding behavior of these plastics, and the brittle behavior of others, makes them unsuitable for structural purposes. But reinforced plastics, such as fiberglass, present acceptable structural characteristics, and their increased use is easily foreseeable.

Modern structural materials, such as steel, are **isotropic:** their resistance does not depend on the direction in which they are stressed. Wood, on the other hand, is **anisotropic,** since it has different strengths in the direction of the grain and at right angles to it. This drawback is remedied by joining, with plastic glues, sheets of wood with grain in different directions. The **plywood** thus obtained presents more homogeneous strength characteristics and moreover can be made weather resistant.

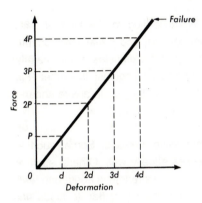

3.5 Brittle behavior.

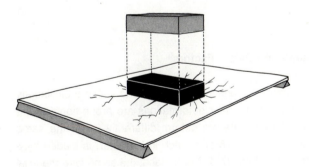

3.6 Brittle failure.

Structural materials can also be classified according to the kind of basic stresses they can withstand: tension, compression, and shear (see Chapter 5). Tension is the kind of stress that pulls apart the particles of the material [Fig. 3.7(a)]. Compression pushes the particles one against the other [Fig. 3.7(b)]. Shear tends to make the particles slide, as they do in a wire sheared by a pair of pliers. [Fig.3.7(c)].

All structural materials can develop compressive stresses. Some, such as steel, stand compressive and tensile stresses equally well. Others, such as stone or unreinforced concrete, do not: their tensile strength is about one tenth of their compressive strength. Their use is necessarily limited to loads and shapes that will not develop tensile stresses. Materials capable of resisting tensile stresses usually resist shearing stresses also; essentially compressive materials, on the other hand, do not have high shear strength (see Section 5.3).

3.2 Material Constants and Safety Factors

For structural purposes, materials are mostly used within their linearly elastic range, and this implies that their deformations are proportional to the loads upon them. But different materials deform differently under the same loads. If a steel wire 5 feet long, 1/16 of an inch in diameter, is loaded by a weight of 1000 pounds, it lengthens by 2/3 of an inch; the same wire made of aluminum stretches three times as much, that is, 2 inches (Fig.3.8).

Steel is tougher in tension than aluminum. The measure of this toughness is a property of each structural material, called its tensile **elastic modulus**. The elastic modulus is the force theoretically capable of stretching elastically a wire, 1 square inch in area, to twice its original length (theoretically, because in actuality the wire will break before stretching that much). The elastic modulus of steel is 30 million pounds per square inch; the modulus of aluminum is 10 million pounds per square inch.

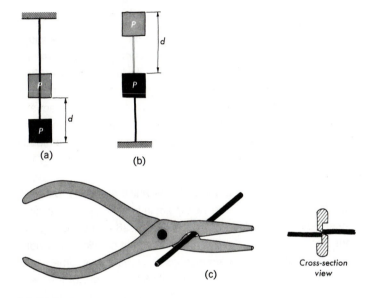

3.7 Basic stresses.

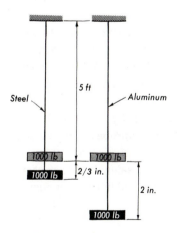

3.8 Tensile deformations.

The modulus in compression differs, in general, from the modulus in tension. The compressive modulus of concrete varies with its composition and has an average value of 4 million pounds per square inch; its tensile modulus has little significance, since its tensile strength is negligible. The compressive modulus of wood varies between 1 million and 2 million pounds per square inch in the direction of the fibers, and is approximately 3/4 million pounds per square inch at right angles to them. Steel and aluminum have the same modulus in tension and compression.

For purposes of safety a knowledge of the stress at which a material will start yielding is of the utmost importance. The yield point in tension or compression for structural steel (and for aluminum) varies between 36 thousand and 50 thousand pounds per square inch. Since structures cannot be allowed to yield under loads lest their permanent deformations accumulate in time, safe stresses are usually assumed as a fraction (usually 60 per cent), of the yield point of their material. Thus, steel and aluminum may be safely stressed in tension or compression to about 20 to 30 thousand pounds per square inch, and concrete to approximately 1 to 5 thousand pounds per square inch in compression. The **safety factors** thus introduced depend on a variety of conditions: the uniformity of the material, its yield and strength properties, the type of stress developed, the permanency and certainty of the loads, the purpose of the building. This last factor is of great importance from a social viewpoint: the safety of a large hall is more critical than the safety of a one-family house, and must be evaluated more conservatively. Factors of safety for buildings of exceptional dimensions, to be occupied simultaneously by large numbers of people, are established today so as to make it **most improbable** that even a predetermined, small number of persons will be killed by a structural failure during the life of the structure. The calculation of such safety factors involves the use of probability theory, and leads to results gauged in terms of human lives.

Safety factors cannot be established on the basis of the yield point whenever the material does not present a well defined yield point, or does not have any. The first case occurs with concrete, which does not have a clear transition from elastic to plastic behavior; the second with brittle materials, which behave linearly up to failure. In these cases safety must be measured directly against failure, as far as the material is concerned. It is thus important to realize that steel will break in tension at a stress of 50 to 300 thousand pounds per square inch, and concrete in compression at a stress of 3 to 12 thousand pounds per square inch. These stresses are called the **ultimate strength** of the material.

The load, or combination of loads, inducing stresses equal to the ultimate strength of an element is called the **ultimate load** for that element. When the design of a reinforced concrete structure is based on ultimate strength (it is then called **ultimate strength design),** the codes specify that certain load combinations should not reach values higher than the ultimate load U. For example, indicating by D the dead load, by L the code live load, and by W the code wind load, the American Concrete Institute 1983 code requires that U be less than $0.75(1.4\,D\,+\,1.7\,L\,+\,1.7\,W)$, or less than $1.4\,D\,+\,1.7\,L$ in the absence of wind. Similar ultimate design formulas are being introduced in steel design.

Some advantage may be had in establishing safety factors on the basis of failure, even when the yield point is clearly defined. These safety factors give direct information on the overload the structure can support **before it collapses,** rather than on the overload that will make the structure unusable because of excessive deformations. A knowledge of both overloads may be useful in establishing higher safety factors for permanent and semipermanent loads on the basis of yield, and lower safety factors for exceptional loads (hurricane winds, earthquakes) on the basis of failure. This criterion is accepted by most codes: a combination of normal gravity loads and of exceptional lateral loads (such as wind or earthquake forces, that have a minimal chance of occurring simultaneously) is usually allowed to stress the structure 33 per cent above the stresses due to gravity loads only.

3.3 Modern Artificial Materials

Iron has been used as a structural material for thousands of years, mainly in combination with other materials. Since the tensile properties of iron and the compressive properties of wood were well known, a combination of wood struts and iron tie-rods was used in the trusses spanning the naves of medieval churches (Fig.3.9).

Increased knowledge in metallurgy, chemistry, and physics has substanitially improved the properties of structural materials during the last 100 years. Stainless steel has eliminated the danger of rust, while rust-resistant steel, such as U.S. Steel's Corten, stops rusting after two or three years and does not require painting. Ultimate tensile stresses of steel alloys have reached values as high as 300 thousand pounds per square inch, and those of minute steel "whiskers," millions of pounds per square inch, forecasting revolutionary developments in steel design. Similarly, some new aluminum alloys have the strength of structural steel and are only one-third as heavy. Plastic glues have transformed wood into a more permanent, practically isotropic material. Glass-reinforced plastics combine the strength of glass with the nonbrittle behavior of plastics.

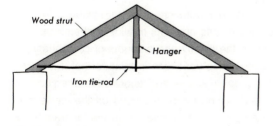

3.9 Wood-and-iron truss.

Possibly the most interesting of artificial structural materials is **reinforced concrete**. Combining the compressive strength of concrete with the tensile strength of steel (see Section 5.4), this material can be poured in a variety of shapes, so as to adapt itself to the architecture of the building and the loads on it. A new freedom in the design of structures has thus been acquired, far greater than that inherent in assembling beams and columns of standard shape, like those of rolled steel sections. The reinforcing steel, like a web of tensile elements, pervades and holds together the mass of cement, sand, gravel (or stone), and water, which sets and hardens to make the structure a single, monolithic entity. (In a recent development, the reinforcing steel bars have been replaced by short glass or metal fibers mixed with the concrete, thus producing elements capable of resisting tension homogeneously.)

The properties of steel depend on the careful check of ore mixtures, furnace and quenching temperatures, and minute amounts of alloyed chemicals. The properties of concrete depend on the quality and amounts of components in the mixture. Concrete is so sensitive to variations in mixture that it must be carefully and scientifically "designed" in specialized laboratories when used in large construction projects. Each batch of concrete used on the job is then tested to guarantee that its strength is in agreement with the laboratory design. The grain size distribution of the sand and gravel aggregates, the quality of the cement, and the quantity of water used may substantially affect the concrete strength and its hardening time. During the "setting" process heat is produced, and unless the concrete is properly cured, i.e., protected from both low and high temperatures, it may set improperly and crack, or have an ultimate strength lower than its design strength. These shrinkage cracks may permit humidity and water to reach the reinforcing steel, which rusts and eventually disintegrates.

The manufacture of concrete is a delicate process, requiring as much care as that of any chemical. The concrete for important construction jobs is seldom mixed at the site; it is manufactured in concrete plants and transported there. On the other hand, because concrete properties vary so much with composition and methods of mixture, many different types of concrete can be obtained, each suited for a specific purpose. Concrete with a compressive strength as high as 12,000 pounds per square inch, rapidly hardening concrete, and concrete with lightweight aggregates, are consistently manufactured. The reader will appreciate the potentialities of this new material after becoming acquainted with some of its applications to structural systems.

Prestressed concrete, either prestressed or post-tensioned, further advances the basic concept of a tensile reinforcement for a nontensile material. In **pre-**

stressed concrete, used mostly in factories for the prefabrication of structural elements, tendons of exceptionally strong piano wire are pulled against the sides of steel forms in which the concrete is poured. Once the hardened concrete grips the tendons, these are cut from the form sides and their frozen tension puts the concrete in compression. In **post-tensioned concrete,** slack tendons are threaded through sleeves set in the concrete forms and, once the concrete hardens, are pulled by outside jacks **against** the hardened concrete, compressing it. Post-tensioning is used mostly at the site and, in large structures, may proceed in stages as required by the stresses in an element, which increase under the increasing dead load. An unloaded beam of prestressed concrete seems unstressed, but "locked-in" stresses compress the concrete and tense the steel. The tensile stresses developed in a beam by the loads (see Chapter 7) reduce, or at most wipe out, the initial compressive stresses due to prestressing, so that the concrete is never in tension, nor does it tend to crack (Fig. 3.10). The prestressing of concrete members was proposed by the very first investigators of reinforced concrete. Unfortunately, the steel available at the time (the middle of the nineteenth century) had a low yield point and could not be stressed high enough to allow the tendons to remain substantially tensed following the plastic flow of the concrete under the prestressing compressive stresses. Only after high-strength steel suitable for this purpose was manufactured at reasonable prices did prestressed concrete become an economic reality.

"Ferrocement" (iron-concrete), a structural material first successfully used by Nervi, is a combination of steel mesh and cement mortar. In Ferrocement a number of layers of wire mesh, with square holes less than half an inch on a side, are packed randomly one on top of the other across the thickness of thin elements and embedded in a mortar of cement, water and sand (Fig. 3.11). The resulting material has the compressive capacity of an excellent concrete and the tensile strength of steel, since the steel is so thoroughly distributed through the mortar as to hold its particles together even when tension is ap-

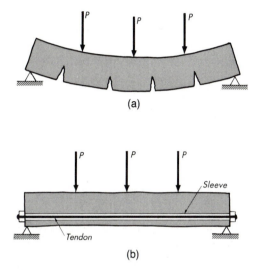

(a)

(b)

3.10 Post-tensioned concrete beam.

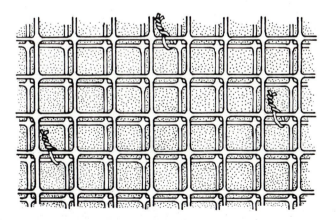

3.11 Ferrocement.

plied to it. One of the most successful applications of Ferrocement is to the construction of small-boat hulls, which Nervi started in the 1920s.

The high compressive strength of ceramic tile may be combined with the tensile strength of steel and the cohesive properties of concrete to create a material similar in behavior to reinforced concrete. Torroja, among others, has shown how imaginatively one may use such material in countries where steel is prohibitively expensive and labor costs are low (see Section 10.6).

Plastics, synthetic materials using organic substances as binders, are finding widening applications in the field of structures because of their varied properties, but, generally, are not used yet as structural materials because of their relatively high costs.

Most structural plastics are glass-reinforced. Glass fibers with a tensile strength of up to 600 thousand pounds per square inch are commonly used to reinforce epoxy resins molded into airplane parts and other structural elements. Glass fabrics give tensile strength to epoxy and polyester resins used to manufacture structural panels, and to polyvinyl and other plastic materials constituting the membranes of large air-supported roofs (see Section 11.3). Urethane and polystyrene foams, with low compressive and tensile strength but sufficient shear strength, are used as cores of sandwich panels of plywood, gypsum, aluminum, steel or plastics, with excellent weight-to-strength ratios and thermal insulating properties (see Section 10.6).

It is easy to forecast that the ever-growing developments in the field of plastics will make these materials more and more competitive with classical structural materials.

The proper use of stuctural materials is essential to correct design, since available materials limit the choice of structural systems in all important structures.

Chapter Four

Structural Requirements

4.1 Basic Requirements

Modern developments in materials production, construction techniques, and methods of structural analysis have introduced new freedoms in architectural design, considerably widening its scope. Subsequent chapters will illustrate the results achieved in this field, describing and analyzing the most commonly used structural systems of contemporary architecture.

These new freedoms do not exempt modern structures from satisfying certain basic requirements which have always been the foundations of good architecture, and which may be listed under the following headings: equilibrium, stability, strength, functionality, economy, and aesthetics.

4.2 Equilibrium

The fundamental requirement of **equilibrium** is concerned with the guarantee that a building, or any of its parts, will not move. Obviously, this requirement cannot be interpreted strictly since some motion is both unavoidable and necessary; but the displacements allowable in a building are usually so small compared to its dimensions that the building appears immovable and undeformed to the naked eye.

The laws governing the motion of bodies, published by Isaac Newton in 1687, are called **Newton's laws.** The particular cases of these laws governing equilibrium, i.e., the **lack** of motion, are of basic importance in structural theory because they apply to **all** structures and are sufficient for the design of **some** of them. Such structures, called **statically determinate,** support loads by developing forces whose values do **not** depend on the material used. Structures that cannot be designed on the basis of Newton's laws only and require a knowledge of material properties are called **statically indeterminate.** Most modern structures are statically indeterminate.

4.1 Equilibrium of vertical forces.

Certain elementary conditions that will ensure the equilibrium of particularly simple structures can be easily visualized. An elevator hanging from a cable is supported by the pull of the cable; the cable, in turn, hangs from the pulley at the top of the building. If the elevator weighs one thousand pounds and is at rest, the cable exerts on the elevator a pull of one thousand pounds. The weight of the elevator and the upward pull of the cable are equal and "balance out": the elevator is "in equilibrium" (Fig. 4.1). Two men pulling on a rope with equal forces do not move: the rope is in equilibrium (Fig. 4.2). But if one of the men exerts a greater pull than the other, he will yank his opponent from his stand, and both the men and the cable will move: equilibrium is lost. Similarly, if a sculpture weighing one thousand pounds is set on a column, the column exerts an upward push of one thousand pounds on the sculpture (Fig. 4.3). If the column exerted a smaller upward push, the sculpture would move down, and there would be lack of equilibrium.

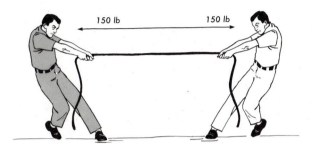

150 lb   150 lb

4.2 Equilibrium of horizontal forces.

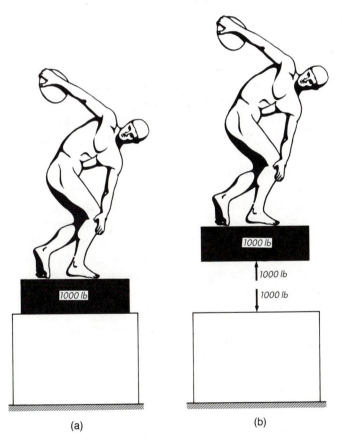

1000 lb

1000 lb

1000 lb

1000 lb

(a)   (b)

4.3 Equilibrium of vertical forces.

These elementary examples show that a body does not move in a certain direction if the forces applied to it in that direction balance out: a force exerted in a given direction must be opposed by an equal force exerted in the opposite direction. Whenever this happens we say that there is equilibrium in that direction, or **translational equilibrium.**

A slightly more complicated situation is presented by the equilibrium in the vertical direction of a bridge while a locomotive crosses it. The bridge rests on piers at its two ends and its weight will be neglected. When the locomotive is at midspan each pier supports half the weight of the locomotive: the weight of the locomotive is "equilibrated" by two equal "support reactions" [Fig. 4.4(a)]. When the locomotive is just entering the bridge from the left, its weight is supported almost entirely by the reaction of the left pier. As the locomotive moves across the bridge the reaction of the left pier decreases and the reaction of the right pier increases [Fig. 4.4 (b)], until they become equal when the locomotive is at midspan. From then on, the right pier reaction increases and the left decreases [Fig. 4.4 (c)] until the right pier carries the entire weight of the locomotive as the locomotive is just leaving the bridge. Whatever its location the bridge transfers to the piers the entire weight of the locomotive. To have vertical equilibrium the two reactions must **always add up** to this weight, but the reactions differ in value depending on the weight's location.

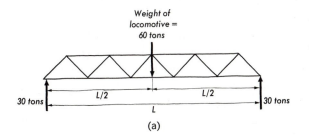

(a)

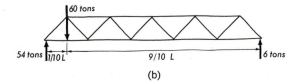

(b)

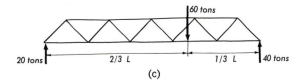

(c)

4.4 Bridge reactions.

Another familiar equilibrium situation is illustrated by two boys of **identical** weight sitting at the end of a seesaw with **equal** arms. The pivot of the seesaw "equilibrates vertically" the weights of the two boys, and "reacts" with an upward push equal to their combined weight [Fig. 4.5(a)]. Equilibrium breaks down when the boys sit at different distances from the point of support: the seesaw **rotates** in the direction of the boy sitting farther away from the pivot [Fig. 4.5(b)]. Such distances from points of support are called "lever arms." In order to guarantee "equilibrium in rotation" when the two boys have equal weights, their lever arms must be equal. If the two boys have different weights, equilibrium in rotation can still be obtained by giving the lighter boy a larger lever arm and the heavier boy a smaller lever arm. In fact, **equilibrium in rotation** requires that the **weight times the lever arm** of each boy have the same value [Fig. 4.5(c)].

Such simple equilibrium principles apply to all structures. Equal and opposite forces guarantee equilibrium in a given direction, and equal and opposite products of forces by lever arms guarantee equilibrium in rotation. Since the product of a force by its lever arm is called the **moment** of the force, we say that equal and opposite moments guarantee rotational equilibrium. In Fig. 4.5(c) the seesaw is in equilibrium in rotation because the clockwise moment about the pivot of the right boy's weight, $60 \times 6 = 360$ foot pounds, equals the counterclockwise moment of the left boy's weight, $90 \times 4 = 360$ foot pounds.

The first applications of the concept of equilibrium are found in the study of the next structural requirement: stability.

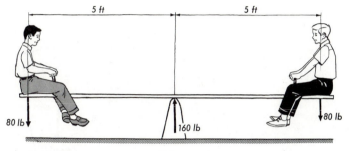

(a)

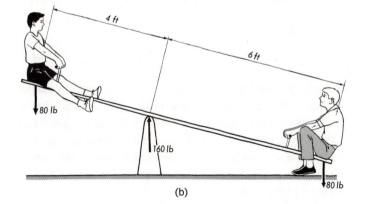

(b)

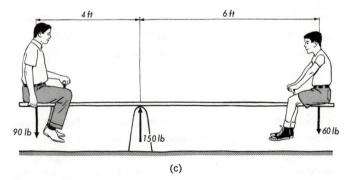

(c)

4.5 Equilibrium in rotation.

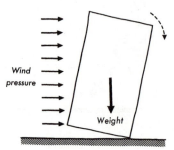

4.6 Instability due to wind.

4.3 Stability

The requirement of "rigid-body" **stability** is concerned with the danger of unacceptable motions of the building **as a whole.** When a tall building is acted upon by a hurricane wind and is not properly rooted in the ground or balanced by its own weight, it may topple over without disintegrating (Fig. 4.6). The building is **unstable** in rotation. This is particularly true of tall narrow buildings, as one may prove by blowing on a slim cardboard box, resting on a rough surface (lest it should slide).

The danger of rotational instability is also present when a building is not "well balanced" or is supported on a soil of uneven resistance. If the soil under the building settles unevenly, the building may rotate, as the Leaning Tower of Pisa still does, and may eventually topple over (Fig. 4.7).

A building erected on the side of a steep hill may, by its own weight, have a tendency to slide down the slope of the hill. This may happen either because the building skids on the soil, or because a layer of soil adhering to the foundations slides on an adjoining layer (Fig. 4.8). The second occurrence is not uncommon in clay soils when water seeps through the ground, transforming the clay into a soapy material.

4.7 Instability due to uneven settlement.

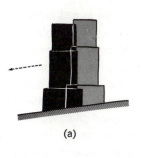

(a)

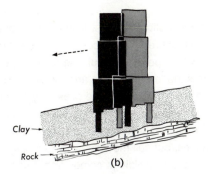

Clay →

Rock →

(b)

4.8 Instability due to sliding.

All these cases of instability are related to the soil, and to the building foundations. From the viewpoint of economy and usage, foundations are a "necessary evil"; moreover, they are out of sight so that the layman is seldom aware of their importance and cost. For example, the foundations of a heavy structure erected on loose sand permeated by water must allow the building to "float" on such a soil: they are built by means of "rafts" which, in structure, are similar to the hull of a ship (Fig. 4.9). A **raft** or a **mat foundation** allow the weight of the building to be spread over a larger soil surface, thus reducing the pressure on soils of low **bearing capacity.** With soils of average bearing capacity the weight of the building is usually supported on isolated rectangular **spread footings** of reinforced concrete.

Elaborate precautions against failures must often be taken to guarantee the stability of structures. Wood, concrete, or steel piles can be driven into the soil to depths which permit the building to be supported either by the friction between the surface of the piles and the soil [Fig. 4.10(a)] or by a deeper layer of solid rock [Fig. 4.10(b)]. The piles may be rammed into the soil or may be made to slide into it by rapid vibrations. Soils may also be consolidated by chemical means. The design of proper foundations is based on thorough soil investigations, but soil mechanics is a complex science and, to this day, most of the damage to buildings comes from faulty foundations, even though their cost may reach 10 per cent or more of the total cost of the building.

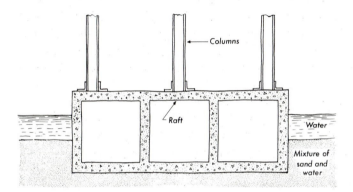

4.9 Raft foundation.

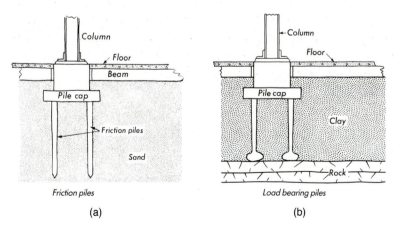

4.10 Foundation on piles.

4.4 Strength

The requirement of strength is concerned with the integrity of the structure and of each of its parts under any and all expected loads. To check strength, the structural system is first chosen, and the expected loads on it are established; the state of stress is then determined at significant points of the structure and compared with the kind and amount of stress the material can safely stand. Factors of safety of varying magnitude are used to take into account uncertainties in loading conditions and material properties (see Section 3.2).

Rigidity should not be confused with strength: two structures may be equally safe, even though one deflects more than the other under the same loads (see Fig. 3.8). Although it is often a measure of strength against loads, rigidity may be a sign of weakness in a structure subjected to temperature changes, uneven settlements, and dynamic loads (see Sections 2.5 and 2.6).

Certain structural weaknesses may lead to modest damage, while others may produce the collapse of the structure. Hence, the designer must check strength under a **variety** of loading conditions to obtain the **worst** stress situation at significant points of the structure. The structural optimist is inclined to believe that a structure collapses only if faulty design is compounded with faulty construction, and helped by an act of God. The cautious pessimist fears, instead, that a structure may collapse at the slightest provocation. In practice, completed structures do collapse, although in relatively small numbers; moreover, owing to the plastic behavior of structural materials (see Section 3.1), most collapses do not occur suddenly and seldom take human lives (see Chapter 13).

The strength of a structure is often evaluated according to the rules and regulations of codes. These procedures are usually safe, although uneconomical when they ignore newly developed systems and materials, but should not be applied blindly, that is, without careful consideration of their original purpose. "Code commentaries" are used to clarify these purposes.

The responsibility for strength rests squarely on the shoulders of the structural engineer. Every day his job is made more complex, and safer, by the increased theoretical knowledge and the improved tools at his disposal. Among the new tools, the electronic computer deserves special mention. These, "electronic brains" allow the performance of otherwise impossibly lengthy calculations in a matter of a few seconds or minutes, and are particularly useful in the kind of basic calculation to be performed daily by the structural engineer. In fact, the electronic computer has already supplanted the engineer in lengthy routine calculations, but at the same time has done much more than that.

The possibility of repeating a long calculation in a matter of minutes allows the consideration of a variety of combinations of shapes, sizes, and materials, and the choice of "the best" among a number of designs. Computers have thus brought about the "partial optimalization" of structural solutions, which until a short time ago was no more than theoretically possible.

Moreover, the computer permits a more accurate analysis of problems of exceptional complexity—for example, those connected with earthquake design—by "mathematical modeling" of the structure. Before the advent of the computer the rigorous analysis of such problems cost so much in both time and money that approximate solutions were mandatory, involving wasteful use of materials. Today large savings and greater safety are obtained by the more detailed and realistic studies computers make possible.

When the mathematical analysis of an exceptionally difficult problem cannot be carried through realistically by mathematical modeling, the designer may solve the problem by means of a test on a structural model of the building. The construction of a reduced-scale model requires a thorough knowledge of material properties, of appropriate scale ratios for lengths and thicknesses (which usually differ), and of correct scale ratios for static and dynamic loads. A number of laboratories, properly staffed and equipped for structural model testing, exist in the world today: dams, bridges, high-rise buildings, and other exceptional structures are sometimes designed on the basis of these tests.

In the rare cases in which doubts may exist even about the reliability of a model test, the engineer may decide to test a full-scale structural member. This procedure is usually adopted when an important component, appearing repeatedly in a structure, does not lend itself to a clear analysis. It is a costly and time-consuming method, and though it yields incontrovertible information on the behavior of a structural element, it is seldom resorted to.

4.5 Functionality

Structural functionality is concerned with the influence of the adopted structure on the purposes for which the building is erected. For example, long-span floors could be built by giving them upward curvature, as in the dome of a church: their thickness and their cost might thus be greatly reduced. But, since the pull of gravity is vertical, floors must be horizontal.

Suspension bridges are rather flexible structures. The Golden Gate Bridge in San Francisco sways laterally as much as 11 feet each side of vertical under strong winds. Such motions obviously must be limited, not only so that fast-traveling cars not be swayed from their paths, but also because the pressure of a steady wind produces aerodynamic oscillations capable of destroying a bridge if it is too flexible (see Section 2.6).

The excessive flexibility of a structure may impair its functionality even under static loads. Thus, most codes limit beam deflections to one 360th of their spans in order to avoid plaster cracks in ceilings. Aluminum, which is three times as flexible as steel, in many cases requires **design for deflection** rather than for strength. Worse conditions may arise under dynamic loads: a stream of traffic may produce a continuous and uncomfortable vibration throughout a flexible adjoining structure, seriously impairing its usefulness. Buildings over subway or railroad tracks are often supported on lead insulation pads to avoid such vibrations.

4.6 Economy

Sometimes economy is not a requirement of architecture. Some buildings are erected for monumental or symbolic purposes: to aggrandize the owners in the eye of the public or to enhance spiritual values. Monuments to the state or to "corporate images" fall in the first category; churches belong in the second. Their cost has little relation to their financial value.

But the utilitarian character of structure is so fundamental that even the structural systems of nonutilitarian buildings are influenced by economy. In other words, a strict structural budget must always be contended with unless the structure **itself** is an advertising display: an aluminum structure may be required, regardless of cost, in order to emphasize the ownership of the building by an aluminum manufacturer.

In the great majority of cases the structural engineer is expected to make comparitive cost studies and, other things being equal, to choose "the most economical structure." In a modern building other engineering costs, particularly those concerning mechanical systems (heating, air conditioning, electrical, and plumbing) and architectural details far outweigh structural costs. The cost of the structure is usually not more than 20 to 30 per cent of the entire cost of a building. Hence, even a substantial reduction in structural costs seldom represents a saving of more than a small fraction of total building costs. It must be always remembered that the adopted structure must produce the greatest economy in the **total** cost of the building and not in the cost of the structure alone. Deeper beams may reduce somewhat the cost of the structure while increasing substantially the cost of the curtain-wall, the partitions, and the mechanical systems, thus increasing the cost of the building.

The cost of the structural design itself represents usually less than 1 per cent of total building costs. The moneys allotted to structural design are subdivided into a budget for the preliminary design, in which the system is established, and one for the final design, which includes preparation of the working drawings and specifications, a check of the shop drawings prepared by the contractor, and, sometimes, inspection or complete supervision during construction. Final drawings are elaborate pieces of workmanship, and may cost many thousands of dollars apiece.

The two largest cost components of a structure are materials and labor. In this connection, two basic types of economy are encountered in the world today. In the first, usually found in the more advanced industrial countries, the cost of materials is relatively low and the cost of labor relatively high. In the second, usually encountered in less developed countries, this ratio is reversed.

The solution of the stuctural problem is influenced in a fundamental way by the ratio of materials to labor costs. In the first type of economy, all kinds of machinery (cranes, conveyors, excavators, compressors, electrical tools) are used to reduce labor costs and to speed construction; easily assembled, prefabricated elements are the rule; steel is often the typical material. In the second, labor is used in large amounts for both transportation and construction; small elements are employed to minimize the use of heavy equipment; masonry, bricks, and concrete are typical materials. But different ratios of materials to labor costs may influence the choice of structural system even in different areas of the same country.

Continuous changes in productivity and economic balance introduce a variety of intermediate conditions, depending on location and time. Concrete is becoming more favored and more competitive in countries where steel reigned until a few years ago. Metallic structures are becoming popular in countries where, up until now, concrete had been the most economical material.

The availability of heavy equipment is one of the main limits upon the use of large prefabricated elements in construction. Some of the most interesting work done in Europe in the recent past was conceived with basic elements not exceeding the capacity of the most readily available cranes, which was of a few tons. On the other hand, elements weighing tens of tons are commonly used in the United States even in construction jobs handled by small contractors.

Availability of skilled manpower limits methods of construction in a variety of ways. Ferrocement as used by Nervi is not economical in the United States at the present time, because of the pouring by hand of cement mortar between the superimposed wire meshes (see Section 3.3). Cement guns commonly used to spray concrete cannot be adopted in this case, because the velocity with which the mortar is ejected makes it bounce off the meshes. The use of specially designed guns may solve the problem. Most of the delicate stone work typical of medieval buildings is ruled out today by the lack of stone masons, whose tradition of apprenticeship has vanished. Similarly, a shortage of certified welders may make it impossible to consider an otherwise economical welded steel structure and require bolted or riveted steel construction instead. Even a lack of equipment to test the execution of the welded joints may rule out such a solution.

Other more subtle factors may also decisively influence cost. At times, the regulations of local codes tip the economic balance in favor of a specific material by imposing restrictions on another. For example, certain codes limit the thickness of flat concrete slabs to no less than a given value. The application of this regulation to curved slabs, which structurally could be much thinner, may make uneconomical the construction of a small reinforced-concrete dome. The inadmissibility of aluminum as a structural material was typical, in the recent past, of the limitations imposed by certain codes.

Fire regulations may favor concrete because of its fire-resistant properties, and comparative fire insurance costs may just as decisively recommend this material.

The initial cost of a structure is but one factor in its economy; maintenance is another. The low maintenance costs of concrete and aluminum structures may swing the balance in their favor, when compared with that of steel structures. Similarly, energy considerations influence the economy of a structure through its **life cycle cost.**

Speed of construction influences the amount of loan interests to be paid during the financially unproductive building period, and is another factor to be considered in the choice of a structural system. Prefabricated elements, whatever their material, allow simultaneous work on foundations and superstructure, and shorten construction time; hence, they are becoming increasingly popular. Governing bodies and labor unions have at times retarded or accelerated the adoption of modern structural systems. Political considerations have had the same effects.

Economy in structure is obtained through the interplay of numerous and varied factors to be weighed carefully in order to develop the most appropriate structural system and method of construction for each set of conditions. This analysis is so complex that, in the case of large buildings, it is entrusted to specialists called **construction managers** who advise the architect and his engineers during the design phase and the contractor during the construction phase.

4.7 Aesthetics

The influence of aesthetics on structure cannot be denied: by imposing his aesthetic tenets on the engineer, the architect often puts essential limitations on the structural system. In actuality, the architect himself suggests the system he believes best adapted to express his conception of the building, and the engineer is seldom in a position to change radically the architect's proposal.

In some cases the architect consults with the engineer from the very beginning of his design, and the engineer participates in the conception of the work, making structure an integral part of architectural expression. The balance of goals and means thus achieved is bound to produce a better structure and a more satisfying architecture.

The influence of structure on architecture and, in particular, on aesthetics is more debatable. It was remarked in Section 1.1 that a totally sincere and honest structure is conducive to aesthetic results, but that some architects are inclined to ignore structure altogether as a factor in architectural aesthetics. Both schools of thought may be correct in their conclusions, provided their tenets be limited to certain fields of architectural practice. No one can doubt that in the design of a relatively small building the importance of structure is limited, and that aesthetic results may be achieved by forcing the structure in uneconomical and even irrational ways. At one extreme, the architect will feel free to "sculpt" and thus to create architectural forms which may be inherently weak from a structural viewpoint, although realizable. Large environmental sculpture involves an even more extreme case of structural design almost entirely influenced by aesthetics.

At the other end of the scale, exceptionally large buildings are so dependent on structure that the structural system itself is the expression of their architecture. Here, an incorrect approach to structure, a lack of complete sincerity, or a misuse of materials or construction methods may definitely impair the beauty of the finished building. The beginnings of an aesthetics of structure itself are being established by **semiotics,** the science of nonverbal communication (see Chapter 14).

The influence of structure on modern architecture is so prevalent that some architects have wondered whether the engineer may not eventually take over the field of architectural design. The growing importance of technical services and of structure suggests such a danger. And a grave danger it would be, since the engineer, as a technician, is not trained to solve the all-encompassing problems of architectural design. But these fears may, after all, be unjustified: the engineer, while participating creatively in the design process, knows that in a group society his role is limited to a collaboration with a design team and its leader. This leader is and, hopefully, will always be the architect, whose role is both that of creator and, more and more, that of coordinator.

4.8 Optimal Structures

A discussion of the basic requirements of structure leads naturally to the question of whether on can satisfy all these requirements and obtain "the best structure" for a given building.

To answer the question we should first clarify "for whom" the structure is to be best. For the user, it should be the most practical or satisfying. For the owner it should, probably, be the least expensive. For labor it should employ the most man-hours. For the supplier of a specific material the best structure should use that material in large quantities. For the structural engineer it might be the easiest to analyze, the most interesting to study, or the most daring, depending on whether he is more interested in profit, theoretical skill, or personal satisfaction and fame.

From the viewpoint of the basic requirements considered in the previous sections, the best structure may be the most stable, the strongest, the most functional, the most economical, or the most beautiful.

Thus it is obvious that the question of establishing the "best" structure does not have a simple, single answer. On the other hand, one may strive for the best structure under a number of specific limitations. For example, optimal solutions have been established in aeronautical engineering under the assumption that minimum weight is the **only** criterion by which structural elements ought to be judged. Similarly, the standard rolled wide flange or W-sections, and the beam I-sections, which are basic elements in all steel structures, have been studied geometrically to approach maximum strength per unit weight when used as beams or as columns (the two shapes are geometrically different).

One may establish more general criteria for "the best" column by considering a variety of shapes and materials and by comparing costs. But it soon becomes apparent that the large number of factors in even a simple problem of this kind makes it practically impossible to establish the values of these factors leading to an "optimal" solution. The column, one of the simplest structural elements, may have a variety of shapes (square, round, I-shaped, boxed); each shape may have a variety of sides- or radii-ratios; the thickness of each side may be different; the length of the column may be large or small compared to its lateral dimensions; the column may be supported on a foundation, or be one of a series of super-imposed vertical columns; the materials to choose from may be many; the load to be supported by the column may be centered, or off center. It is understandable that the group of structural specialists of the Column Research Council has been at work for decades in the United States in order to establish simple criteria of strength and design for columns of steel and aluminum.

A question of common concern is the determination of the "lightest structural system," which supposedly spans the "longest distance" with the "minimum weight" of materials. Even considering a single material, simple studies show that different structural systems do not vary in weight as much as one may believe. The weight saved by the use of certain structural elements is often found to be required in their connections. Sometimes a system appears lighter than others, until a check of its flexibility shows that additional material is needed to stiffen it and make it functional.

The evolution of structural systems is a slow and delicate process. This should not discourage the serious student from investigating new possibilities or the practicing engineer from adopting new techniques. Let them simply be aware that a field as old and tried as Structures does not bear new fruits without the lavishment of incomparably more effort than that required by a routine application of established principles.

Chapter Five

Basic States of Stress

5.1 Simple Tension

Structures change shape whenever loaded. Although these deformations can seldom be seen by the naked eye, the corresponding stresses have measurable values. Stress patterns may be quite complex; each, however, consists at most of only two basic states of stress: tension and compression.

Tension is the state of stress in which the particles of the material tend to be pulled apart. The steel cables lifting or lowering an elevator have their particles pulled apart by the weight of the elevator (see Fig. 4.1). Under the pull of the weight the cables become longer: lengthening is typical of tension. The elongation of a **unit length** of cable is called its **tensile strain** (Fig. 5.1).

Provided the material is not stressed beyond its elastic range (see Section 3.1), the lengthening of the cable depends only on its cross section, its length, and the load. The larger the diameter of the cable, the smaller the unit elongation: in the elastic range the tensile strain is proportional to the load carried by each unit area of the cable cross section, or the **tensile stress** in the cable (Fig. 5.2). The ratio of tensile stress to tensile strain is a characteristic of the material called its **elastic modulus** in tension (see Section 3.2).

For a given strain the lengthening of the cable is proportional to the length of the cable: if the cable elongates by 1/4 inch when the elevator is at the top floor of an eight-story building, the cable will elongate eight times that much, or 2 inches, when the elevator is at the ground floor (Fig. 5.3).

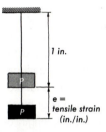

1 in.

P

e =
tensile strain
(in./in.)

5.1 Tensile strain.

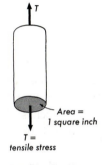

T

Area =
1 square inch

T =
tensile stress

5.2 Tensile stress.

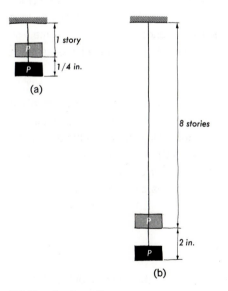

1 story

P

1/4 in.

(a)

8 stories

P

2 in.

(b)

5.3 Tensile elongation.

87

Certain materials, such as concrete, may be easily torn apart by tension with little elongation; others, such as steel, are capable of substantial tensile elongation and are very strong in tension. For example, a high-strength steel cable, 1 square inch in area (1.13 inches in diameter) can safely carry a load of 100,000 pounds and will break only under a load of 200,000 pounds or more. Since the unit weight of steel is 3/10 of a pound per cubic inch, a length of 333,000 inches, or 5 1/3 miles of such a cable would weigh 100,000 pounds and hence could hang safely, developing a maximum tensile stress at the top of 100,000 pounds per square inch. A cable of aluminum alloy, with the tensile strength of steel and a unit weight one-third that of steel, could be three times as long: it could hang for 16 miles. Because it would be three times as long and, moreover, because aluminum stretches under tension three times as much (see Section 3.2), the aluminum cable would stretch nine times as much as the steel cable.

Elongation is the most important, but not the only, deformation accompanying simple tension. Careful measurements of the cable before and after the application of the load show that as the load increases and the cable elongates, its diameter decreases. This lateral change in dimension was first discovered by the French physicist Poisson at the beginning of the nineteenth century. The ratio of the lateral to the longitudinal strain is called Poisson's ratio: it is about one-third for steel.

5.2 Simple Compression

Compression is the state of stress in which the particles of the material are pushed one against the other [see Fig. 3.7(b)]. A column supporting a weight is under compression: its height shortens under load. Shortening is typical of compression. In the elastic range the shortening of a unit length of column, or its **compressive strain,** is proportional to the load per unit of column area, or its **compressive stress**: the ratio of compressive stress to compressive strain is the **elastic modulus** in compression (see Section 3.2).

Deformations in compression are opposite to those in tension: shortening takes place in the direction of the load and lengthening at right angles to it, due to Poisson's phenomenon. Thus, a column of structural steel capable of developing a safe stress of 20,000 pounds per square inch, theoretically could safely carry its own weight up to a height of 66,000 inches or about one mile [if prevented from buckling (see page 90)]. Since the elastic modules of steel have the same value in tension and in compression, this column would shorten as much as a one mile rod made out of the same steel would lengthen in tension under the same stress.

Structural elements developing simple compression are very common because, eventually, all loads must be channeled down to earth: they appear in modern steel buildings and in Greek stone temples.

Materials incapable of resisting tension are often strong in compression: stone, mansonry, mortar, and concrete can develop high compressive stresses. A column of marble could be built to a height of 10,000 feet before failing in compression; a concrete column could reach a height of 8,000 feet. Modern materials with high compressive strength, such as steel, can be used to build columns much slimmer than those of stone or concrete, but their slenderness introduces an important new type of limitation in the design of compressive elements.

The reader may be familiar with the early movies of Charlie Chaplin in which he is often seen leaning on a cane, a slim bamboo rod: whenever the little fellow leans heavily on his cane, the cane bends outward (Fig. 5.4). The same behavior is typical of all long, **slender** structural elements under compression. As the compression load is slowly increased, a value is reached at which the slender element, instead of just shortening, "buckles out," and **usually breaks**. This dangerous value is called the **buckling load** of the element. It becomes a basic design factor whenever the material is strong enough in compression to require only a small cross-sectional area, thus leading to the use of slender elements.

The buckling phenomenon may be usefully visualized from another viewpoint. A slender column shortens when compressed by a weight applied to its top, and, in so doing, lowers the weight's position. The tendency of all weights to lower their position is a basic law of nature. It is another basic law of nature that, whenever there is a choice between different paths, a physical phenomenon will follow the "easiest" path. Confronted with the choice of bending out or shortening, the column finds it easier to shorten for relatively small loads and to bend out for relatively large loads. In other words, when the load reaches its "buckling" value the column finds it easier to lower the loads by buckling and bending, rather than by shortening.

5.4 Buckling under compression.

It must be realized that, theoretically, the column will bend out even if the load is perfectly centered and the column perfectly homogeneous. In practice, small imperfections in the centering of the load and/or flaws in the material will facilitate buckling.

The danger of buckling is not related to the stressing of the material above a safe compressive stress or to its flowing under a state of plastic stress. The value of the compressive load for which a slender column will buckle may produce stresses **below** the safe values determined on the basis of the compressive strength of the material. Buckling is, in a sense, similar to resonance: if an otherwise safe load oscillates in step with the structure, the structure deflects more and more until it fails; if an otherwise safe compressive load is near the buckling load, the column becomes **unstable** and bends out more and more until it breaks.

The buckling load of a column depends on its material, its length, the shape of its cross section, and the restraints applied to its ends. The buckling load is proportional to the elastic modulus of the material: a column of steel is three times stronger against buckling than an identical column of aluminum. The buckling load is inversely proportional to the square of the column length: a column twice as long as another, and with identical cross section, has a buckling load four times smaller (Fig. 5.5).

To be strong against buckling and still be efficient, compression members must not be slender and yet must have a small area so as to use a limited amount of material. The wide-flange sections, with a thin web and wide flanges, the boxed section, and, in general, cross sections with most of the material away from the center of the section are well suited for this purpose.

The buckling load increases with the restraints at the ends of the compressed member. A cantilevered column [Fig. 5.6(a)] buckles as the upper half of a column twice as long free to rotate at both supported ends; hence, its buckling load is four times smaller than that for the same "simply supported" column [Fig. 5.6(b)].

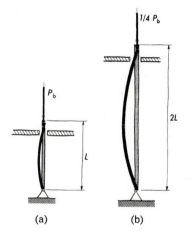

5.5 Buckling load versus length.

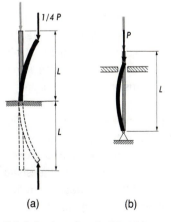

5.6 Influence of end restraints
on buckling load.

5.3 Simple Shear

Shear is the state of stress in which the particles of the material slide relative to each other [see Fig. 3.7(c)]. Rivets in riveted connections tend to shear (Fig. 5.7). A hole puncher uses shear to punch out holes in a sheet of paper (Fig. 5.8) since the lever arm of the shear is very small. The weight of a short cantilever beam built into a wall tends to shear off the beam from the wall at its "root" (Fig. 5.9).

Shear introduces deformations capable of changing the shape of a rectangular element into a skewed parallelogram (Figs. 5.7, 5.8, 5.9). The **shear strain** is measured by the skew angle of the deformed rectangle (Fig. 5.9) rather than by a change in unit length, as in the case of tension or compression.

The forces producing this deformation act on the planes along which the sliding takes place, and when measured on one square inch (Fig. 5.10) are called **shear stresses**. In the elastic range of behavior the deformation is proportional to the force and, hence, the shear strain is proportional to the shear stress. The ratio of shear stress to shear strain is called the **shear modulus**. It is a characteristic of the material and is less than half as large as the elastic modulus in tension or compression: steel, for example, has a shear modulus of 11.5 million pounds per square inch.

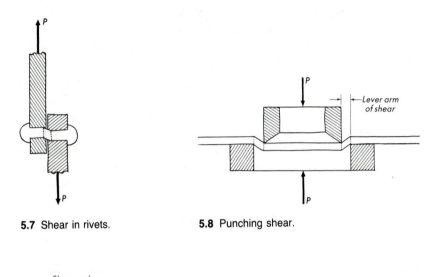

5.7 Shear in rivets.

5.8 Punching shear.

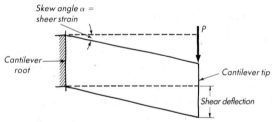

5.9 Shear strain in cantilevered beam.

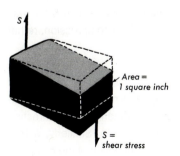

5.10 Shear stress.

One of the essential characteristics of shear is to produce sliding along not one but **two planes,** which are always **at right angles** to each other. If a square element is isolated at the root of a cantilevered beam it is seen that, due to the action of the beam weight, equal and opposite vertical shearing forces act on its vertical faces to maintain vertical equilibrium (Fig. 5.11). These forces also have a tendency to rotate the element, just as the pull and push of the driver's arms tend to rotate the steering wheel of a car. If the isolated element is to be in equilibrium in rotation (see Section 4.2), as it is in the actual beam, two equal and opposite forces must act on its horizontal faces to counteract the rotating action of the vertical forces (Fig. 5.12). The horizontal forces required by rotational equilibrium produce a shearing tendency in horizontal planes. Thus, shear stresses in vertical planes **necessarily** involve shear stresses in horizontal planes, **and vice versa**. Moreover, to maintain rotational equilibrium (Fig. 5.12) the horizontal and vertical shear stresses must have equal magnitudes.

The existence of the horizontal shearing forces may also be inferred by analyzing the deformation of the square element. The skewing of the element produces a lengthening of one of its diagonals and a shortening of the other. Since lengthening is always accompanied by tension and shortening by compression, the same deformation could be obtained by compressing the element along the shortened diagonal and tensioning it along the other (Fig. 5.13). Thus, shear may also be considered as a combination of tension and compression at right angles to each other in directions making an angle of 45 degrees with the shear directions.

The tensile and compressive diagonal forces "result" by combining the horizontal and vertical shears first along the lengthened and then along the shortened diagonals (Fig. 5.13). It is in this sense that in Section 5.1 it was stated that the **basic** states of stress are two, tension and compression, rather than three.

The consideration of shear as equivalent to compression and tension at right angles to each other is of great practical importance. A material with low tensile strength cannot be strong in shear, as it will fail in tension in a direction at 45 degrees to the directions of shear (see Section 7.2). Similarly, a **thin** sheet cannot be strong in shear as it will buckle in the direction of the compressive equivalent stress.

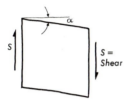

5.11 Vertical shears.

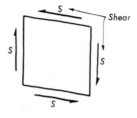

5.12 Shears required for
equilibrium in rotation.

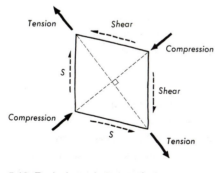

5.13 Equivalence between shear
and tension and compression.

The tendency to slide, characteristic of shear, is found in structural elements twisted by applied loads. Consider a bar of circular cross section, on the surface of which is graphed a square mesh of circles and straight lines [Fig. 5.14(a)]. If this bar is twisted so that one end section rotates in relation to the other, the squares on its surface become skew rectangles [Fig. 5.14(b)]. Since the same kind of deformation can only be due to the same kind of stress, twisting must produce shear strains and, hence, shear stresses in the cross section of the bar and, for equilibrium, also in the radial planes perpendicular to the cross section. This state of stress, although consisting of pure shear, is called **torsion**.

Since torsion develops shear stresses, it must be equivalent to tension and compression at right angles. The housewife who wrings the wet rag before hanging it proves this to be true: the torsion-induced compression squeezes the water out of the rag.

Torsion occurs in a structural element whenever the loads tend to twist it. For example, the eccentric loads transferred by a floor beam to a **spandrel** beam induce torsional stresses in the spandrel (Fig. 5.15). Rigidity against torsion involves the shear modulus. The most efficient cross sections against torsion are hollow, giving the shear stresses the greatest possible lever arm in rotation around the axis of the bar.

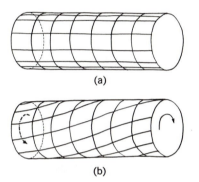

(a)

(b)

5.14 Shear in torsion.

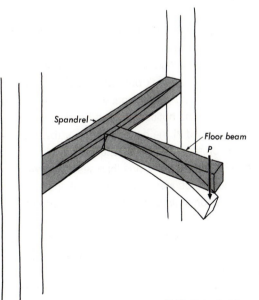

Spandrel

Floor beam

P

5.15 Spandrel beam under torsion.

5.4 Simple Bending

It was stated in Section 5.1 that all complex states of stress are combinations of no more than two basic states of stress: tension and compression. Compression and tension in different fibers of the same structural element is perhaps the commonest of these combinations: it is called **bending,** and plays an essential role in most structural systems.

Consider a plank supported on two stones with equal lengths cantilevered out (Fig. 5.16). If two boys of equal weight stand at the ends of the plank, the plank ends move downward, while the portion of plank between the stones moves upward: the curve assumed by the plank between the stones can be shown to be an arc of a circle. By drawing evenly spaced vertical lines on a side of the straight plank [Fig. 5.17(a)] and noticing that on bending the plank these lines open up at the top and crowd at the bottom [Fig. 5.17(b)], we see that the plank's upper fibers lengthen, its lower fibers shorten, and its middle fibers maintain their original length. But the plank has thickness, and **all** of its fibers must become curved. Hence, the bending up of the plank induces tension in its upper fibers and compression in its lower fibers. Moreover, the tension and compression may be seen to increase in proportion to the distance of the fibers from the middle or **neutral** fibers. (This behavior, carefully described in the sixteenth century by Leonardo da Vinci, was rediscovered only in the nineteenth century by the French physicist Navier.) The state of stress in which the stress varies as a straight line from a maximum tension to an equal maximum compression is called **simple bending**.

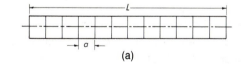

5.16 Simple bending.

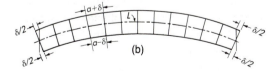

5.17 Strains in bending.

Bending stresses curve along the arc of circle of the deformed plank, but this deformation is so small in comparison with the length of the plank that the vertical weights of the two boys may be said to produce in the plank practically horizontal stresses. **Bending** may thus be considered a structural mechanism capable of channeling **vertical** loads to the supports in a **horizontal** direction or, more generally, in a direction at right angles to the loads. The weights of the boys are transferred horizontally to the two stones supporting the plank by bending stresses.

In view of the compressive strength of most structural materials, it is relatively easy to channel loads **vertically** down to earth. The fundamental structural problem consists, instead, in transferring vertical loads **horizontally** in order to span the distance between vertical supports. Bending is thus seen to be of prime importance as a structural mechanism.

A good bending material must have practically equal tensile and compressive strengths. This explains the historical predominance of wood among natural structural materials, and the long unrivaled role of steel in modern structures. Reinforced concrete is a man-made material with bending properties comparable to those of steel. In this material the compressive strength of concrete is used in the compressed fibers of the element, and the tensile strength of steel in the tensioned fibers. If the plank considered above were built of reinforced concrete, it would have reinforcing bars near its top (Fig. 5.18), since this is the region in which tensile stresses develop.

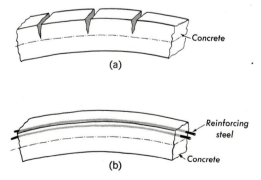

5.18 Reinforced concrete beam in bending.

Chapter Six

Tension and Compression Structures

6.1 Cables

The high tensile strength of steel, combined with the efficiency of simple tension, makes a steel cable the ideal structural element to span large distances.

Cables are flexible because of their small lateral dimensions in relation to their lengths. Flexibility indicates a limited resistance to bending. Because uneven stresses due to bending are prevented by flexibility, the tensile load in a cable is evenly divided among the cable's strands, permitting each strand to be stressed to the same safe, allowable stress.

In order to understand the mechanism by means of which a cable supports vertical loads, one may first consider a cable suspended between two fixed points, located at the same level, and carrying a single load at midspan. Under the action of the load the cable assumes a symmetrical, triangular shape, and half the load is carried to each support by simple tension along the two halves of the cable (Fig. 6.1).

The triangular shape acquired by the cable is characterized by the **sag,** the vertical distance between the supports and the lowest point in the cable. Without sag the cable could not carry the load, since the tensile forces in it would be horizontal, and horizontal forces cannot balance vertical load. The inclined pull of the sagging cable on each support may be split into two components: a downward force equal to half the load, and a horizontal inward pull, or **thrust,** (Fig. 6.2). If the supports were not fixed against horizontal displacements, they would move inward under the action of the thrust, and the two halves of the cable would become vertical.

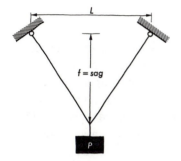

6.1 Symmetrical load on cable.

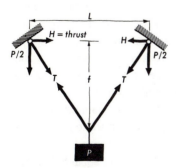

6.2 Cable thrust.

Holding in each hand one end of a thread with a weight attached at its middle, the reader may sense physically that the string develops no thrust when the hands are joined, while an increasing thrust is developed as the hands are moved apart, thus decreasing the string sag. The thrust may be shown to be inversely proportional to the sag: halving the sag doubles the thrust (see Fig. 6.3). For vertical equilibrium the vertical pull on the hands is always equal to one half of the load and independent of the sag. Hence, as the sag decreases, the tension the cable exerts on the hands increases because of the increase in the thrust. If the thread used is weak enough, there comes a point when it snaps, indicating that, as the sag diminishes, the tension eventually becomes larger than the tensile strength of the thread.

The cable problem just considered raises an interesting question of economy. A larger sag increases the cable length, but reduces the tensile force in the cable and, hence, allows a reduction of its cross section; a smaller sag reduces the cable length, but requires a larger cross section because of the higher tension developed in the cable (Fig. 6.3). Hence the total volume of the cable, the product of its cross section and its length, is large for both very small and very large sags and must be minimum for some intermediate value of the sag. The optimal or "most economical sag" for a given horizontal distance between the supports equals half the span and corresponds to a symmetrical, 45-degree-triangle cable configuration with a thrust equal to half the load (Fig. 6.4).

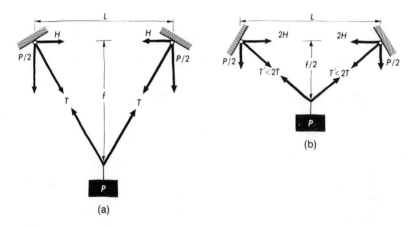

6.3 Variation of cable thrust with sag.

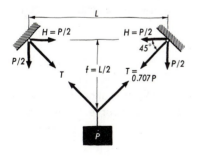

6.4 Optimal sag.

If the **load is shifted** from its midspan position, the **cable changes shape,** and adapts itself to carrying the load in tension by means of straight sides with different inclinations [Fig. 6.5(a)]. The two supports develop different vertical reactions, but equal thrusts, since the cable must be in equilibrium in the horizontal direction. The value of the thrust differs from the value for a centered load, but still varies inversely as the sag. The reader may sense this by shifting the load along the hand-supported thread.

If two equal loads are set on the cable in symmetrical locations, the cable again adapts itself, and carries the loads by acquiring a new configuration, with three straight sides [Fig. 6.5(b)]. If the number of loads is increased, the cable acquires new equilibrium configurations with straight sides between the loads, and changes in direction at the points of application of the loads. The shape acquired by a cable under concentrated loads is called a **funicular polygon** [Fig. 6.5(c)] (from the Latin word **funis** for rope, and the Greek words **poly** for many and **gonia** for angle): it is the **natural** shape required to carry loads in **tension.**

As the number of loads on the cable increases, the funicular or **string polygon,** acquires an increasing number of smaller sides and approaches a smooth curve. If one could apply to the cable an infinite number of infinitesimally small loads the polygon would become a **funicular curve.** For example, the funicular polygon for a large set of equal loads evenly spaced **horizontally** approaches a well-known geometrical curve, the **parabola** [Fig. 6.6(a)]. The optimal sag for a parabolic cable equals three-tenths of the cable span.

110

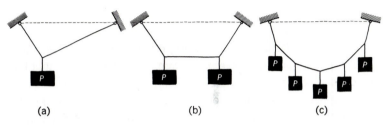

(a)   (b)   (c)

6.5 Funicular polygons.

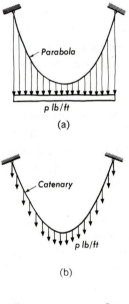

Parabola

p lb/ft

(a)

Catenary

p lb/ft

(b)

Parabola

Catenary

(c)

6.6 Funicular curves.

If the equal loads are distributed evenly **along the length** of the cable, rather than horizontally, the funicular curve differs from a parabola, although it has the same general configuration: it is a **catenary,** the natural shape acquired by a cable of constant cross section or a heavy chain (**catena** in Latin) under their own weight, which is uniformly distributed along their lengths [Fig. 6.6(b)]. The optimal sag for the catenary is about one-third of the span; for such sag ratio the catenary and the parabola are very similar curves [Fig. 6.6(c)].

A cable carrying its own weight (the dead load), and a load uniformly distributed horizontally, acquires a shape that is intermediate between a catenary and a parabola. This is the shape of the cables in the central span of suspension bridges, which carry their weight and that of the stiffening trusses on which the roadway is laid (Fig. 6.7).

A cable would span the **largest** possible distance if it could just carry its weight, but would break under the smallest additional load. Assuming an optimal sag-span ratio of one-third to minimize the weight of the cable, it is found that such a steel cable with a strength of 200,000 pounds per square inch could span a distance of 17 miles. (This maximum distance is independent of the cable diameter, since both the weight of the cable and the tension in it are proportional to the area of the cross section.) Obviously, actual cable spans are built to carry loads, which are usually much heavier than the cables themselves; hence, cable spans are much shorter that the limit span of 17 miles. The longest American suspension bridge to date (1986), the Verrazano Narrows Bridge at the entrance of New York harbor, spans 4260 feet between the towers, a length over two-and-a-half times that spanned by the Brooklyn Bridge (built in 1883). The Humber Bridge in Great Britain, 4626 feet between towers, is the longest in the world to date (1986). The Akashi-Kaykio Bridge in Japan, designed with a span between towers of 5800 feet, will become the longest in the world when completed before the end of the century. Such spans are rapidly approaching limiting values, beyond which it is not practically conceivable to go with the types of steel available today. Only an improvement in cable strength will make substantially larger spans possible.

6.7 Suspension bridge.

One may wonder why the efficiency and economy of steel cables does not make them more frequently used in smaller structures. The limitations in the application of cables stem directly from their adaptability to changing loads: cables are unstable, and stability is one of the basic requirements of structural systems. The trusses hanging from the cables of a suspension bridge have the purpose not only of supporting the roadway but also of stiffening the cables against motions due to changing or moving loads.

Stiffening trusses are usually rigid in the direction of the bridge axis, but less so in a transverse direction: this explains the fairly large displacements of suspension bridges caused by lateral winds. Moreover, the long roadway and the shallow trusses constitute a thin ribbon, so flexible in the vertical direction that it may develop a tendency to twist and oscillate vertically under steady winds (see Section 2.6). Modern suspension bridges are made safe against such dangers by the introduction of stiffening guy wires (like those used in the Brooklyn Bridge in New York, designed in 1867) and by an increase in the bending and twisting rigidity of their roadway cross section.

In so-called **stayed bridges** of the "harp" or "fan" type [Fig. 6.8(a), (b)] the guy wires, or **stays,** have the double role of supporting the truss and of stabilizing it. Their elegance and economy has made them popular for middle-range spans.

A cable is not a self-supporting structure unless ways and means are found to absorb its tension, which in large spans may reach values of the order of millions of pounds. In suspension-bridge design this result is achieved by channeling the tension of the main-span over the towers to the side spans, and by anchoring the cables in the ground. The heavy anchoring blocks of reinforced concrete are usually poured into rock, and resist tension both by the action of their own weight and by the reaction of the adjoining rock (Fig. 6.9). Under these circumstances the optimal sag to minimize the cost of the entire structure is approximately 1/12 of the span, since a 3/10 sag-span ratio leads to very tall, expensive towers. Compression in the towers, bending in the trusses, and shear in the anchorages are essential to the stability and strength of the tensile cables of suspension bridges. In **self-anchored** bridges the cables are anchored to the ends of the stiffening trusses thus compressing them, while the ends of the trusses are anchored to the piers to develop downward reactions (see Fig. 6.7).

More complex cable structures and other tensile structures are considered in Section 6.2.

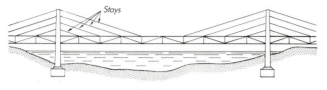

Stays

Harp type

(a)

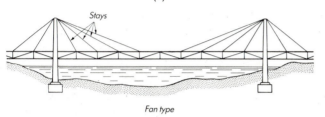

Stays

Fan type

(b)

6.8 Stayed bridges.

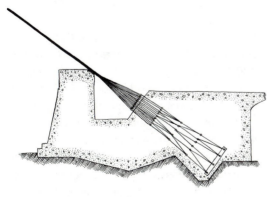

6.9 Anchorage of suspension bridge cables.

6.2 Cable Roofs

The exceptional efficiency of steel cables suggests their use in the construction of large roofs. This relatively recent development has brought about a number of new solutions, in which tensile cables are the basic element in what may be otherwise a complex structural system. All these solutions are essentially aimed at stabilizing the cable system.

The simplest tensile roof consists of a series of cables hanging from the tops of columns or buttresses, capable of bending resistance, or passing over the tops of compressive struts and anchored to the ground. Straight beams or plates connect the parallel cables, thus creating a polygonal or inverted barrel roof surface (Fig. 6.10). The simplicity and low cost of this suspension-bridge scheme would make it popular, but for the fact that the straight elements connecting the cables are usually light and tend to oscillate or "flutter" under the action of the wind. To avoid flutter, the roofing material must be relatively heavy, or the cables must be stabilized by guy wires or stiffening trusses.

The suspension-bridge principle has been adopted in a structure designed by Nervi and Covre for a manufacturing plant (Fig. 6.11). The reinforced concrete towers of each roof section (100 feet wide and 830 feet long) are inclined posts supported by shorter compression struts. The horizontal roof consists of reinforced concrete beams and slabs, prefabricated on the ground, and is suspended from the cables by means of wire hangers. This structure permitted the economic roofing of areas of 10,000 square feet without intermediate supports. The peripheral walls are independent of the roof structure and must be supported by vertical columns capable of resisting the wind forces. The relatively heavy horizontal concrete roof acts as stiffening truss and, moreover, stabilizes the cables by its own weight.

116

6.10 Polygonal cable roof.

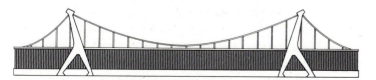

6.11 Suspension-bridge roof.

A similar principle was used by Saarinen in the Yale University skating rink (Fig. 6.12). The cables are suspended from a central arch, with inverted curvature at the ends, and are anchored to the heavy, peripheral, curved walls of the rink. The roofing material is wood: its relatively light weight does not stabilize the cables entirely.

The solution suggested by Nowicki for the roof of the Raleigh, North Carolina, arena consisted of two inclined intersecting arches of concrete, supported by and tensioning by their weight a series of main cables (Fig. 6.13). Cables at right angles to the main cables formed a mesh on which a tent roof could slide. In its present form, the roofing consists of lightweight corrugated metal plates, permanently anchored to the cable mesh. The arches, essentially supported by vertical columns, resist in compression the thrust of the upward curved main cables, which are stabilized by the tension of the downward curved cables. The surface defined by the cables resembles a saddle, and is more stable under wind loads than a barrel-shaped roof. Notwithstanding the shape of the roof, in order to avoid flutter of the lightweight corrugated plates, these had to be stabilized by guy wires connecting a number of internal mesh points to the outer vertical columns.

In designing the roof for a stadium in Montevideo, Uruguay, Viera invented an inexpensive stable system, well suited to roof large circular areas (Fig. 6.14). In this roof a series of radial cables connects a lower, central tension ring of steel to an outer compression ring of concrete, which is supported by the thin, cylindrical, exterior concrete wall of the stadium. The decking consists of a large number of prefabricated, wedge-shaped concrete slabs, which are supported on the radial cables by the hooked ends of their own reinforcing bars. To reduce instability, the slabs are first loaded with a ballast of bricks or sandbags, temporarily over-tensing the cables, and then the radial and circumferential gaps between the slabs are filled with cement mortar. Once the mortar sets, the entire roof becomes a monolithic concrete "dish." When the temporary ballast is taken off the dish, the cables tend to shorten, but are prevented from doing so by the monolithic concrete roof in which they are embedded (see also Section 12.7). The inverted roof is thus prestressed by the cables, and shows little tendency to flutter. Similar roofs, like that of Madison Square Garden in New York City, have been successfully and economically built in the United States and elsewhere on this principle, which Viera has also applied to suspension bridge design. The drainage of the Viera type roofs is obtained by pumping the rainwater to drain pipes located on the outer rim of the roof.

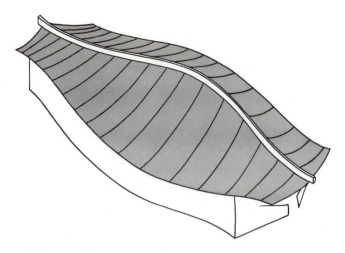

6.12 Cable roof with arch rib.

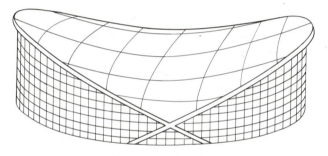

6.13 Cable roof with saddle shape.

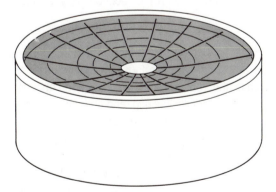

6.14 Viera's prestressed cable roof.

In the design of airplane hangars it is essential to provide large front doors which slide open smoothly. These sliding doors cannot be supported by columns and are usually hung from a top beam, longer than the hangar opening. The structural problem to be solved for this type of building consists in covering a rectangular area having columns on not more than three of its sides. A solution, realized by Ammann and Whitney, uses a scheme in which a cantilevered span is equilavent to one half of a stayed bridge (Fig. 6.15). The space between "tower" and "anchorage" is used for offices or shops, while the cable-supported cantilevered roof consists of "folded-plate" reinforced concrete construction (see Section 10.7). The limited weight and high resistance to bending and compression of folded plates, together with the tensile strength of cables, make such structures capable of economically cantilevering as much as 125 feet.

A similar solution has been adopted by Tippets-Abbett-McCarthy and Stratton in roofing the Pan-American arrival building at John F. Kennedy International Airport in New York. In this case the roof consists of reinforced-concrete plates supported by radial beams, an outer elliptical ring, and an inner elliptical ring (Fig. 6.16). The beams are cantilevered from the outer ring, and supported by cable stays going over compression struts at the outer ring, and anchored at the inner ring. The outer ring is supported by compression columns; the inner ring is anchored to tension struts attached to heavy concrete blocks in the ground. The cantilevers, 150 feet long, permit the sheltering of the planes during the embarkation and debarkation of the passengers.

120

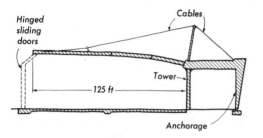

6.15 Cable-suspended cantilevered roof.

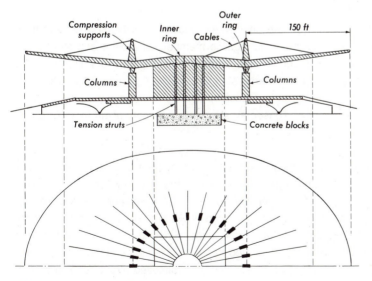

6.16 Cable-suspended elliptical roof.

In 1948 the sculptor Kenneth Snelson exhibited his first **Tensegrity** sculpture, consisting of a space truss with tensile members of prestressed steel cable and compressive members of steel pipe. In the following years his sculptures assumed the dimensions of large structures (Figs. 6.17 and 6.18). The Tensegrity principle has been successfully applied to large tensile roofs since 1955, but the theory of Tensegrity structures was only given in 1972 by G. Minke.

A notable example of such a structure, built by means of radial tensile elements, and tensile and compressive rings, is the bicycle wheel. The two sets of spokes are tensed between the tensile circular hub and the compressed circular rim, forming a structure with high "locked-in" stresses, which is stable against both in-plane and transverse loads. Since the circle is the funicular curve for a compression arch acted upon by radial forces (see Section 6.4), the entire (unloaded) wheel is a funicular prestressed structure. The roof of the auditorium in Utica, New York, designed by Zetlin in 1955, is based on the

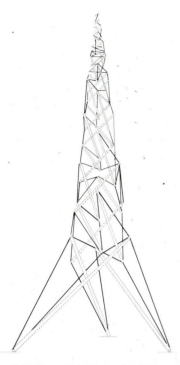

6.17 Tensegrity Tower by Snelson at the Hirschorn Museum, Washington, D.C.

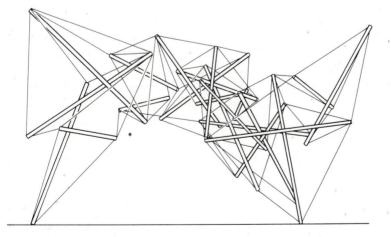

6.18 Tensegrity sculpture by Snelson at the Storm King Art Center, Mountainville, N.Y.

bicycle-wheel principle (Fig. 6.19). Two series of cables, of different cross section, connect the outer compression ring to the upper and lower rims of a central hub, consisting of two seperate tension rings connected by a truss system. The cables are kept separate and post-tensioned by compression struts of adjustable length. Each pair of cables can be correctly tensed by turning the turnbuckles of the struts, and the roof, covered by a series of prefabricated metal plates, is practically free of flutter because the high tension in the cables makes them more rigid than if they were free-hanging.

David Geiger designed Tensegrity **domes** spanning up to 800 feet, the first of which for St. Petersburg, Florida, covers a circular stadium with a seating capacity of 43,000 people and a diameter of 680 feet. Its structure consists of radial trusses (see Section 6.3) with diagonals and chords of steel cables, prestressed against verticals of steel piping, which span between an inner tensile ring of steel and an outer compressive ring of reinforced concrete (Fig. 6.20). The vertical pipes, sheathing the continuous cables, are supported by the tensed diagonals, and kept vertical by concentric steel rings connected to their foot and inclined stays connected to their top of concentric steel rings. Radial tensed cables, running between the compression and the tension rings along the vertical pipes' bottoms, constitute the lower chords of the trusses. Similar radial cables (the "ridge cables") running along their tops constitute the upper chords of the trusses (Fig. 6.21). The prestress in the radial ridge cables increases the tension in the lower chords due to the roof loads, and is high enough to wipe out the compression in the upper chords due to these loads. A third set of prestressed radial cables (the "valley cables") runs from the compression to the tension ring along the "valleys" formed by the intersections of the inclined stays at the concentric steel rings (Fig. 6.21). All the components of the structure can be bought "off the shelf." The roof ondulated surface is a membrane of silicone fiberglass fabric wrapped over and attached to the ridge and valley cables. Since the tension ring is at a higher level than the compression ring, these roofs are **shallow tensile domes** similar in principle to "bicycle-wheel" roofs. They can also be considered as membrane roofs supported by trusses rather than air pressure: elimination of the fan system and the revolving doors reduces the cost of these roofs in comparison with that of pneumatic roofs (see also Section 12.14).

Pneumatic roofs present one of the most interesting applications of cables to the reinforcing and stiffening of membranes. They consist of air-supported or air-inflated plastic fabrics stretched over a network of cables and can span hundreds of feet. They are described in detail in Section 11.3.

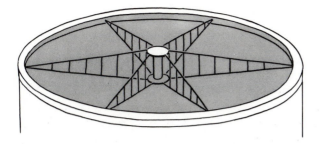

6.19 Bicycle-wheel roof of Utica, N.Y., auditorium.

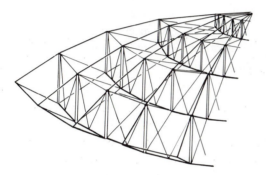

6.20 Geiger's tensile dome, St. Petersburg, Fla.

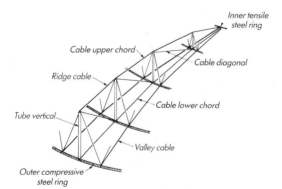

6.21 Tensegrity trusses of Geiger's tensile dome.

125

The tensile solutions mentioned above are just a few of the most recently adopted to roof large areas. Whereas the largest span covered by a compressive roof, to date, is 760 feet [in the C.N.I.T. double concrete shell in Paris (see Section 12.7)], tensile roofs can easily span much larger distances. In view of the exceptional potentialities of cable roofs it is to be expected that their use will increase with the increasing dimensions of the areas to be covered.

6.3 Trusses

A flexible cable supporting a load at midspan was found to be a pure tensile structure [Fig. 6.22(a)]. Consider now the structure obtained by flipping the cable up and stiffening its inclined sides to make them capable of resisting compression. The "negative sag" or **rise** changes the nature of the stresses, and the upped cable becomes a pure compressive structure: it is the simplest example of a **truss** [Fig. 6.22(b)].

The load at the top of the truss is channeled by the compressed struts to the supports, which are acted upon by downward forces equal to half the load, and by **outward** thrusts [Fig. 6.22(b)]. The thrust can be absorbed by buttresses of a compressive material, such as masonry, or by a tensile element, such as a wood or a steel **tie-rod** (see Fig. 3.9). Such elementary trusses, of wood with iron tie-rods, were built in the Middle Ages to support the roofs of churches, and there is reason to believe that the Greek temples were covered by wooden structures of similar design. As spans became larger, it was found practical to hang the tie-rod from the top of the truss to eliminate the large sag of this relatively flexible element (see Fig. 3.9). A similar triangular truss may be built with a "positive sag," using steel rods for the tensile bars and wood for the compressive "tie-rod" (Fig. 6.23).

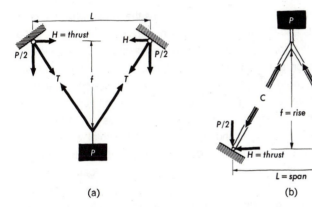

(a)　　　　　　　　　　(b)

6.22 Triangular truss.

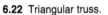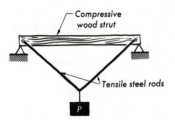

6.23 Truss with compressive strut.

Trusses capable of spanning large distances by means of tension and compression elements only are obtained by combining triangular elementary trusses, whose bars are considered **hinged,** that is, free to rotate at their ends. For example, if two triangular trusses with their vertices down are joined at an upper **joint** [Fig. 6.24(a)], they cannot support a load unless a tensile bar prevents the vertices from moving apart. A truss with two triangular fields capable of spanning a greater distance is thus obtained [Fig. 6.24(b)]. A similarly built triangulated truss with the bars of the **upper chord** and the **verticals** in compression, and the bars of the **lower chord** and the **diagonals** in tension is shown in Fig. 6.25. The middle load W_1 is channeled along the tension diagonals to the upper points A and B. (The dashed vertical OO' does not carry load, because at O' the horizontal forces of bars O'A and O'B could not equilibrate it.) The compressive upper tie-rod AB absorbs the thrust, while the compressed verticals AC and BD transfer the vertical reactions at A and B, equal to half W_1, down to the points C and D. The tension diagnol CE channels both the transferred reaction at C and the additional load W_2 to E, and introduces tension in the lower chord member CO. The compression tie-rod EA absorbs the thrust at E, and the compressed vertical EG transfers the vertical reaction to G. This channeling mechanism occurs in all other panels of the truss until the last compressed verticals, IL and MN, carry half the total weight of the truss to each support L and N. If, as is desirable, the loads on the truss are applied only at the **panel points** O, C, D, etc., and the dead load of the truss members is negligible, all the truss members are only tensed or compressed. When loads are applied **between** the panel points and the dead load is not negligible, the truss bars develop some bending also (see Section 7.4).

It is sufficient to reverse the inclination of the diagonals to have these bars work in compression, and the verticals in tension. Thus, in Fig. 6.26 the load W_1 is transferred up by the tensioned vertical from O to O', and down the compression diagonals from O' to C and D. CD is a tension tie-rod. The triangular truss CO'D rests on the adjoining panels at C and D; here the additional loads W_2 and W_3 are picked up, transferred to A and B by the tension verticals, and down the compression diagonals to G and H. The diagonals GA and HB compress the bars AO' and O'B. CG and DH are again tension tie-rods. The channeling of the loads may be continued until the last compression diagonals carry the load to the supports. In this truss the verticals IL, MN, and the last upper chord bars are unnecessary. Similarly, the end verticals and the last lower chord bars would have been unstressed if the truss of Fig. 6.25 had been supported at I and M. The scheme of Fig. 6.26 is commonly used in highway bridges, that of Fig. 6.25 in railroad bridges, where the truss is often below the roadway. Additional insight on truss behavior may be gained by analogy with beam behavior, as shown in Section 7.2.

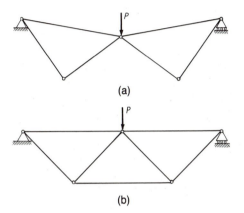

(a)

(b)

6.24 Truss built of two triangular trusses.

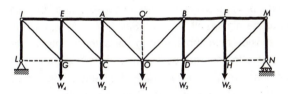

6.25 Triangulated truss with tensed diagonals.

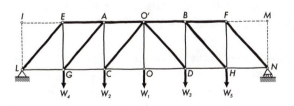

6.26 Triangulated truss with compressed diagonals.

Upper chord members, verticals, and diagonals may buckle under compression unless properly designed. One of the first studies on the buckling of trussed bridge structures was prompted by the failure in buckling of a Russian railroad bridge at the end of the nineteenth century. Since, moreover, moving loads may produce either tension or compression in the same member, depending on their location, some trusses are built with both tension and compression diagonals, so that loads may be always carried by tension diagonals with purposedly slender compression diagonals inactive when buckled.

The combinations of tension and compression bars capable of producing practical trusses are extremely varied. The reader may wish to follow the channeling mechanism in the elementary examples given in Figs. 6.27(a) and 6.27(b), and thus visualize how such structures work.

The bars of a truss are joined by being riveted, bolted, or welded to a "gusset plate" at their intersection (Fig. 6.28). In either case the restraint against relative rotation produced by the gusset plates transforms the truss bars from pure tension or compression members into elements developing a minor amount of additional bending and shear stresses. These so called **secondary stresses** are considered in Section 7.4.

130

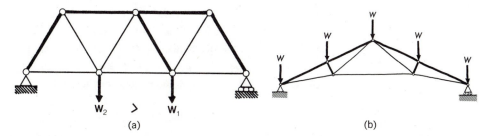

(a)

(b)

6.27 Load channeling of trusses.

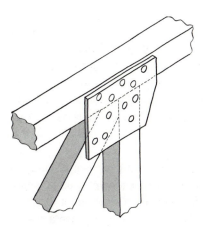

6.28 Gusset plate.

6.29 Composite truss bridge.

Trusses are used in bridge design to span hundreds of feet between supports. They may be cantilevered from piers and in turn carry other simply supported trusses (Fig. 6.29). Bridge trusses with curved top chords behave very much like suspension bridges (Fig. 6.30). Parallel trusses are commonly used in steel design to cover large halls (Fig. 6.31). **Open web joists** are "off the shelf" light trusses used to span small distances, either as roof or as floor structures (Fig. 6.32). Vertical trusses are used in highrise steel buildings to stiffen their frames against wind and earthquake forces (see Section 8.3).

Although not as popular today as they were in the 1800s, at the beginning of the structural steel era, trusses are to this day one of the essential components of large structures.

6.4 Funicular Arches

The parabolic shape assumed by a tensed cable carrying loads uniformly distributed horizontally may be inverted to give the ideal shape for an arch developing only compression under this type of load (Fig. 6.33). The arch is an essentially compressive structure; it was developed in the shape of a half-circle by the Romans, the greatest road builders of antiquity, to span large distances, but it is also used in a variety of shapes to span smaller distances. The arch is one of the basic structural elements of all types of architecture.

The ideal shape of an arch capable of supporting a given set of loads by means of simple compression may always be found as the overturned shape of the funicular polygon for the corresponding tension structure: it is by this method that the Spanish architect Gaudí determined the form of the arches in the Church of the Sacred Family in Barcelona.

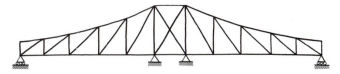

6.30 Truss with curved top chord.

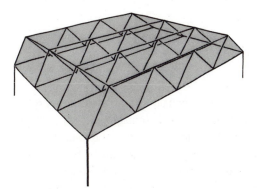

6.31 Parallel-chord truss roof.

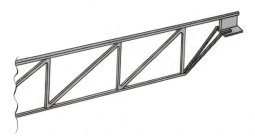

6.32 Open web joist.

6.33 Funicular arch.

The funicular polygon for a set of equal and equally spaced loads **converging toward** or **diverging from** a common point is a regular polygon, centered about this point [Fig. 6.34 (a) and (b)]. At the limit, when the loads become infinite in number and infinitesimally small, the funicular polygon becomes the funicular curve for a **radial pressure** or **suction,** and is a circle [Fig. 6.34 (c)]. Since arches can obviously be funicular for only the set of loads, the circle cannot be the funicular curve for a vertical load uniformly distributed either along the horizontal or along the circular arch. Hence, the Roman arch develops some bending and, although a compression structure, is not **uniformly** compressed across its depth.

The shape of a masonry arch is usually chosen to be the funicular of the dead load. But whenever an arch is used in a bridge, a variety of moving loads must be assumed to travel over the arch, and a state of stress other than simple compression is bound to develop; the arch also develops some bending stresses. A cable can carry any set of loads in tension by changing shape; a rigid arch cannot change shape and, hence, cannot be funicular for all the loads it is supposed to carry. The stability of the arch implies lack of adaptability. The relative importance of bending stresses in arches is considered in Section 8.4.

The channeling of vertical loads along a curve by means of compression is today such an elementary concept that it is hard to realize how slow its evolution has been. Practically unknown to the Greeks, it produced the daring and lovely lines of the Gothic cathedrals as well as those of modern bridges (see Section 8.4). The ultimate consequences of the use of **curved** structural elements are even more recent and interesting: they are considered in Chapters 11 and 12.

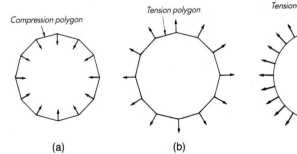

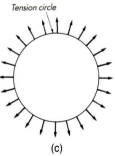

6.34 Funicular polygon for equal radial loads.

Chapter Seven

Beams

7.1 Cantilevered Beams

Since a majority of loads are vertical and a majority of usable surfaces horizontal, structural elements are commonly needed to transfer vertical loads horizontally. Beams are such elements. Their mechanism involves a combination of bending and shear. **Cantilevered beams** will be considered first.

By experimenting with a thin steel ruler clamped between the fingers, the reader may verify the following facts:

(a) The deflection of the loaded tip of the cantilevered ruler increases rapidly with the cantilevered length; doubling the length increases the deflection by a factor of eight, which is the cube of the lengths ratio (Fig. 7.1).

(b) The tip deflection is much larger when the width of the ruler is kept horizontal than when it is kept vertical. Accurate measurements show that the deflection is inversely proportional to the horizontal side of the ruler's cross section, and to the **cube** of its vertical side. If the ruler has a width of two and a thickness of one, in the first case the deflection is inversely proportional to 2 times 1 cubed, i.e., 2; in the second to 1 times 2 cubed, i.e., 8: the deflections are four times smaller in the second case than in the first (Fig. 7.2).

(c) The deflections under the same load of two identical rulers made of different materials, such as steel and aluminum, are inversely proportional to the elastic moduli of the materials. The aluminum ruler deflects three times as much as the steel ruler (Fig. 7.3).

(d) Finally, the tip deflection of the cantilevered ruler increases as the load moves from the root toward the tip of the cantilever (Fig. 7.4).

7.1 Influence of length on cantilever deflection.

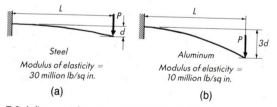

7.2 Influence of depth and width on cantilever deflection.

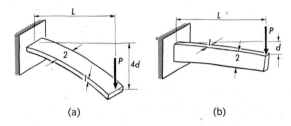

Steel
Modulus of elasticity =
30 million lb/sq in.

(a)

Aluminum
Modulus of elasticity =
10 million lb/sq in.

(b)

7.3 Influence of material on cantilever deflection.

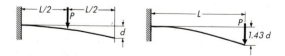

7.4 Influence of load location on cantilever deflection.

Another geometrical factor influences the magnitude of the beam deflections and merits detailed consideration: the shape of the beam's cross section. We shall first consider a beam of rectangular cross section.

The deflection of the loaded tip of the cantilever is due to the deformation of the originally straight beam into a slightly curved element. Such deformation requires the elongation of the upper fibers and the shortening of the lower fibers of the beam, and produces the state of stress defined in Section 5.4 as **simple bending**. The bending stresses in a cantilever beam vary linearly from a maximum tensile value at the top fibers to a maximum compressive value at the bottom fibers, and vanish at the middle fibers, the so-called **neutral axis** of the beam [Fig. 7.5(a)]. The load, through its lever arm about any section of the cantilever, tends to rotate the beam clockwise; the bending stresses, through the lever arm of their "resultants" T and C (which equals two-thirds of the beam depth h), tend to rotate the beam counterclockwise, and establish equilibrium in rotation [Fig. 7.5(b)]. The deeper the beam, the larger the lever arm of the bending stresses; hence, for a given value of the allowable stress at the top and bottom fibers, the deeper beam is capable of equilibrating a larger load. Since stresses are constant across the width of the beam, an increase in depth is more profitable than an increase in width: how profitable is shown by the decrease in deflection with the **cube** of the depth (see Fig. 7.2).

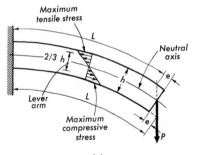

(a)

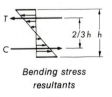

Bending stress
resultants

(b)

7.5 Bending of cantilever beam.

The behavior described above is typical of beams with a length at least **twice** their depth. **Deep beams,** that is, beams with a length less than twice their depth, support the load mostly by shear and do not exhibit a linear variation of stress across their depth.

From the viewpoint of use of material a beam of rectangular cross section is obviously inefficient in bending, since most of its fibers are not stressed up to the allowable stress; usually, only its top and bottom fibers at one section reach maximum values, while all other fibers are unavoidably understressed. This cross-sectional inefficiency can be remedied by relocating most of the beam material near the top and bottom of the beam. The cross section of an I beam or of a "W section" (as rolled steel sections are usually called), with most of the material in **flanges** connected by a thin **web,** has this characteristic (Fig. 7.6). The large areas of the flanges develop maximum tensile and compressive stresses up to the allowable limit with a lever arm almost equal to the full depth of the beam, and contribute substantially to the bending action. The smaller web area is nearer the neutral axis and contributes negligibly to bending. If **all** the material of a beam of rectangular cross section could be shifted toward its top and bottom, creating an "ideal I section" without web, its rigidity would increase by a factor of three (see also page 150). This means that deflections and stresses would decrease by a factor of three, or, to put it the other way around, that the beam could support three times as much load with the same allowable stress and deflection (Fig. 7.7).

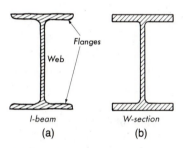

7.6 Rolled steel sections.

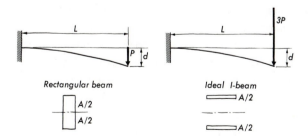

7.7 Variation of strength with cross-section shape.

Splitting the web of an I beam in two and shifting the material laterally produces another cross section just as efficient in bending and more efficient in torsion, the "box section" (Fig 7.8). The symmetrical I section and the box section are typical of materials with equal strength in tension and compression; different shapes become more logical when these strengths differ. For example, the compressive strength of concrete is approximately one-tenth of the tensile strength of structural steel; hence, in a reinforced concrete beam the area of the compressed concrete must be much larger than the area of the tensed steel. This leads to a T section, in which the horizontal compression flange is made of concrete, and the steel is concentrated in the web. In the case of cantilevered beams, the T beam is inverted: the flange is at the bottom and the web at the top of the beam, since the compressed fibers are at the bottom of the beam (Fig. 7.9). The reinforced-concrete T beam acts very much like an I beam in which the area of one of the flanges is shrunk because its material is stronger, but T beams of steel, obtained by connecting two "angles" or cutting an I section in two, are also used, mainly to facilitate connections with other beams (Fig. 7.10).

The bending stiffness of a cross-sectional shape is gauged by a quantity called its **moment of inertia**. The moment of inertia is proportional to the area of the cross section, i.e., to the amount of material used, but also, and more significantly, to the square of a length, called its **radius of gyration,** that measures the moving of the material away from the neutral axis. The deflections and bending stresses in a beam are inversely proportional to the moment of inertia of its cross section. Moments of inertia for various types of cross sections appear in standard section tables, so that the designer can gauge the strength and rigidity of a given beam without lengthy calculations.

The bending stresses and deflections of a cantilever depend on the location of the loads. The greater the lever arm of the load, the greater the bending stresses (tension and compression) it produces, since for equilibrium in rotation (see Section 4.2) the moment of the tension and compression forces must equal the moment of the load (see Fig. 7.5). Consequently, the largest stresses occur at the root of the cantilever, the point farthest from the load, where the load develops the largest moment. For example, if the same total load instead of being applied at the tip of the cantilever is evenly distributed over the beam, the bending stresses are reduced in the ratio of two to one and the deflections in the ratio of eight to three (Fig. 7.11).

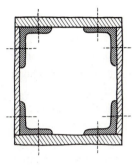

7.8 Box section.

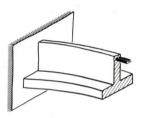

7.9 Reinforced-concrete T section.

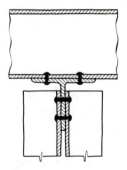

7.10 T beam connection.

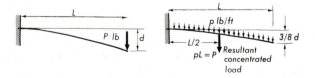

7.11 Deflections due to concentrated and distributed loads.

The influence of the lever arm of the load on the stresses introduces another type of inefficiency in the bending mechanism of beams, even when I sections are used. The I section was seen to stress most of the section fibers to maximum value. But these maximum stresses can equal the allowable stress only at the **most stressed** beam section, that is, at the root; elsewhere the stresses are bound to be smaller because the lever arm of the load is smaller. Maximum stresses are developed only in the top and bottom fibers of a small portion of the beam near its root, while everywhere else even the extreme fibers of the beam are understressed. Efficiency may be restored somewhat by varying the cross section of the beam from its tip to its root. Although this is not practical for small cantilevers, it becomes mandatory for large ones. The change in section may be obtained either by increasing the area of the flanges from tip to root while maintaining the beam depth constant, or by maintaining the area of the flanges constant but increasing the beam depth, or by increasing both the flange area and the beam depth (Fig. 7.12). Thus, as the lever arm of the load increases, either the tensile and compressive **forces** in the flanges increase or else their lever arm also increases, keeping the beam in equilibrium without a substantial increase in **stress**. The sloping bottom of tapered cantilever beams is the visual evidence of the increased lever arm of the flange forces necessary to counterbalance the increasing lever arm of the loads.

Whenever depth limitations permit, it is economical to set the flanges of an I beam as far apart as possible, thus reducing their area to a minimum, but it must be also remembered that **any** thin compressed element has a tendency to buckle (see Section 5.2). If the compression flange or the web of an I beam is too thin, it may buckle. The compression flange buckles by bending out in its own horizontal plane, since the web prevents its otherwise easier buckling in a vertical plane. When the web buckles its compressed fibers, located below the neutral axis, bend out of the vertical plane. In either case the cross section of the beam rotates and the beam twists (Fig. 7.13). Such buckling of an entire cross section, due to the buckling in compression of some of its fibers, may take place during construction when very long I beams are gripped at midspan and lifted, so that each half of the beam acts as a cantilever. In order to prevent this bending-and-twisting buckling, called **lateral buckling,** the beam cross section must be sufficiently strong in horizontal bending and in torsion (see Section 5.3).

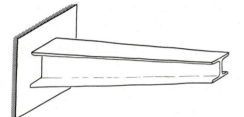

7.12 Tapered cantilevered beam.

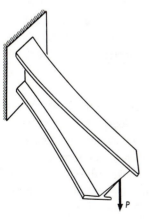

P

7.13 Lateral buckling.

So far only the bending effects of a tip load have been considered. But as pointed out in Section 5.3, this load also tends to shear the beam, for example, at the point where it is clamped into the supporting wall. Actually the tendency to shear occurs everywhere in the beam and is independent of the beam length: if the beam were clamped nearer its tip, the load would have the same tendency to shear it there (Fig. 7.14). When the load is evenly distributed on the cantilever instead of being concentrated at its tip, the amount of load on the beam, and hence the tendency to shear, increases from the tip to the root of the beam (Fig. 7.15).

The presence of vertical shear in the beam becomes evident if one notices that a vertically sliced beam is unable to carry vertical loads, but that its carrying capacity is restored if the vertical slices are sewed together by horizontal wires, so as to prevent their relative sliding. The reader may perform an experiment of the same nature by trying to lift a row of books: he will not be able to do so unless he presses the books together, thus creating between them a large amount of friction, that is, shear, which prevents their sliding (Fig. 7.16).

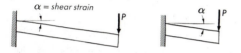

7.14 Deformation due to shear only.

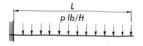

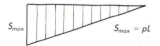

7.15 Shear distribution along cantilever beam uniformly loaded.

7.16 Vertical shear in a row of books.

It was shown in Section 5.3 that vertical shear is always accompanied by horizontal shear (see Fig. 5.12). The influence of horizontal shear on the rigidity of a rectangular beam may be visualized by considering the beam "sliced" horizontally into a number of rectangular beams of limited depth. Under the action of a tip load, this assemblage of superimposed beams presents large deflections, because each slice, free to slide with respect to the others, acts as a shallow, flexible beam (Fig. 7.17). The sliding of the various slices shows the tendency of the beam fibers to shear along horizontal planes. This tendency is prevented by shear stresses along the horizontal planes, obtained either by gluing the various slices together or by sticking vertical pins across the entire depth of the parallel slices. When shear resistance is developed, the slices act as a single beam, and the deflections under the same load are considerably reduced. Remembering that the moment of inertia of a rectangular beam is proportional to the cube of its depth, the ratio between the moment of inertia of the monolithic beam, considered of depth equal to one, and that of four identical slices of depth one-fourth, equals the ratio between the cube of one, which is one, and four times the cube of one-fourth, which is four times one sixty-fourth or one-sixteenth; the monolithic beam is sixteen times more rigid than the separate four slices (Fig. 7.17).

The essential function of the web in the I section is to develop the shear stresses necessary to have the two flanges work together. Without web, each flange of an "ideal I beam" would act as a **separate** shallow beam, and the moment of inertia of the cross section would be small. The flanges connected by the web act monolithically so that the I section acquires a large moment of inertia. It is thus seen that **the transmission of shear through the web from flange to flange is essential to the bending action of the flanges,** and that shear and bending are interdependent beam actions.

The bending stresses are distributed linearly across the depth of the beam section whatever its cross-sectional shape (see Fig. 7.5). The shear stresses may be shown to be distributed parabolically across the depth of a rectangular beam, with a maximum value at the neutral axis (Fig. 7.18) This maximum is one and a half times the average shear stress, that is, one and a half times the shear force divided by the area of the cross section. In I beams bending action is essentially provided by the flanges and shear action by the web: the maximum shear stress is approximately equal to the load divided by the area of the web. The shear stresses increase from the tip to the root in proportion to the accumulated load, and hence are usually maximum at the root (see Fig. 7.15).

150

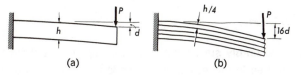

7.17 Superimposed shallow beams.

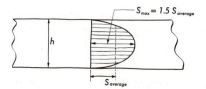

7.18 Shear-stress distribution across rectangular beam depth.

7.2 Simply Supported Beams

A beam is said to be **simply supported** when it is supported at both ends, so that its ends are free to rotate, **and** the beam is free to expand or contract longitudinally (Fig. 7.19).

A simply supported beam transfers a load applied at midspan half to one support and half to the other. It bends and deflects. Because of symmetry, the midspan section moves downward but remains vertical. Hence, each half of the beam acts as an upside-down cantilever half the length of the beam, loaded by half the load at its tip (Fig. 7.20). Since cantilever deflections are proportional to the tip load and to the cube of the length (see Section 7.1), the deflection of the simply supported beam is one-half of one-eighth, or one-sixteenth that of a cantilever of equal length under the same load at its tip. By the same token, the half load reaction acting through a lever arm half the length of the beam produces maximum bending stresses one-fourth of those in the cantilever. A simply supported beam is stronger and stiffer than a cantilever of the same length: it can carry at mid-span a load four times as large and will deflect only one-fourth as much under this larger load than the tip-loaded cantilever.

When the same load is evenly distributed over the beam, the stresses in the beam become one-half and the deflections five-eighths as large as when the load is concentrated at midspan (Fig. 7.21).

In a uniformly loaded beam the bending stresses are also **maximum at midspan,** the point corresponding to the roots of the two half beams considered as upside-down cantilevers. The shearing action is maximum in the neighborhood of the supports, where the support reactions tend to move the beam up while the **total** load tends to move it down. The shear **vanishes at midspan,** where there is no tendency for adjoining sections to slide either up or down with respect to one another. The vanishing of the shearing action at the point where bending stresses are greatest is a characteristic of beam behavior for any and all types of beams.

152

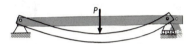

7.19 Simply supported beam.

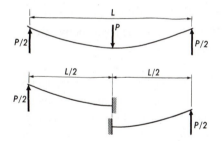

7.20 Concentrated load on simply supported beam.

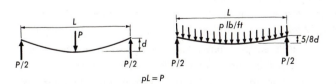

$$pL = P$$

7.21 Distributed load on simply supported beam.

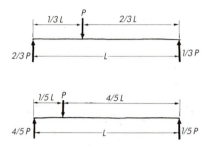

7.22 Reactions due to unsymmetrical load.

Unsymmetrical loads produce similar bending and shearing actions in a simply supported beam. Concentrated loads near the supports have a reduced bending influence, owing to the reduction of their lever arms, but an increased shearing effect. In fact, as a load approaches one of the supports, a larger fraction of the load is transferred to this support, while the other is gradually unloaded (Fig. 7.22). When the load is in the immediate neighborhood of a support, the shearing force equals the total load, whereas it was equal to only half the load when the load was at midspan.

It was noted in Section 5.3 that shear may be considered as a combination of tension and compression at right angles. The presence of maximum shearing effects near the supports of a beam is clearly shown by 45-degree cracks appearing near the supports of reinforced-concrete beams that have inadequate shear reinforcement. Isolating a beam element in this region and applying to it the corresponding shear stresses or the equivalent tensile and compressive stresses at 45 degrees (see Section 5.3), it is seen that the cracks are perpendicular to the direction of the equivalent tensile stress (Fig. 7.23). In order to avoid them, reinforcing bars must be added toward the supports, running at a 45-degree angle and capable of absorbing the tensile stresses due to shear [Fig. 7.24(a)]. Alternatively, the horizontal shear stress may be resisted by "sewing together" horizontal beam layers by means of vertical steel hoops called **stirrups** [Fig. 7.24(b) and (c)]. Similarly, a beam element of the thin web of a steel beam near its support may buckle, as shown by a wavy deformation in a direction perpendicular to that of the equivalent compressive stresses. To prevent such buckling, the web must be strengthened by **vertical stiffeners** (Fig. 7.25).

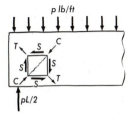

7.23 Shear cracks near beam supports.

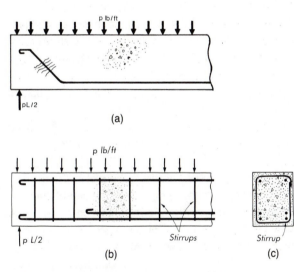

(a)

(b)

(c)

7.24 Reinforced concrete simply supported beam.

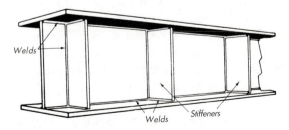

7.25 Plate girder with stiffeners.

The influence of the cross section's shape on stresses or deformations is the same for simply supported beams as for cantilevers or any other type of beam. Small beams may be built with a uniform cross section; large beams usually have a variable cross section, obtained by increasing the area of the flanges near the center of the beam (where the bending stresses are usually larger) rather than by increasing the depth of the beam at midspan. **Built-up girders** or **plate girders** are beams with variable flange areas, built of plates, and used to carry heavy loads over spans of fifty or more feet (see Fig. 7.25).

Simply supported beams under downward loads develop tension in the bottom fibers and compression in the top fibers. The reinforcing bars in a concrete simply supported beam run along its bottom and, if necessary, are increased in numbers or in area toward the center of the beam (see Fig. 7.24).

In steel beams the compressive stresses, usually highest at midspan, may produce lateral buckling of the upper flange and of the upper part of the web, thus causing a twist of the entire cross section. For example, one of the large rolled W sections used as beams in the United States is 36 inches deep and weighs 300 pounds per foot. (This section, when made out of high-strength structural steel, may carry a load of 6000 pounds per foot, besides its own dead load, over a span of 50 feet) The largest distance such a W section could span is one for which the beam carries safely its own dead load, but no additional live load. For an allowable bending stress of 30,000 pounds per square inch this maximum span is 271 feet. But this distance can be spanned only if the twisting of the beam in buckling is prevented by the restraint of adjoining structural elements, such as transverse beams or slabs. When the beam is free to twist, the danger of lateral buckling reduces the maximum span to about **one-half** the previous value, or 150 feet.

Twisting action is also induced by loads displaced sideways over the upper flange of a beam, due to their lever arm with respect to the web (Fig. 7.26).

7.26 Twist producing loads.

The large amount of material inefficiently used in the neighborhood of the neutral axis of a beam suggests the elimination of some of it by cutouts, which would also make the beam lighter (Fig. 7.27). As the cutouts become larger, the beam gradually is transformed into a truss. Thus, in a truss considered as a beam with cutouts, the upper and lower chords act as the upper and lower flanges of an I beam, while the diagonals and the verticals absorb the shearing forces and act as a discontinuous web. By varying the distance between the chords, or by properly distributing the area of the chord members according to the variation of the bending action, and by locating the verticals according to the variation of the shear, trusses could be theoretically designed for maximum efficiency (Fig. 7.28), but, in practice, the verticals of a parallel chord truss are usually spaced equally for economy of fabrication.

Beams must be designed for stiffness as much as for strength. It is customary to limit beam deflections to about one 360th of their span in buildings, and one 800th in bridges. Thus a plate-girder bridge 200 feet long, should not deflect more than three inches under maximum loads, while a beam 30 feet long is unacceptable if it deflects more than 1.2 inches. When the dead load represents the largest share of loads, beams may be built with a **camber,** that is, an upward deflection equal to the downward deflection due to the dead load; the live load alone then induces smaller deflections, easily contained within acceptable limits.

Combinations of beams with different support conditions are often used to span long distances. The longest reinforced concrete bridge in the world, the Maracaibo Bridge in Venezuela, designed by Morandi, has main spans consisting of beams continuous over a support with cantilevered stayed sections, and of intermediate beams simply supported at the tip of the cantilevers (Fig. 7.29). Thus an efficient combination of tensile and bending structures allows the spanning of 1386 feet between towers, while the effects of thermal expansion are eliminated by the use of a rocker connection between the stayed and the cantilevered spans.

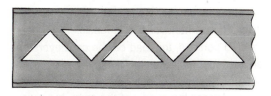

7.27 I-beam with openings.

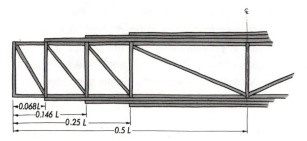

-0.068L-
--0.146 L--
---0.25 L---
----0.5 L----

7.28 Maximum-efficiency truss.

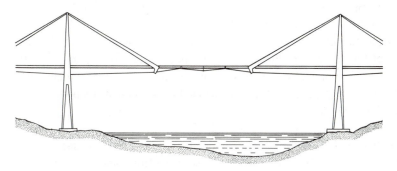

7.29 Combination of simply supported and stayed cantilevered beams.

7.3 Fixed Beams and Continuous Beams

It was noted in the preceding section that a uniformly loaded, simply supported beam is an inefficient structure, because the bending stresses in it reach their allowable value only in the extreme fibers at midspan, where the beam fibers, that have upward curvature all along the beam, present their greatest curvature (Fig. 7.30).

An obvious way of improving the beam efficiency would consist in shifting the supports toward the center of the span, whenever this is feasible. The beam would thus acquire two cantilevered portions, the load on the cantilevers balancing in part the load between the supports. When this is done, the deflection at midspan is reduced and the curvature near or over the supports reversed; the beam may or may not curve up toward the middle of the span, but always curves down toward its ends [Fig. 7.31(b), (c)].

It is interesting to examine the beam behavior as the length of the cantilevers decreases. When both supports become a single support at the midspan section, the two halves of the beam are cantilevered, and the curvature is down everywhere. The largest stresses occur at the support, and are equal and opposite in value to those developed at mid-span in the simply supported beam [Fig. 7.31(a)].

When the ratio of cantilevered length to supported span is 1 to 2, the center deflection is small but upward and the entire beam has still a downward curvature. The largest stresses occur over the supports, and are about four times smaller than those in the beam supported at the ends [Fig. 7.31(b)].

When the ratio of cantilever to span lengths is approximately 1 to 2.5 **the sections of the beam over the supports do not rotate;** the stresses over the supports are about twice the stresses at midspan but of opposite sign, and about five times smaller than the stresses in the same beam supported at the ends [Fig. 7.31(c)].

When the ratio of cantilever to span lengths is 1 to 3 the stresses over the supports are **equal** and opposite to those at midspan and about six times smaller than in the beam supported at the ends [Fig. 7.31(d)]. This is the **smallest value** of maximum stresses that may be obtained.

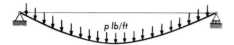

7.30 Deflected beam axis.

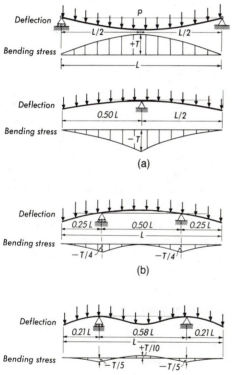

(a)

(b)

(c)

(d)

+T =Tension
−T =Compression

7.31 Bottom fiber stress T and deflections in beam with cantilevered ends.

When the ends of a beam are built into a **rigid** element and are thus prevented from rotating (but not from moving horizontally one relative to the other), the beam behaves as the supported span of a beam with cantilevers in the ratio of 1 to 2.5 [Fig. 7.31(c)]. Such a uniformly loaded, **fixed-end beam** has the largest bending stresses at the built-in ends. These stresses are twice as large as the stresses at midspan, and two-thirds as large as the stresses in the same span simply supported (Fig. 7.32). Provided the beam can develop tensile and compressive stresses both at top and bottom, it can carry a load **50 per cent higher than an identical simply supported beam** (whenever shear does not govern). Moreover, the fixed beam is **five times stiffer** than the simply supported beam: its midspan deflection is one-fifth that of the simply supported beam. Fixed beams of concrete must have the tensile reinforcement at the bottom near midspan, and at the top near the supports (Fig. 7.33).

The deflected axis of a fixed beam changes from downward to upward curvature at two points, called **inflection points,** where bending stresses vanish, and a stress reversal occurs [Fig. 7.32(b)]. The lack of bending stresses at inflection points indicates that the beam behaves as if it were simply supported at such points, since bending stresses vanish at the hinged ends of a simply supported beam. Thus a beam with fixed ends behaves as a simply supported beam of **shorter** span supported on two short cantilevers, and this explains its greater load capacity and its greater rigidity [Fig. 7.32(b)].

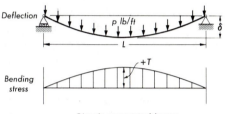

Simply supported beam

(a)

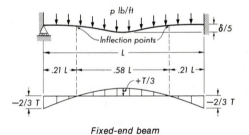

Fixed-end beam

(b)

7.32 Bottom fiber stress T and deflections in simply supported and fixed-end beams.

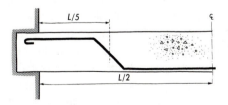

7.33 Fixed-end beam of reinforced concrete.

Fixed beams present the added advantage of a greater resistance to both longitudinal and lateral buckling when compressed. Whereas in a simply supported beam the top fibers are entirely compressed, in a fixed beam only about 58 per cent of their length is in compression at the top and 42 per cent at the bottom. Remembering that the buckling load is inversely proportional to the square of the compressed length, a compressed fixed beam and, hence, a fixed-end column are found to be four times as strong in longitudinal buckling as a simply supported beam or column (see Section 5.2). The resistance to **lateral** buckling is inversely proportional to the beam length between inflection points. A fixed beam is only about twice as strong against lateral buckling as an identical simply supported beam.

Simply supported and fixed-end beams present two extreme cases of support conditions. The first allows the unrestrained rotation of the beam ends; the second completely prevents such rotation. In practice, any intermediate condition may prevail. The wall into which the beam is built may not prevent the rotation entirely, or the beam may be continuous over more than two supports. In the last case each span, if cut from the others, usually deflects down and curves up as a simply supported beam [Fig. 7.34(a)]. Continuity with the other spans reverses the curvature near or over the supports and restrains the rotation of the ends common to two spans [Fig. 7.34(b)]. Depending on the relative lengths and rigidities of the beams in the various spans, the rotations at the supports are more or less prevented, and each beam develops stresses and deflections intermediate between those of simply supported and fixed-end spans.

The continuity of a beam over many supports introduces new characteristics in its behavior. If each span were simply supported and only one span were loaded, the load would be supported exclusively by the bending and shear stresses of the loaded span [Fig. 7.34(c)]. Continuity makes the loaded span stiffer by restraining its end rotations and introduces bending and shear in the unloaded spans. The entire beam participates in the load-carrying mechanism, and some of the load may be considered as transferred to the unloaded spans [Fig. 7.34(d)]

164

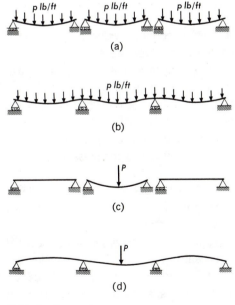

7.34 Continuous beam.

The stresses due to continuity peter out as one moves away from the loaded span. The curvature in the continuous beam is greatest **under** the load and is "damped out" by the supports, so that stresses become practically negligible two or three spans away from the loaded span [Fig. 7.35(a)]. Continuity increases the resistance of a beam to concentrated loads, but its effect diminishes rapidly, becoming negligible a few supports away from the load.

It may finally be noticed that, depending on the location of the load, the curvature of a given span may change from downward to upward, or vice versa [Fig. 7.35(b)]. Hence, continuous beams of reinforced concrete may require tensile reinforcement at both top and bottom whenever loads may be located on different spans, as is the case, for example, with moving loads on bridges.

7.4 Secondary Bending Stresses

Compressive and tensile stresses of **constant value** over the entire cross section of a structural element are called **direct stresses** to distinguish them from bending stresses, which vary linearly through its depth from a maximum compression to a maximum tension. Direct stresses allow a more efficient use of the material than bending stresses because they develop the same stress in every fiber of the element. The hinged bars of a truss, for example, develop their maximum resistance at all points of their cross sections, since they are acted upon by simple tension or simple compression.

One of the essential characteristics of direct stress is to develop displacements that are extremely small in comparison with bending displacements. The shortening of a ruler by a compressive load cannot be gauged by the naked eye [Fig. 7.36(a)]; but the bending deflection of the tip of the cantilevered ruler under the same load can be noticeable [Fig. 7.36(b)]. The bending deflection is often two or three thousand times larger than the compression shortening due to the same load; in other words, a structural element is much stiffer in tension or compression than in bending.

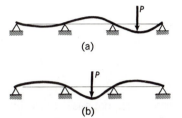
(a)

(b)

7.35 Change in curvature in continuous beam under moving loads.

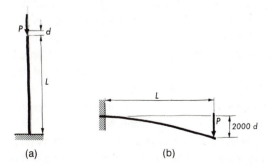

(a)   (b)

7.36 Compressive and bending displacements.

Unfortunately, pure compression or tension elements are not easily realizable in practice, as the example of a simple truss will clearly indicate.

The triangular bracket of Fig. 7.37 is acted upon by a vertical load at its tip; it supports the load as an elementary truss by tension in the inclined bar and compression in the horizontal bar. Direct stresses develop in these bars only if their ends are free to rotate; otherwise the lower bar, for example, would behave as a cantilevered beam and carry part of the load by bending action (Fig. 7.38). Ideally, the bars of a truss should be connected to the supports and to one another by joints allowing unrestrained rotations, or so-called **hinges**.

Some of the truss bridges of the nineteenth century were actually built with hinged bars. But because of weathering, rusting, and painting, the hinges often became locked, and the bars of modern trusses are all bolted, riveted or welded in order to avoid prohibitive maintenance costs. In this case, even if the small amount of bending due to the dead load of the bars is neglected, it may easily be seen that additional bending stresses are introduced by the welding, bolting, or riveting of the bar ends. In the bracket of Fig. 7.37, under the action of the load the upper bar elongates and the lower bar shortens. If the bars were hinged, they would rotate so as to bring the tips of the lengthened and shortened bars together again, and these rotations would change the angle between the bars (Fig. 7.37). Such angle changes are prevented by the rigid welded, riveted, or bolted connection. In order to maintain the angle unchanged, the bars must bend, and develop bending stresses (Fig. 7.39). These so-called **secondary** bending stresses may reach values as high as 20 per cent of the direct stresses.

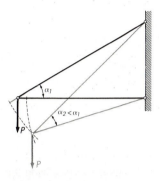

7.37 Truss bracket.

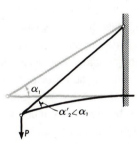

7.38 Bending action in bracket.

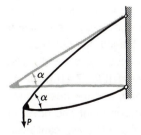

7.39 Bending deformations of bracket hinged to wall.

The presence of bending stresses can always be detected by visualizing the deformation of a bar. In a continuous beam on four supports, loaded on the middle span only, the deflection shows that the center span develops bending stresses with tension at the bottom and compression at the top, towards midspan, while the outer spans and the portions of the middle span nearer the supports have inverted stresses [see Fig. 7.34(c)]. Similarly, in the bolted bracket the bending stresses produce tension in the outer fibers and compression in the inner fibers of both bars, if the ends connected to the wall are hinged (see Fig. 7.39). When the connections to the wall are fixed, the horizontal bar behaves very much like a beam with fixed ends, and its stresses change from tension to compression at both the outer and the inner fibers (Fig. 7.40).

The visualization of deflections is most useful in determining a state of locked-in stresses not caused by loads. Such is the state of stress due to the uneven settlements of the foundations of a building (see Section 2.5). If the right support of a simply supported beam settles more than the left, the beam adapts to this situation by rotating around the hinges and acquiring a slightly tilted position, but remains straight and hence **unstressed** [Fig. 7.41(a)]. If the beam has fixed ends, the end rotations are prevented, and the beam bends [Fig. 7.41(b)]. Its midspan section presents an inflection point and does not develop bending stresses. The two beam halves behave like two cantilevers carrying a load at their tip [Fig. 7.41(c)].

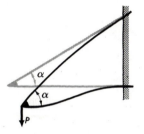

7.40 Bending deformations of bracket fixed to wall.

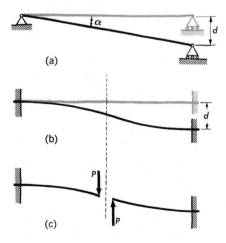

(a)

(b)

(c)

7.41 Uneven settlements of beam ends.

The advantages of fixed-end beams are thus balanced by some disadvantages; fixed-end beams are more sensitive to settlements, which may not be easily assessed beforehand. Whenever the danger of foundation settlements is present, a structural system should be chosen capable of adapting to such conditions without straining and stressing.

Considerations of the same kind hold for **differential deformations due to temperature**. The outer columns of a tall building elongate when the temperature of the outside air rises, while the interior columns and the core do not if the building is air-conditioned. The ends of a beam connecting an outer to an inner column or to the core acquire different levels, and may develop additional bending stresses (Fig. 7.42). Here again, a flexible structural system capable of adapting itself to deformations by developing minor stresses is superior to a rigid system.

Both rigidity and flexibility have their place in structural design, but must be given different weight depending on the loading conditions to be considered. Rigidity is well adapted to fight loads; flexibility, to fight deformations.

172

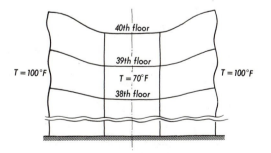

7.42 Thermal deformation of building frame.

Chapter Eight

Frames and Arches

8.1 Post and Lintel

From time immemorial the problem of sheltering human beings from the weather has been solved by an enclosure of walls topped by a roof. In prehistoric times walls and roof were made of the same material, without any distinction between a supporting "structure" and the protecting "skin." A separation of the supporting and protecting functions leads to the simplest "framed" system: the **post and lintel** (Fig. 8.1).

The **lintel** is a beam simply supported on two posts and carrying the roof load. The **posts** are vertical struts compressed by the lintel. The posts must also resist some horizontal loads, such as the wind forces; this resistance stems from a bending capacity in the case of wooden or steel posts, from their own weight in stone or masonry piers. Some connection between post and lintel must also be provided, lest the wind blow the roof away.

The foundations of the posts carry the roof and post loads to the ground by means of **footings** which spread the load and guarantee that soil settlements will be limited (Fig. 8.1). In any case, the posts and the foundations are essentially under compression, and this is characteristic of the post-and-lintel system.

Post-and-lintel systems may be built one on top of another to frame multistory buildings. In this case the lintels are supported by vertical columns, or bearing walls of stone or masonry as high as the entire building (Fig. 8.2). Construction of this type, while capable of carrying vertical loads, is not well suited to resist horizontal loads, and is easily damaged by hurricane winds and earthquakes. This happens because masonry or stone elements have little bending resistance, and a strong connection between the horizontal and the vertical structural elements is not easily developed.

8.1 Post and lintel.

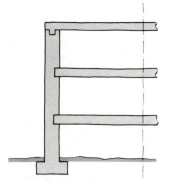

8.2 Multi-story post-and-lintel system.

8.2 The Simple Frame

The action of the post-and-lintel system changes substantially if a rigid connection is developed between the lintel and bending-resistant posts. This new structure, the **simple** or **single-bay frame,** behaves monolithically, and is stronger than the post-and-lintel against both vertical and horizontal loads (Fig. 8.3).

Under a uniform load the lintel of a post-and-lintel system deflects, and its ends rotate freely with respect to the posts, which remain vertical. In order to grasp the action of the rigid frame under the same load, one may first consider the horizontal beam as simply supported at its ends, and the columns as rigidly connected to the rotated ends of the beam, so as to stick out in a straight, inclined position [Fig. 8.4(a)]. In order to bring back the feet of the columns to their supports, the columns must be forced inward by horizontal forces, and the ends of the beam must rotate partially backwards. In their final position both the beam and the columns of the frame are curved and develop bending stresses [Fig. 8.4(b)]. The beam has partially restrained ends, and behaves like the center span of a continuous beam on four supports [see Fig. 7.35(b)].

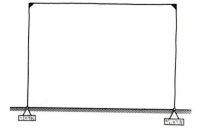

8.3 Simple hinged frame.

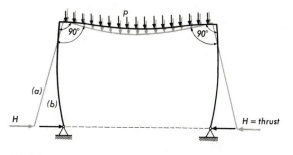

8.4 Hinged-frame deflection.

Three consequences of rigidly connecting the horizontal and vertical elements of the frame are immediately apparent: (a) the beam has partially restrained ends, it becomes more rigid, and is capable of supporting a heavier load in bending (see Section 7.3); (b) the columns are subjected not only to the compressive loads of the beam and of their own weight, but also to bending stresses due to the continuity with the beam; (c) a new **horizontal** force is required to maintain the frame in equilibrium under vertical loads, the **thrust,** which brings back the columns to their bent vertical position, and, through the columns, introduces compression in the beam. The thrust is typical of frame action. It may be provided by the resistance of the foundation to lateral displacements, e.g., by the natural buttressing action of rock [Fig. 8.5(a)]; by buttresses of stone or masonry built for this purpose [Fig. 8.5(b)]; or by a tie-rod, which does not permit the frame to open up under the action of vertical loads [Fig. 8.5(c)].

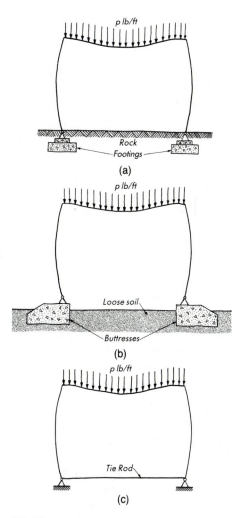

8.5 Thrust absorption.

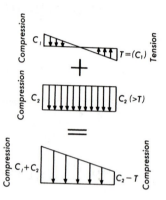

8.6 (a) Stresses due to compression and bending in right column of simple frame.

All three members of a simple frame under vertical loads are bent **and** compressed. Simple bending develops a linear stress distribution across the depth of the element, with maximum tensile and compressive stresses of equal value; compression adds a constant compressive stress, which develops the resultant trapezoidal stress distributions shown in Fig. 8.6. Usually compression prevails in the columns so that their stresses are entirely compressive [Fig. 8.6(a)]; bending prevails in the beam, so that tensile stresses are developed in some parts of the beam [Fig. 8.6(b)].

The foot of the column may be either "hinged" or "fixed." In steel frames the first type of connection may be provided by an actual hinge [Fig. 8.7(a)] or by suitably located anchor bolts; in reinforced-concrete frames it is provided by crossing the reinforcing bars so as to reduce the bending capacity of the section [Fig. 8.7(b)]. The deformation of the frame under vertical load shows that a hinged frame usually has smaller compressive stresses on the outer column fibers than on the inner fibers [Fig. 8.6(b)].

182

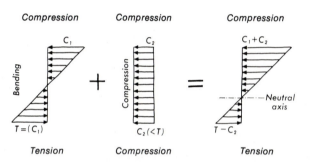

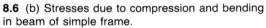

8.6 (b) Stresses due to compression and bending in beam of simple frame.

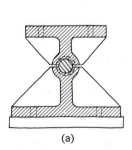

(a)

(b)

8.7 Steel and reinforced-concrete hinges.

The deformations of a fixed frame under vertical loads show that the columns develop inflection points (Fig. 8.8). Since an inflection point is a point of no curvature, it is equivalent to a hinge where no bending stresses are developed. Hence, the fixed frame is roughly equivalent to a hinged frame with shorter columns and is stiffer than the hinged frame. The thrust in the fixed frame is **greater** than in the hinged frame, since it takes a larger force to bring back (even if partially) its shorter, stiffer equivalent columns.

Frames are stronger against vertical loads than post-and-lintel systems, but their action is even more advantageous in resisting lateral loads. A post loaded by a horizontal load, such as the wind pressure, acts as a single cantilevered beam without any collaboration from the lintel or the opposite post [Fig. 8.9(a)]. In the frame, instead, continuity with the beam transfers part of the wind load to the opposite column, as shown by the fact that both columns bend [Fig. 8.9(b)]. Even if the beam were hinged at the tops of the columns, because of its rigidity in compression it would carry half the wind load to the leeward column, and cut in half the bending stresses in the columns (Fig. 8.10). Since, moreover, the rigidity of the frame connections compels the beam to bend together with the columns, an additional restraint is introduced in the columns, which become stiffer [Fig. 8.9(b)]. Their deflection is reduced, and so are their bending stresses.

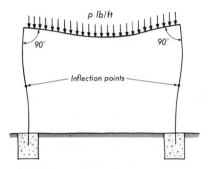

8.8 Simple fixed frame.

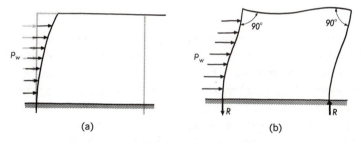

(a)   (b)

8.9 Post-and-lintel and fixed frame under wind load.

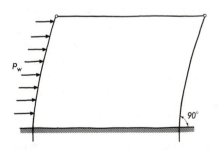

8.10 Wind load on frame with hinged bar.

The tendency of the frame to turn over due to the pressure of the wind is balanced by additional reactions in the columns: tensile in the windward column and compressive in the leeward column [see Fig. 8.9(b)]; but these forces are usually small because their lever arm, equal to the width of the frame, is large compared to the lever arm of the wind pressure, which is half the frame height. The lateral displacement or **sidesway** produced in a frame by lateral loads is also present when unsymmetrical vertical loads are applied to the frame (Fig. 8.11).

Whenever the beam of a fixed frame is much stiffer in bending than the columns, under lateral or unsymmetrical loads the inflection points in the columns appear approximately at midheight; the shortened legs of the equivalent hinged frame show that the fixed frame is stiffer than the hinged frame against lateral loads also (Fig. 8.12). In either type of frame lateral loads must be considered acting from either side of the frame, so that the reinforcement of concrete frames must be located along both the inner and the outer fibers of the posts, and the top and bottom fibers of the beam.

The bending-strength requirements of the columns are often so small as to make the entire frame flexible. If for functional reasons an open bay is required, a substantial increase in lateral rigidity of the frame can be achieved only by increasing the bending rigidity of its columns. On the other hand, lateral rigidity is inexpensively obtained by tensile or compressive elements; hence, tensile or compressive diagonals may be used to stiffen the frame with little increase in material (Fig. 8.13) and with a large reduction of bending stresses in the columns and beam. In general, structural systems with rectangular meshes, such as frames, are more flexible than triangulated systems, but triangulated systems seldom meet the functional requirements of a modern building.

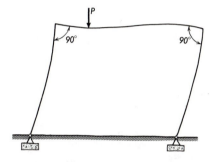

8.11 Sidesway under vertical load.

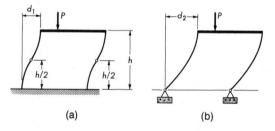

(a)   (b)

8.12 Deformation of hinged and fixed frames with stiff beam under unsymmetrical load.

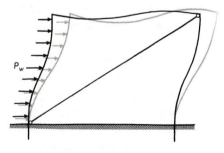

8.13 Diagonally stiffened frame.

8.3 Multiple Frames

The advantages of continuity can be compounded by the use of **multiple frames,** in which a horizontal beam is supported by, and rigidly connected to, three or more columns.

In view of the rigidity of compressed elements (see Section 5.2), the vertical deflections of the columns of a multiple frame are small, and the behavior of its beam, when loaded vertically, is similar to, although not identical with, that of a continuous beam on rigid supports (see Section 7.3). Under the action of loads concentrated on one span the multiple frame develops curvature not only in all other spans, as a continuous beam, but in all columns as well. The frame as a whole also exhibits a lateral displacement, the so called **sidesway,** which is absent in the continuous beam (Fig. 8.14).

If the spans and the vertical loads of the multiple frame do not differ substantially from bay to bay, the thrusts in adjoining frames act in opposite directions and tend to cancel each other. Theoretically only the two outer bays need to be tied or buttressed. In practice, some means must always be provided to take care of uneven loadings on the various spans of the multiple frame: the excess thrust on each column is often resisted by the action of the soil on the foundations.

Multiple frames are efficient in resisting lateral loads. The rigidity of the beam against compressive loads makes the lateral deflections of the tops of all the columns practically identical. Hence, if the columns are identical, the lateral load is carried equally by all the columns of the frame, each acting as a cantilever and additionally stiffened by the bending rigidity of the beam. The overturning tendency due to wind action is equilibrated by tensile reactions on half the frame columns on the windward side, and by compressive reactions on the half on the leeward side. In view of the greater number of column reactions and their large lever arms, these forces are relatively small. Multiple frames in the external walls or in the core walls of a building are often used to carry the wind load on the faces perpendicular to these walls.

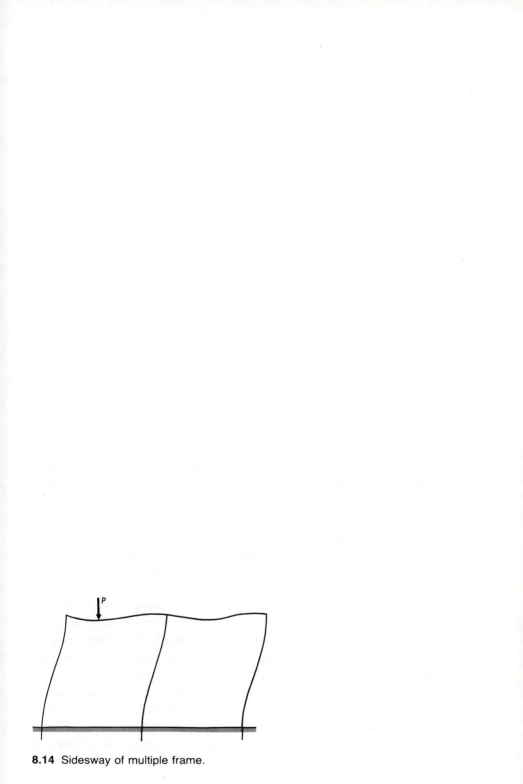

8.14 Sidesway of multiple frame.

A single-bay frame with a beam rigidly connecting the feet of the columns is a closed structural element capable of carrying vertical and horizontal loads [Fig. 8.15(a)]. A multiple-bay frame with continuous beams at the top and the bottom of the columns is also a closed system, and may be used as a truss to span large distances [Fig. 8.15(b)]. In this case, the multiple frame may be thought of as a beam with compression and tension flanges, in which the shear is resisted by the columns. The "secondary" bending stresses in the horizontal and vertical elements of such truss-frames (see Section 7.4) are much greater than in the members of triangulated trusses, but the simplicity of their connections and their unencumbered bays have made these truss-frames popular. Such **Vierendeel trusses,** named after their Belgian inventor, are commonly used in bridge design. They are also used in buildings when the structure is supported on wide spans and unencumbered bays are essential. In this case, the truss consists actually of the columns and floor beams of the building (Fig. 8.16). **Multistory** frames are commonly used in tall structures. Their action against vertical loads is similar to that of single-bay frames, with the added advantage that the horizontal beams act both as load-carrying elements for a given floor and as tie-rods for the frame above it.

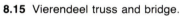

(a)

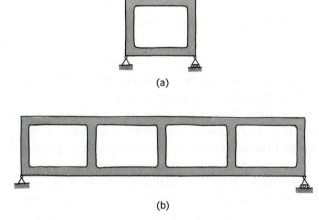

(b)

8.15 Vierendeel truss and bridge.

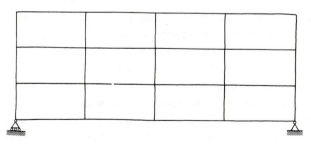

8.16 Vierendeel truss structure.

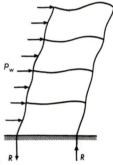

8.17 Multi-story frame under lateral loads.

The action of a single-bay, multi-story frame under lateral loads is similar to the action of a cantilevered Vierendeel truss: the leeward columns are in compression and bending, the windward columns are in tension and bending, while the floor beams or slabs transmit the shear from the tension to the compression elements (Fig. 8.17). One may also think of a multi-bay, multi-story frame as a gigantic I beam, cantilevered from the ground, in which the depth equals the width of the frame and the floor beams act as a discontinuous web. The continuity between the floor beams and the columns makes the entire structure monolithic and introduces bending in both the horizontal and the vertical elements. A concentrated vertical load is felt in the entire structure, each part of which collaborates in carrying it (Fig. 8.18).

As the height and the width of the building increase, it becomes practical to increase the number of bays so as to reduce the beam spans and to absorb horizontal loads more economically. The resisting structure of the building thus becomes a frame with a number of rectangular meshes, allowing free circulation inside the building, and capable of resisting both vertical and horizontal loads. A number of such frames, parallel to each other and connected by horizontal beams, constitute the cage structure encountered in most steel or concrete buildings today. These **three-dimensional frames** act integrally against horizontal loads coming from any direction, since their columns may be considered as part of either system of frames at right angles to each other (Fig. 8.19).

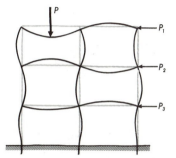

8.18 Multi-story frame under concentrated load (sidesway prevented by imaginary lateral forces).

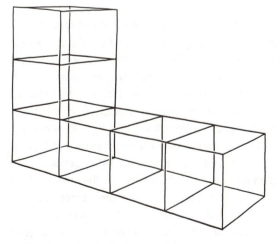

8.19 Three-dimensional frame.

The **high-rise building,** or skyscraper, is one of the great conquests of modern structural design, made possible by the multi-story frame and the high strength of steel and concrete. The Empire State Building in New York, built in 1930, has 102 floors and is 1050 feet high, not including the 200-foot upper tower originally designed to anchor dirigibles, and the 222-foot TV antenna. The John Hancock Insurance Company building in Chicago (Fig. 8.20), the twin towers of the World Trade Center in New York, and the Sears building also in Chicago (Fig. 8.21), the tallest building in the world to date (1986), all built in the 1970s, have heights of between 1200 and 1450 feet and steel structures consisting of frames with bays of narrow width on the outside of the building. Such structures behave essentially as cantilevered **steel tubes** of rectangular cross section. Tubular high-rise steel buildings have also been built by "bundling" a number of tubular frames and with other than rectangular cross section, e.g., triangular.

8.20 The John Hancock Insurance Company building in Chicago.

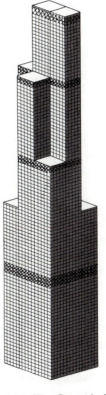

8.21 The Sears building in Chicago.

195

Reinforced concrete skyscrapers cannot reach the height of steel skyscrapers, but have been built to heights of over 800 feet: the tallest to date (1986) is the 895-foot Water Tower Building in Chicago. They usually consist of outer frames and of an inner core built by means of concrete walls. The lateral stiffness of the boxed core is usually so large relative to that of the outer frame that the lateral forces due to wind or earthquake are predominantly resisted by the so-called **shear walls** of the core. (These walls resist the horizontal loads as cantilevered beams in bending; their misleading name indicates that they resist the wind shear.)

Because of their lateral stiffness, concrete core walls are also used in high-rise buildings with outer steel frames (Fig. 8.22), thus combining the advantages of smaller steel columns to resist vertical loads only and of concrete walls to resist lateral loads. The steel frame of the core of a steel building may also be stiffened by steel diagonals or by prefabricated concrete panels inserted in its bays.

A skyscraper is nothing but a slender, vertical, cantilevered beam resisting lateral and vertical loads. The vertical floor loads accumulate from the top to the bottom of the building, requiring larger columns as one moves down. Were it not for the high compressive strength of modern structural materials, the area of the columns would encroach on the usable floor area to the point where this might become nil.

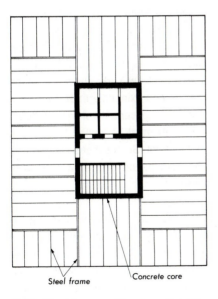

Steel frame   Concrete core

8.22 Steel frame with concrete core.

The efficiency of frame and shear-wall action is required by skyscrapers to resist large horizontal wind loads with minor deflections. A constant wind pressure of 46 pounds per square foot (due to a 113 miles per hour wind) represents a total load of 12 million 500 thousand pounds on the 1350 foot cantilever of one of the World Trade Center Towers in New York; under the action of this wind load the top of the building sways approximately three feet each side of vertical. In order to avoid discomfort to the occupants of the top floors of a high-rise building, the top deflection or **drift** must be limited to between one thousandth and one five-hundredth of its height. Such stiffness is required because human discomfort is severe when the period of the swaying is in resonance with the period of the human insides.

The columns, beams, and walls of a framed structure are its resisting "skeleton." In order to enclose the space defined by the skeleton and to make it usable, the exterior of the building is covered with a "skin" and the floor areas are spanned by horizontal floor systems. The skin of modern buildings is often made of metal or concrete, and glass, and called a **curtain wall.** A curtain wall of prefabricated concrete or brick panels may also be used to enclose buildings and must be connected to the structure so as to allow expansion and contraction of the panels under differences in temperature between the exterior and the interior of the buildings. The floor structure consists of long-span beams connecting the outer frames to the core, of secondary beams or joists spanning the distance between the main beams, and of slabs of concrete or steel decks spanning the distance between the secondary beams. Floor systems are analyzed in Chapter 10.

8.4 Gabled Frames and Arches

All three members of a single-bay frame under vertical loads are subjected to compressive and bending stresses. The columns are compressed by the loads on the beam and bent by the rotation of the joint connecting them rigidly to the beam. The beam is bent by the loads on it and compressed by the thrust from the foot of the columns. With the usual proportions of beam and columns, compression prevails in the columns and bending in the beams, since the columns are relatively slender and the beam is relatively deep.

Whenever for functional reasons the top member of the frame must be horizontal, this type of design is efficient and economical, but it may be improved when the upper member does not have to be horizontal. In **gabled frames** the top member consists of two inclined beams. If these were hinged at top and bottom, they would act as the compressed struts of a triangular truss, and the columns would be bent by the thrust from the upper members, besides being compressed by their vertical reactions (Fig. 8.23). Continuity between the gable and the columns introduces bending in the gabled member, so that the frame transfers loads by a combination of compression and bending in all its members (Fig. 8.24). The higher the rise of the gable, the smaller the thrust and hence the bending in it and in the columns. The load-carrying capacity of the gable may be split between the two mechanisms of compression and bending, gaining in efficiency and saving material in comparison with a beam in bending.

The principle used in gabled frames may be extended. The columns may be shortened and the upper member folded so as to have more than two straight sides, with an increase in compression and a reduction in bending (Fig. 8.25). In the limit, the polygonal frame with an infinite number of infinitesimally short sides becomes an **arch.**

It was noted in Section 6.4 that for each set of loads there is a particular arch shape (the so-called funicular shape) for which the entire arch is under simple compression. Such shape can be determined by hanging the arch loads from a cable and by turning the resulting curve upside-down.

8.23 Hinged gabled frame.

8.24 Continuous gabled frame.

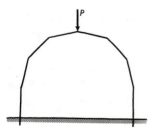

8.25 Polygonal frame.

Funicular arches are at one end of the structural scale, where there is uniform compression and no bending; beams are at the other, where there is bending and no uniform compression. Any other downward curved structural member will carry loads by a combination of compression and bending. Even if an arch is funicular for **one** set of loads, it cannot be funicular for **all** sets of loads it may have to carry: a combination of compression and bending is always present in an arch.

In masonry design the arch is heavy and loaded by the weight of walls; its shape is usually the funicular of the dead load, and some bending is introduced in it by the live loads. In large steel arches, the live load represents a greater share of the total load than in masonry arches and introduces a larger amount of bending; but bending is seldom critical, in view of the tensile strength of steel.

The arch thrust is absorbed by a tie-rod whenever the foundation material is not suitable to resist it. When the arch must allow the free passage of traffic under it, whether it is a bridge or the arched entrance to a hall, its thrust is absorbed either by buttresses or by tie-rods buried under ground.

The stationary or moving loads carried by the arch of a bridge are usually supported on a horizontal surface. This surface may be above or below the arch, connected to it by compression **struts** [Fig. 8.26(a)] or tension **hangers** [Fig. 8.26(b)]. The compression struts are often restrained laterally against buckling by diagonals or transverse beams, particularly when the arch is deep.

The shape of an arch is not chosen for purely structural reasons. The half circle, exclusively used by the Romans, has convenient construction properties that justify its use. Similarly, the pointed Gothic arch has both visual and structural advantages (it develops lesser thrusts), while the Arabic arch, typical of the mosques and of some Venetian architecture, is "incorrect" from a purely structural viewpoint, but often only visually so because it masquerades a Gothic arch (Fig. 8.27).

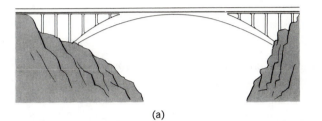

(a)

(b)

8.26 Bridge structures.

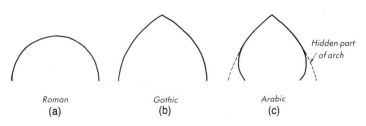

Roman
(a)

Gothic
(b)

Arabic
(c)

Hidden part
of arch

8.27 Arch shapes.

The shape of the arch may be chosen to be as close as possible to the funicular of the heaviest loads, so as to minimize bending. On the other hand, it is often more important to minimize the arch thrust so as to reduce the dimensions of the tie-rod, or to guarantee that the soil will not move under the pressure of the abutments. The thrust may be shown to be proportional to the total load and to the span, and inversely proportional to the rise of the arch. To minimize the thrust for a given distance to be spanned, the arch must be as light as possible, and have a rise as high as economically feasible (Fig. 8.28).

The arch may have hinged or fixed supports. The hinged supports allow the rotation of the arch at the abutments under load or temperature changes. Hinged arches are relatively flexible, and do not develop high bending stresses under temperature variations or soil settlements. Steel hinges are used at the abutments of most steel arches [see Fig. 8.7(a)]. Reinforced-concrete hinges were developed by the French engineer Mesnagier, who first crossed the reinforcing bars to create a section where the bending resistance is substantially weakened by the lack of lever arm between the steel bars [see Fig. 8.7(b)].

Fixed arches are built both in steel and in concrete. They are stiffer than hinged arches and consequently are more sensitive to temperature stresses and settlements of the supports.

If temperature or settlement stresses are to be entirely avoided, a third hinge may be introduced, usually at the **crown** of the arch: the **three-hinge arch** is entirely free to "breathe" or to settle unevenly without bending deformation of its two halves (Fig. 8.29). Such arches, commonly used at the end of the nineteenth century, have lost their popularity because of the improved knowledge of arch behavior.

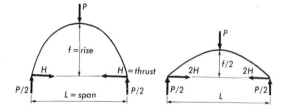

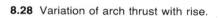

8.28 Variation of arch thrust with rise.

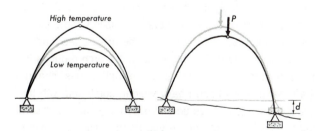

8.29 Three-hinge arch displacements.

When bending materials were costly and easily deteriorated by adverse weather conditions, the arch was the structural member most commonly used to span even modest distances. Roman and Romanesque architecture are immediately recognized by the circular arch motive. The Gothic, high-rise arch and the buttresses required to absorb its thrust are typical of one of the greatest achievements in architectural design, the Gothic cathedral (Fig. 8.30). In these magnificent structures, built of stone capable of resisting compression only, a combination of arches and vaults channels to the ground the loads of roofs spanning up to one hundred feet. The high rise of the arch reduces the thrust, and lightened **flying buttresses,** in the shape of half-arches, channel it from the inner to the outer pillars whose heavy weight, combined with that of the pinnacles, deflects it to an almost vertical direction. A Gothic cathedral is essentially a framed building in which the curved frame elements develop almost exclusively compressive stresses.

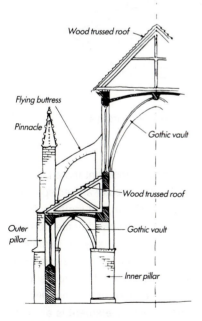

Wood trussed roof

Flying buttress

Pinnacle

Gothic vault

Wood trussed roof

Outer
pillar

Gothic vault

Inner pillar

8.30 Section of Gothic cathedral.

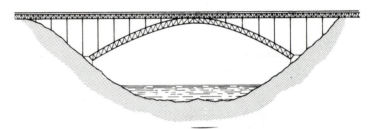

8.31 The New River Gorge Bridge in West Virginia.

It was only with the development of modern bending-resistant materials that greater structural achievments were obtained. Roman circular arches spanned about 100 feet and medieval stone bridges up to 180 feet, but the New River Gorge Bridge in West Virginia, the longest steel-arch span in steel to date (1986) spans 1700 feet (Fig. 8.31). The largest single-arch span in reinforced concrete built to date is the 1280 foot span Krk Bridge in Yugoslavia (Fig. 8.32). Combinations of trussed arches with cantilevered half-arches connected by trusses were built to span as much as 1800 feet in the Quebec Bridge in 1917 (Fig. 8.33). To this day no other structural **element** is as commonly used to span large distances as the arch.

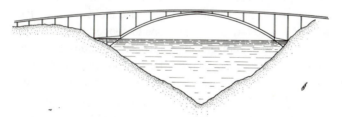

8.32 The reinforced-concrete Krk Bridge in Yugoslavia.

8.33 The Quebec Bridge, the longest cantilever span in the world.

8.5 Arched Roofs

It was seen in the previous section that the roof of a Gothic cathedral is a combination of arches and vaults, capable of channeling the roof load to the ground.Arches are used in a variety of combinations to support curved roofs. One of the simplest is a series of parallel arches connected by transverse elements and roofed by plates, which constitute a **barrel roof** (Fig. 8.34). The connecting elements transmit the roof load to the arches by bending or arch action, and these channel the load to the ground mostly by compression. This is the mechanism used in the medieval, Romanesque church roofs, and in the modern cylindrical concrete hangars, first built in Europe in the 1920's and in the United States in the 1940's. The shape of the arches is chosen to be the funicular of the dead load; any additional load due to wind or snow produces a certain amount of bending in the arches. The element connecting the arches is a brick vault in the medieval churches, and a concrete curved plate in the modern hangars. Barrel roofs supported by steel arches are also common in modern factory roof design.

Rectangular areas are often covered by structures in which the arches span the diagonals rather than the sides of the rectangle (Fig. 8.35). Typical of this kind of structure are the vaults over the transept of medieval churches, and some reinforced-concrete structures used in large halls, as in the air terminal at St. Louis, Missouri, designed by Yamasaki.

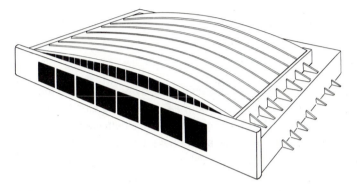

8.34 Arched barrel roof.

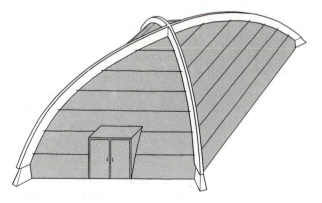

8.35 Diagonal-arch roof.

Areas with circular or otherwise curved boundaries may be covered by arches converging toward the center of the curved area, as in some Gothic chapels or modern wood roofs (Fig. 8.36). In this case the arches butt against a central ring or plate and may be restrained by a peripheral tension ring; their action is more integral than in the case of parallel arches. Arched domes of steel, wood and of reinforced concrete have been used in modern times as roofs of exceptionally large halls for a variety of functional purposes (see Chapter 12).

In the **lamella cylindrical roof** structure a series of parallel arches, skewed with respect to the sides of the rectangular covered area, is intersected by another series of skew arches so that an efficient interaction is obtained between them [Fig. 8.37(a)]. This system does away with the beams connecting parallel arches and constitutes a **curved space frame.** It is particularly efficient when the lengths of the sides of the rectangular area do not differ appreciably, since in this case the arches near the corners have small spans and are very rigid, thus reducing the effective span length of the arches butting into them (see also Section 10.3). Lamella roofs of wood, steel, and concrete are used to create barrel-shaped roofs. Among the largest concrete roofs of this kind are the hangar roofs designed and built by Nervi in the 1940's which spanned 1080 feet by 427 feet and consisted of prefabricated concrete elements, connected by welding the reinforcing bars at the mesh points of the roof and concreting the joints. None of these hangars exists today, since they were dynamited during World War II, but it is interesting to notice that after being dropped to the ground from a height of 40 feet, these roofs remained integral, except for a few among the many hundreds of joints.

In the **lamella dome** the intersecting ribs are spirals [Fig. 8.37(b)]. Arched ribbed roofs behave structurally in a manner analogous to shells; their load-carrying mechanism will be better understood after reading Chapter 12.

8.36 Radial-arch roof.

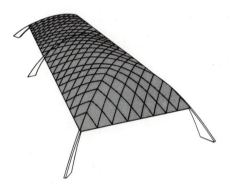

8.37 (a) Lamella cylindrical roof.

8.37 (b) Lamella dome.

Chapter Nine

Some Fine Points
of Structural Behavior

9.1 How Simple Is Simple Stress?

The structural systems considered in the previous chapters react to external loads with states of stress called "simple." A cable develops "simple tension," a funicular arch "simple compression," a beam "simple bending," or "simple bending" combined with "simple shear." A more careful look at the ways in which loads are actually carried by even the simplest element will prove, instead, that the stresses developed in a structure are most of the time anything but simple.

If a weight is to be suspended from a cable, a connection must be developed between the weight and the cable. One of the devices most commonly used to achieve this purpose is called a "conical connector," and consists of a short cylinder with a slightly tapered inner surface, within which are located three conical segments (Fig. 9.1). The cable is gripped by the three segments, which are pulled into the cylinder by the friction developed between the cable and the segments; the larger the pull of the cable, the greater the friction developed. The greater friction pulls the segments deeper into the cylinder, and they develop a tighter grip on the cable. The conical connector is a self-locking device.

The section of cable gripped by the connector is acted upon by frictional shears parallel to its surface, and by compressive stresses perpendicular to its surface (Fig. 9.2). The compressive stresses squeeze the cable, and the ·frictional shears actually transfer the load from the cable in tension to the connector. In the neighborhood of the connector the stresses in the cable present a complicated pattern of compression and surface shear, but they **rapidly** merge into a simple-tension pattern away from the connector (Fig. 9.2).

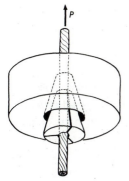

9.1 Conical connector.

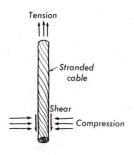

9.2 Stresses in cable due to conical connector.

As shown by the French engineer de St. Venant, the tendency of complicated stress patterns to **become** simple occurs often in correctly designed structural elements, and justifies the elementary approach to stress used in the preceding sections. The stresses in the portion of cable gripped by the connector are complicated, but at a distance from the connector equal to two or three times the diameter of the cable, the stress pattern, to all practical purposes, is one of simple tension. The cable is designed for simple tension because only a small portion of it is under a more complicated state of stress. On the other hand, the stresses in the portion of cable gripped by the connector may be much higher, and of a more dangerous kind than simple tension, and cannot be ignored.

A condition similar to that existing in the cable arises in a truss bar under tension. The connection between the bar and the gusset plate is often bolted. The bolts develop compressive stresses on part of the inner surface of the bar holes, and shears due to friction between the gusset and bar surfaces; these stresses are transformed into simple tension away from the connection (Fig. 9.3). Truss bars are designed as if they were under simple tension or compression, but the complicated stress pattern in the neighborhood of the gusset plate must be taken into careful account.

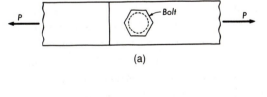

(a)

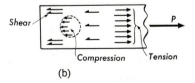

(b)

9.3 Stresses in bolted joint under tension.

9.2 The Largest Stress

It was shown in Section 5.3 that pure shear is equivalent to compression and tension at right angles to each other and at 45 degrees to the direction of the shear. Some essential implications of these equivalent states of stress must now be considered.

Since shear stresses develop on the horizontal and vertical sides of a square element cut out of a beam, and tension and compression on the sides of a square element cut out of the same beam at 45 degrees to the horizontal, one may inquire as to what stresses are developed on the side S of a square element oriented to any other angle (Fig. 9.4). It seems natural to investigate **how the stress on one of its sides,** say AB, **varies as the cut out square element is rotated,** since for an angle equal to zero (horizontal position of the side AB) the stress is pure shear, for an angle of 45 degrees it becomes compression, for an angle of 90 degrees it is shear again, and for an angle of 135 degrees it becomes tension (Fig. 9.4).

A general analysis of this question shows that, **whatever the stress pattern in the beam,** as the element is rotated: (a) the direct stress (tension or compression) on the sides varies from a maximum to a minimum value; (b) the maximum and minimum direct stresses occur on sides at right angles to each other; (c) shear is **never** developed on the sides of the element for which **the direct stress is maximum or minimum;** (d) both shear **and** direct stress are developed for any other orientation of the sides. In the elementary case of "simple shear" of Fig. 9.4 the maximum stress is tension (equal in magnitude to the shear stress) at an angle of 135 degrees; the minimum stress is compression (considered as **negative** tension) at an angle of 45 degrees; and there is no shear on the side of the elements in these two orientations.

The perpendicular directions for which the direct stresses become maximum or minimum are called **the principal stress directions;** the corresponding values of the stresses are called their **principal values.**

9.4 Stress variation with orientation of element.

The principal directions of stress allow a visualization of complex stress patterns. In general, the two principal stress directions vary from point to point of a stress pattern and may be indicated by small crosses. Lines may, then, be drawn paralled to the principal directions at each point of the stress pattern. There are two families of such lines and they intersect at right angles (Fig. 9.5); they are called the **principal stress lines,** or **isostatic lines**. The stresslines pattern indicates the flow of stress within the structural element, and is useful in visualizing complex stress situations, like that due to a tension load applied to a plate through a bolt (Fig. 9.5).

Figure 9.6 illustrates the stress lines in a dam loaded by the pressure of water on its vertical side. Since water exerts only normal pressure on the vertical wall, the dam elements at the wall do not develop shear. Hence, the principal stress directions at the wall are vertical and horizontal. The family of compression isostatics starts horizontally at this wall. The inclined dam wall is altogether free of stress, and, in particular, of shear stress. Hence the direction of the inclined wall is one of the principal directions there, and the other is perpendicular to it. The heavy stress lines show how the pressure of the water is channeled down the dam to its foundation. The light stress lines of the tension family cross the compression lines at right angles, and show that in these directions the dam acts as a series of cables in tension. Thus, the action of the dam is seen to be a combination of tension and compression at right angles, in varying directions.

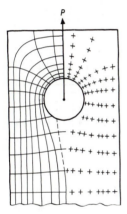

9.5 Principal stress lines (isostatics) in tension plate.

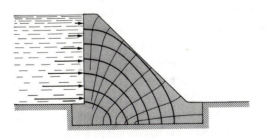

9.6 Isostatics of dam.

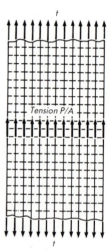

9.7 (a) Isostatics of tension bar.

The stress lines for a flat bar in simple tension constitute a mesh of vertical tension lines, and of horizontal compressive lines due to Poisson's phenomenon (see Section 5.1) [Fig, 9.7(a)]. If a hole is introduced in the bar, the straight tensile lines cannot go through the hole and are diverted around it. In so doing the tensile stress lines crowd in the neighborhood of the hole, and the compression lines bend so as to remain perpendicular to the tension lines [Fig. 9.7(b)]. The flow of the tensile stresses is similar to the flow of water in a river: the flow pattern is made up of parallel lines when the river banks are parallel and there is no obstruction in the river, but the lines curve when a circular pile is embedded in the current, compelling the water to move around the pile. The similarity between these two flow patterns is quite significant: just as the water of the river increases its speed to move through the reduced section created by the obstruction, the tensile stress increases its value because of the obstruction created by the hole. Thus, the tensile stress across the two sections at the sides of the hole is not uniform, but higher near the hole than

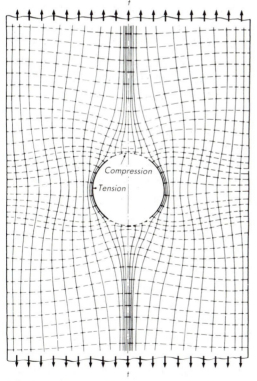

9.7 (b) Isostatics of tension bar with hole.

at the boundary of the bar (Fig. 9.8). Such increases in stress due to holes, sharp notches, and other abrupt changes in cross section are called **stress concentrations**. Stress concentrations may increase the value of the stress above its average value by large factors, thus bringing the stress not only above the elastic limit, but above the ultimate strength of the material. For example, when the edge of a bolt of cloth is nicked, a high stress concentration is developed under tension, and the material tears as the stress concentration moves along the cut. Without the nick, it is practically impossible to tear the material. Similarly, to cut plate glass the glazier scratches it with a diamond and bends the plate at the scratch, creating stress concentration on the tensile side of the plate.

Figure 9.9(a) gives the stress lines for a simply supported beam under uniform load. The bending and shear stress pattern considered in previous sections is shown by the stress lines to be equivalent to a set of arch stresses, indicated by the heavy compression lines, combined with a set of cable stresses, indicated by the light tension lines, at right angles to each other. The bottom fiber of the beam is in tension, and if a notch is cut out of the beam at midspan, stress concentration arises, because the tensile stress lines must go around the notch and crowd at its top [Fig. 9.9(b)]. When the load on a beam, made of a material stronger in compression than in tension, is increased beyond safe values, compressive arch action carries more of the load to the supports as the fibers in tension fail. Thus, the beam at first carries the load by bending but changes its mechanism to compression as soon as failure in tension makes bending impossible. This readjustment of stress cannot be counted upon for normal loads, since it is accompanied by large displacements and the partial failure of the beam, but is useful in preventing or retarding the total collapse of a structure under exceptional loads.

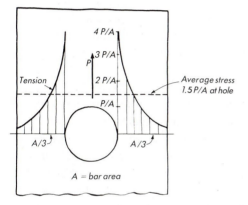

9.8 Stress concentration in tension bar.

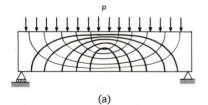

(a)

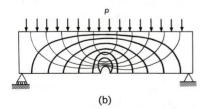

(b)

9.9 Isostatics of simply supported beam.

9.3 The Importance of Plastic Flow

It was stated in Section 3.1 that most structural materials have an elastic stress range, followed by a plastic range, and that under normal loading conditions stresses are kept below the elastic limit in order to avoid the accumulation of permanent deformations, which may occur through plastic flow. On the other hand, plastic flow plays an essential role in the behavior of all structural elements.

In the post-and-lintel system it is generally assumed that the lintel rests on the post, and that a uniform compression is developed between their contact surfaces. This assumption would be correct if the two surfaces were ideally smooth; in practice, instead, both are uneven and present small irregular bumps. If two bumps coincide (Fig. 9.10), the contact is limited to a small area and the compressive stress on it may be many times greater than if the contact took place over the entire surface. But, if the high stress developing at the bumps is above the yield point, the material flows, the bumps flatten, the contact area increases, and the stress decreases to acceptable values. Thus, **plastic flow eliminates stress concentrations** due to the roughness of the surfaces, and brings about a stress situation nearer the ideal one on which the design was based. Post-and-lintel systems of brittle materials (see Section 3.1) could not readjust, and would fail owing to high stress concentrations.

Besides the unavoidable presence of small irregularities, another cause of stress concentration exists at the inner edge of the post. As the lintel bends under the applied loads it tends to rest on the inner portion of the contact area with the post, and, at the limit, on its inner edge alone [Fig. 9.11(a)]. If the post were made of a brittle material, the partial contact would increase the contact stresses and the edge of the post would cut into the lintel or shear off. In practice, plastic flow comes to the rescue. The rotation of the lintel produces a stress concentration at the inner edge of the post, and the elastic-plastic material of the post flows together with the lintel material. Plastic flow increases the contact areas between these two elements until the stresses are reduced to acceptable values, and flow stops [Fig. 9.11(b)].

228

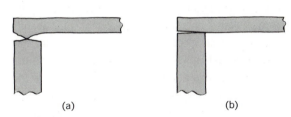

9.10 Stress concentration and flow.

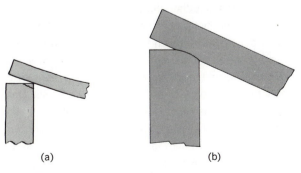

9.11 Redistribution of stress by flow.

The stress concentrations at the ends of the horizontal diameter of the hole in a tension bar (Fig. 9.8) are similarly relieved by plastic flow. In the neighborhood of these points flow spreads until the stress lines acquire greater radii of curvature, and do not crowd as much as they did when compelled to go around a hole of small radius. The analogy with the flow of water may be carried one step further: in order to reduce the pressure on the piles of a bridge, piling guards are set up which divert the flow of water in a smoother fashion. The plastic areas (Fig. 9.12) around the stress concentration points perform the same role, and ease the stress flow of elastic stresses.

Stress redistribution due to plastic flow is responsible for the **reserve of strength** exhibited by beams, frames, and other structures in which loads are carried essentially in bending. It was found in Section 7.2 that the midspan section of a simply supported beam develops the highest bending stresses under symmetrical loads. The heaviest loads the beam can safely carry are those for which the upper and lower fibers at midspan are stressed up to the allowable stress for the given material, which is a fraction (usually 60 per cent) of its elastic limit. If under increased loads the extreme fiber stresses reach the elastic limit, the stress distribution through the beam depth is still linear and all but the extreme fibers are stressed below the elastic limit [Fig. 9.13(a)].

If the loads on the beam are increased further, the extreme fiber stresses cannot grow any higher, since the elastic limit is practically the value of the stress at which plastic flow starts; but the other beam fibers may help support the additional loads by increasing **their** stress up to the elastic limit. The stress distribution in the beam stops being triangular, and follows the diagram of Fig.9.13(b). The loads may be increased until all fibers reach the elastic limit, at which point the stress distribution is rectangular [Fig. 9.13(c)], the beam reaches its **ultimate load** capacity, and all fibers flow, the upper fibers in compression and the lower in tension. The beam fails at this point, because its two halves rotate about the middle section **as if the beam had a hinge at midspan,** and the **plastic hinge** makes the beam into a three-hinge moving

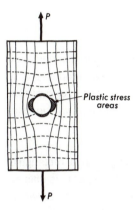

9.12 Plastic flow at edge of hole in tension bar.

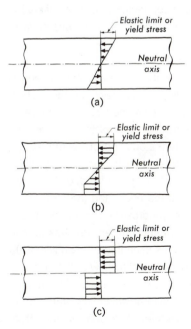

Elastic limit or
yield stress

Neutral
axis

(a)

Elastic limit or
yield stress

Neutral
axis

(b)

Elastic limit or
yield stress

Neutral
axis

(c)

9.13 Plastic flow in beam section.

mechanism (Fig. 9.14). For a rectangular cross section the ultimate load is 50 per cent higher than the load at which flow starts; plastic flow introduces a 50 per cent reserve of strength which may prevent collapse in case of exceptional loads. (See Section 10.7 for the added strength reserve in beams with longitudinally restrained ends.)

A simply supported I beam is more efficient in bending than a rectangular beam, but does not have such high reserve of strength. The I beam is efficient **because** most of its area is concentrated in the top and bottom flanges, where the stresses are highest. But as soon as the flanges flow, the only fibers that can help carry additional loads by increasing their stresses are those in the web; and the web has such a small area that the corresponding increase in load is small. Practically, the I beam develops a plastic hinge soon after the flanges reach the elastic limit. Wide-flange steel sections have a reserve of strength of about 15 per cent against collapse, because their flanges have almost no reserve of strength.

The reserve of strength is greater for beams with fixed ends. It was seen in Section 7.3 that a fixed-end beam under uniform load develops the highest bending stresses at the supports. If the load is increased beyond the value that brings such stresses up to the elastic limit, the fibers of the end sections flow progressively until the stress distribution at the end sections is that shown in Fig. 9.13(c). At this point the end sections develop plastic hinges (Fig. 9.15). As the load keeps increasing, the beam, although originally fixed, behaves under the additional loads as if it were hinged at the ends, and the stresses at the middle section (b) start increasing until they progressively reach the elastic limit. At this point the beam develops **three plastic hinges,** reaches its ultimate capacity, and collapses (Fig. 9.15). It is thus seen that a beam with fixed ends has a two-fold source of strength reserve: the plastic flow of the end sections, and the plastic flow of the middle section. The ultimate load for a fixed beam of rectangular cross section is twice the load at which flow starts at the extreme fibers of the end sections. Such a beam has a reserve of strength of 100 per cent.

9.14 Plastic hinge in simply supported beam.

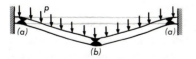

9.15 Plastic hinges in fixed beam.

An I beam of constant cross section cannot substantially redistribute stresses **at a section,** but has a reserve of strength of more than 33 per cent when its ends are fixed. As soon as the higher stresses at the flanges of the end sections reach the elastic limit and hinges are developed there, the lower stresses in the flanges of the midspan section grow until they develop a third hinge. **Redistribution** of stress occurs **between end and midspan sections,** rather than at any **one** section.

Stress redistribution due to plastic flow occurs in any framed structure, since the loads produce maximum stresses only at a few at critical sections; as soon as one of these sections develops a plastic hinge, stresses start growing at other sections. Continuity between the various bars of a frame allows such redistributions to occur at a number of sections (Fig. 9.16). Thus, continuity insures strength reserve and develops in the frame a "democratic structural action"; understressed sections come to the help of more severely stressed ones as soon as these have reached their ultimate capacity. Continuity is one of the best guarantees against collapse, even if, under certain loads, it may produce higher elastic stresses at particular points.

Large amounts of flow should usually be avoided, since they introduce permanent, and often increasing, deformations in the structure. On the other hand, small amounts of plastic flow are necessary to smooth out local stress concentrations, which otherwise might endanger the stucture. Plastic flow is the mechanism through which a structure redistributes stresses and is made safe against a sudden collapse. It is thus clear that no material may be properly used structurally unless it exhibits some plastic flow under high loads.

A structure is only capable of redistributing stresses **between** its elements if it can stand up when one or more of its elements are cut out or removed. For example, a fixed beam has such capacity because if we cut it through its middle section, it may still carry loads as two cantilevers [Fig. 9.17(a); a simply supported beam does not, because, if cut at midspan, it collapses [Fig. 9.17(b)]. A structure so designed as to be capable of stress redistribution between its elements is called **redundant:** it is **always** a statically indeterminated structure (see Section 4.2). Redundancy is an essential guarantee of safety against structural collapse and should be the basis of design for all important structures (see Section 13.3).

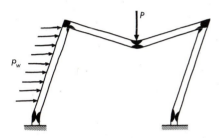

9.16 Plastic hinges in simple frame.

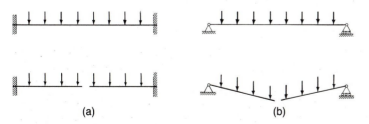

(a)   (b)

9.17 Results of stress redistribution for (a) fixed
beam and (b) simply supported beam.

235

Chapter Ten

Grids, Plates, Folded Plates, and Space-Frames

10.1 Load Transfer in Two Directions

The structural elements considered so far have in common the property of transferring loads in one direction. A load set on a cable or a beam is channeled to the supports along the cable line or the beam axis; an arch, a frame, and a continuous beam produce the same type of "one directional load dispersal." These structures are labeled **one-dimensional resisting structures,** because they can be described by a straight or curved line, along which the stresses channel the loads. (Lines are said to have only one dimension, because a **single** number—for example, the distance from one end of the line—is sufficient to define the position of a point on the line.)

One-dimensional resisting elements may be used to cover a rectangular area, but such an arrangement is usually impractical and inefficient. For example, a series of beams, all parallel to one of the sides of the rectangle, serves this purpose; but a concentrated load on such a system is carried entirely by the beam under the load, while all other beams are unstressed (Fig. 10.1). The system is impractical because one beam deflects while the other beams remain horizontal, and inefficient because it does not work as a whole in carrying the load. The load transfer occurs always in the direction of the beams, and the loads are supported by the two walls at their ends, while the walls parallel to the beams remain unloaded. This may be a proper solution when unloaded walls are needed for functional purposes, but it becomes inefficient when all the walls enclosing the space can be used to support loads.

These considerations suggest that in the example given above it would be structurally more efficient to have "in-plane two-way load dispersal." Such dispersal is obtained by means of **grids** and **plates, two dimensional resisting structures** acting in a plane.

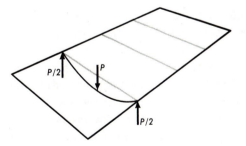

10.1 Concentrated load on one-dimensional system of beams.

10.2 Rectangular Beam Grids

If two identical, simply supported beams at right angles to each other, placed one on top of the other, are connected at their intersection and a concentrated load is applied there, the load is transferred to the supports at the ends of **both** beams and thus **dispersed in two directions** (Fig. 10.2). This mechanism involves the loading of a beam and its consequent deflection, the deflection of the first beam by the connection to the other, and the sharing of the load-carrying action between the two beams. Since the two beams are connected, they are bound to have the same deflection; and, because they are identical, these equal deflections must be due to equal loads. Hence, each beam must carry half the load (Fig. 10.2). Thus each support reaction equals one-fourth of the load, and "two-way dispersal" reduces the loads on the supports to one-half the value they would have if only one-way dispersal took place.

Two beams at right angles must deflect by the same amount at their intersection even if they have different lengths or different cross sections. However, a greater load is required to deflect a stiffer beam by the same amount as a more flexible one. Hence, the stiffer beam will support a greater share of the load than the more flexible beam, and the loads on the two beams will not be equal. The stiffness of a beam under a concentrated load is inversely proportional to the cube of its length. Thus if two beams of **identical cross section** have spans in the ratio of one to two, their stiffnesses are in the ratio of eight to one. Consequently, the short beam will carry eight-ninths of the load and the long beam one-ninth of the load (Fig.10.3).

240

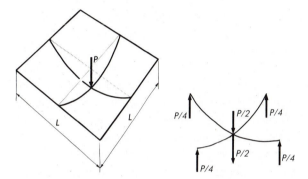

10.2 Two-way load dispersal by equal beams.

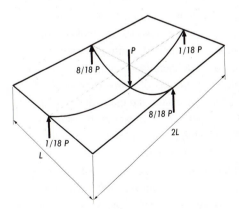

10.3 Two-way dispersal by different beams.

This example shows that true two-way transfer takes place only if the two beams are of equal, or almost equal, stiffness. As soon as one beam is much stiffer than the other, the stiffer beam carries most of the load, and the transfer occurs essentially in its direction. To obtain an efficient two-way transfer in the case of unequal spans, the longer beam must have either a substantially stiffer cross section, that is, a greater moment of inertia (see Section 7.1), or "stiffer" support conditions. For example, if two identical beams have lengths in the ratio of 1 to 1.59, which is the cube root of 4, their midspan deflections under the same load would be in the ratio of $(1.59)^3$ to 1, i.e., 4 to 1. But if the longer beam is fixed, its deflection becomes four times smaller and, since the deflections of the two beams are now equal, the simply supported shorter beam and the longer fixed beam connected at midspan carry equally a load concentrated there.

The sharing of one concentrated load between two beams may be extended to a series of concentrated loads by setting beams in two or more perpendicular directions, one under each load. Once again, the intersection points must deflect by the same amounts. In the arrangement of Fig. 10.4 the deflections of an unsupported long beam at the quarter points would be smaller than the deflection at midspan. Hence, if three, equally spaced, shorter cross-beams of equal stiffness support it, the middle beam deflects more and takes a greater share of the load than the side beams. For beams of identical cross section, and cross-beams one-half as long as the long beam, the loads at the supports have the values shown in Fig. 10.4. The **greater** dispersal in the direction of the **shorter,** stiffer span is evident: the two long sides of the boundary support 94 per cent of the total load. With a long beam eight times stiffer, the long sides still carry about 65 per cent of the total load. The loads tend to move to the support along the shortest possible paths and two-way action vanishes as soon as the ratio of the sides of the rectangle, its so called **aspect ratio,** is greater than 1.5.

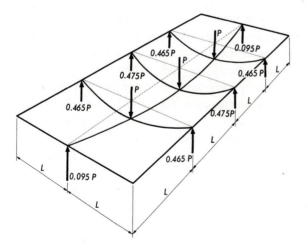

10.4 Two-way dispersal of three loads.

Finally, one may cover a rectangular area by a **grid** of beams at right angles, and obtain the two-way dispersal of loads located at any grid intersection (Fig. 10.5). If all the beams of the grid running in one direction are not connected to, but just set **above** the beams running in the other, any one of the upper beams acts as a continuous beam on flexible supports provided by the lower beams. In this grid an uncentered load may produce upward deflections of an upper beam, and lift it from its supports (Fig. 10.6). A better interaction of the two beam systems is obtained by "weaving" the beams so as to have their relative positions change at each intersection (Fig. 10.7). In this case the grid system is capable of giving support from both below and above: a beam moving up is pulled down by the cross-beam set above it, while a beam moving down is pushed up by the cross-beam under it. In practice, this behavior is obtained by means of welded, bolted, or riveted connections between the beams of steel grids and occurs naturally in reinforced-concrete grids, due to their monolithic construction.

The substitution of trusses for beams transforms grids into rectangular **space frames,** which exhibit the same two-dimensional behavior (see Section 10.9).

244

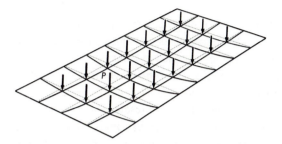

10.5 Rectangular grid.

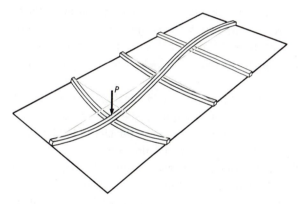

10.6 Uplift of upper beam of grid.

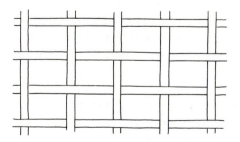

10.7 Woven grid.

Rigid connections between the beams of the two systems introduce another structural action in the grid. When two perpendicular beams connected at mid-span are deflected by a concentrated load at their intersection, their midspan sections [Fig. 10.8, (a)], move downward, but **remain vertical** because of symmetry. When the intersection of the two beams does not occur at mid-span, the beam sections [Fig. 10.8, (b)] deflect and **rotate,** and the continuity introduced by the rigid connection transforms the **bending** rotation of one beam into a **twisting** rotation of the other. The stiffness of the grid is greater when the beams are rigidly connected than when they are simply supported over one another; this indicates that the twisting mechanism is capable of transferring part of the load to the supports, thus producing smaller displacements in the grid. The reader may use a simple grid model with "woven" beams to show that the partially rigid connections introduce a certain amount of twist in the beams, and that the woven grid is stiffer than the unwoven grid.

Grid systems are seen to be particularly efficient in transferring concentrated loads, and in having the entire structure participate in the load carrying action. This efficiency is reflected not only in the more even transfer of the loads to the supports, but in the reduced **depth-to-span ratio** required in rectangular grids. Systems of parallel beams used in ordinary construction have depth-to-span ratios of the order of one-tenth to one-twentieth. This ratio varies some-what with the beam material: steel beams may be somewhat shallower than prestressed concrete beams; reinforced concrete beams deeper; wood beams still deeper; but the depth-to-span ratio cannot go much below one-twentieth, if the beams are to be practically acceptable from the viewpoints of both strength **and** deflection. Sufficiently stiff rectangular grid systems with aspect ratios near unity may be designed with depth-to-span ratios of as little as one-thirtieth to one-fortieth. When accumulated over a large number of floors, this reduction in depth lowers structural and other costs, by reducing the height of the building.

Notwithstanding their interesting properties, it is well to remember that, in practice, two-way grid systems are seldom more economical than one-way beam systems when they require connections, because these are always costly.

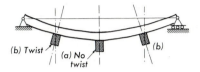

10.8 Grid action with twist.

10.3 Skew Grids

An additional saving in floor depths may at times be achieved by the use of skew grids, in which the beams of the two systems do not intersect at right angles (Fig. 10.9). The advantages thus obtained are twofold.

In the case of rectangular areas with one side much longer than the other, most of the beams of a skew grid span equal distances, and the loss of two-way action is substantially reduced. Moreover, the beams diagonally across the corners of the rectangle, shorter and stiffer than the other beams, give stronger support to the beams intersecting them. For loads concentrated around the center of the plate, and even under uniformly distributed loads, these stiff supports create a reversal of curvature in the longer beams, which behave very much as if they were fixed rather than simply supported at those ends (Fig. 10.10). Since a beam with a fixed end has a load-carrying capacity for uniform loads 120 per cent greater than an identical simply supported beam, skew grids have a somewhat greater structural efficiency. Their depth-to-span ratios may be as low as one-fortieth to one-sixtieth.

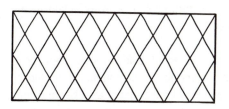

10.9 Skew grid.

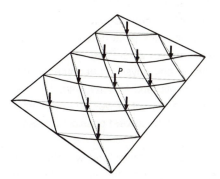

10.10 Reversal of curvature in skew grids.

10.4 Plate Action

The two-way action of beam grids is due to the pointwise connection of the two beam systems at their intersections. Such action is even more pronounced in practice, because the openings in the grid are plugged with slabs or plates, thus making the roof or floor an almost monolithic structure. The advantages of an entirely monolithic structure having two-way action **at all points** would be even more pronounced.

A **plate** or **slab** is a monolithic structural element of relatively small depth covering an area which at first we shall assume to be rectangular. Any strip of plate parallel to one side of the rectangle may be thought of as a beam acting in that direction; any strip at right angles to the first may also be considered as a beam, and since the two perpendicular beams act together, bending of one produces twisting in the other [Figs. 10.11(a) and 10.8]. The action of a plate is analogous to that of a welded beam grid with an infinite number of infinitesimally narrow beams near to one another; but the beams of this grid may be considered to act in **any** direction, since the plate may be ideally divided into perpendicular or skew strips supported at any two points on its boundary [Fig. 10.11(b)]. Since, moreover, in any physical phenomenon nature follows the easiest path, structural elements tend to carry loads by their most efficient mechanism, and a plate acts as the set of welded grid beams transferring the load to the supports by means of the **lowest** possible stresses.

The analogy with a beam grid shows that a plate under load will bend and twist at every point. Bending produces beam-action, that is, bending and shear stresses; twisting produces torsional shears (see Section 5.3).

(a)   (b)

10.11 Equivalent grids in plate action.

It is easy to visualize the role of bending, shear, and torsional stresses in the transmission of a concentrated load by **plate action.** If the plate consisted of a series of independent parallel beams, only the beam under load would deflect, thus transferring the load to the supports by bending and shear [Fig. 10.12(a)]. But the "beams" of a plate are all cemented together so that the loaded beam is partially supported by the two adjacent parallel beams and transfers **part** of the load to them. This transfer occurs through the shears developed between the vertical sides of the adjacent beams, and produces bending and shear in the adjoining beams [Fig. 10.12(b)]. The two adjacent beams, in turn, transfer **some** of their load to the adjoining beams through vertical shears; the **difference** between the downward shears coming from the loaded beam and those upward transferred to the adjoining beams produces the twisting action [Fig. 10.12(c)]. Thus, a combination of shearing and twisting transfers load at **right angles** to the loaded beam, while bending and shear transfer load in the direction of the loaded beam. Since a plate may be considered as a rectangular grid of beams, the transfer mechanisms just described take place not in one but in **two directions,** and plate action is equivalent to beam action in two perpendicualr directions **plus** twisting action in these two directions [Fig. 10.12(d)].

Load carrying by twisting action characterizes plates, and differentiates them from beams and grids, since even welded grids cannot develop substantial twisting action. In this connection, it is interesting to notice that the plate twist is responsible for a good percentage of its load-carrying capacity. For example, in a square plate uniformly loaded and simply supported along its four sides, twisting action is responsible for approximately 50 per cent of the load transfer to the supports. In a rectangular grid weak in twist, 80 to 90 per cent of the load is transferred to the supports by beam action.

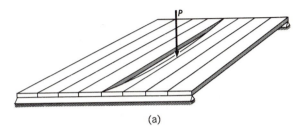

(a)

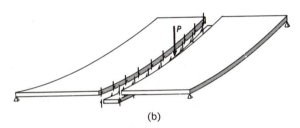

(b)

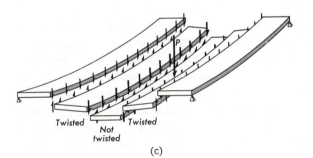

Twisted — Twisted
Not
twisted

(c)

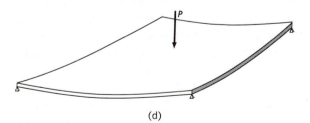

(d)

10.12 Plate action.

It was noticed above that a plate may be considered capable of developing grid action in any direction. This means that any point in the plate may be considered as the intersection of two beams of a rectangular grid system, and that any number of rectangular grid systems may be thought of as passing through a plate point (see Fig. 10.11). The bending stresses at the same point will vary depending on the direction of the imaginary grid system considered, because the beam spans to reach the boundaries change with the beam directions. An evaluation of the bending stresses in different directions **at the same point** of a plate shows that there are two perpendicular directions for which these stresses are, respectively, maximum and minimum, and that for these directions the torsional shears are zero. These are the **principal directions,** which were encountered in other stress situations earlier (see Section 9.2). Indicating the principal directions at various points in the plate by crosses, one may plot the **principal stress lines** or **isostatics,** which show the flow of bending stresses in the plate. Since no torsional shears are developed along the isostatics, the plate may also be thought of as a grid of beams **curved** in the plane of the plate, which meet at right angles, but do not transmit loads to the adjoining beams by twisting action. The isostatics for a simply supported square plate under uniform load are shown in Fig. 10.13(a) and for a rectangular plate in Fig. 10.13(b).

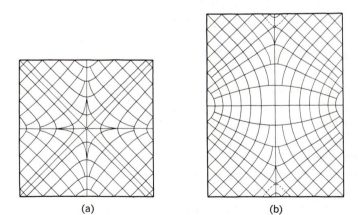

(a)   (b)

10.13 Isostatics of simply supported plates
under uniform load.

The deflections of the plate of Fig. 10.13 (a), shown in Fig. 10.14, explain visually the structural behavior of the plate. The center strips of the plate deflect very much as simply supported beams. At the corners, the two sides of the plate are compelled to remain horizontal by the boundaries, assumed capable of reacting both up and down, and the entire corner areas are stiff; the ends of the diagonal strips are thus prevented from rotating, and these strips behave as fixed-end beams with a reversal of curvature at the ends.

A peculiarity of plate behavior occurs at the corners if a rectangular plate is simply supported over a hole with boundaries that can provide only **upward-**acting reactions: the plate corners curl up [Fig. 10.15(a)]. In order to have the entire plate boundary in contact with the supports, the corners must be pushed down by concentrated corner forces, which must be added to the load carried by the plate in computing its support reactions. For a square plate under a load concentrated at the center, the four corner forces add about 50 per cent to the total plate reactions [Fig. 10.15(b)].

The stiffness of a simply supported, uniformly loaded square plate may be compared to the stiffness of simply supported beams having spans equal to the sides of the plate. The center deflection of the plate is 42 per cent smaller than the corresponding beam deflections. The bending stresses in the plate are 29 per cent smaller than in the beams. The reversed bending stresses at the corners of the plate are two and a half times smaller than the stresses in the fixed diagonal beams connecting opposite plate corners. Although the bending-stress distribution **across the thickness** of the plate is the linear distribution typical of beam bending, and as such is not ideally efficient, the two-way plate action reduces the maximum stresses by substantial amounts.

256

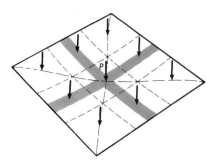

10.14 Deflections of simply supported square plate under uniform load.

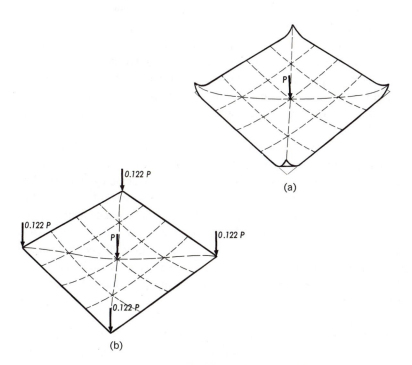

(a)

(b)

10.15 Curling up of plate corners.

A knowledge of maximum and minimum stresses, or reversed stresses, and of the directions in which the torsional shear stresses become maximum in a plate is essential in placing the reinforcement in **concrete slabs.** Maximum shears always occur in directions at 45 degrees to the principal bending directions; in the corners of the plate shear acts in the upper half of the plate as shown in Fig. 10.16 (a), and diagonal reinforcing bars should be oriented as shown in Fig. 10.16(b) in order to absorb directly the equivalent tensile stress.

It was shown in Section 10.2 that rectangular grid systems lose most of their two-way action as soon as one of the sides of the rectangle is much longer than the other. Plates exhibit the same behavior, as indicated in Fig. 10.17 for the case of a uniformly loaded rectangular plate with sides in the ratio of two to one. The center deflection of the plate is only 15 per cent smaller than the deflection of beams parallel to its short sides, while it was 42 per cent smaller for a square plate. The largest stress in the plate is only 20 per cent smaller than in the short equivalent beam. Since the short span is much stiffer than the long span, approximately two-thirds of the load is carried to the long side supports.

What has been said of plates with simply supported sides is true of plates with fixed sides. Such plates are stiffer and behave like a rectangular, welded grid of fixed beams.

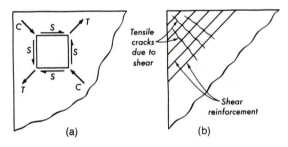

10.16 Shear reinforcement at plate corners.

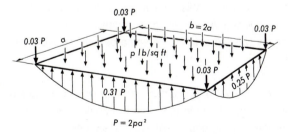

10.17 Action in simply supported rectangular plate.

10.5 Plate Structures

Plates of many shapes and with different support conditions find application in construction, mostly as **floor slabs.**

The conditions of support may differ on the four sides of a plate. A plate may have two simply supported parallel sides and two fixed parallel sides. In this case an increased rigidity of the long spans, due to their fixity, may compensate for a large aspect ratio; the plate exhibits two-way action comparable to that of a square plate with all sides simply supported (Fig. 10.18). Similarly, a **corner balcony plate** may have two adjacent sides simply supported and the other two sides completely unsupported or free. Obviously, no simply supported "unwoven" grid could be built in this fashion, since the beams of the lower system would be unsupported. A "woven" grid, instead, would be capable of carrying load mostly by twisting action. The same behavior is exhibited by the plate (Fig. 10.19).

A stiffer corner balcony plate with two unsupported adjacent sides is obtained by fixing the other two sides (Fig. 10.20); in this case the analogy with a grid system holds, since each beam of the equivalent system is cantilevered, and bending action prevails again.

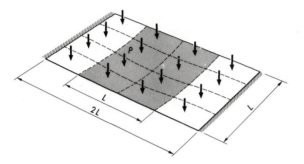

10.18 Plate with opposite simply supported and fixed sides.

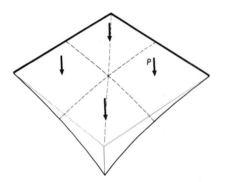

10.19 Plate with adjacent simply supported and free sides.

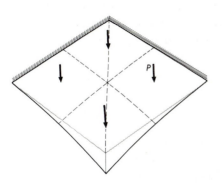

10.20 Corner balcony plate.

Rectangular plates may be supported on more than one type of boundary. In modern office-buildings it is common to support the floor slabs on an outer wall or a series of columns, and on an inner "core," inside of which run the elevators, the air-conditioning ducts, and other parts of the mechanical, electrical, and plumbing systems (Fig. 10.21). A completely free floor area is thus obtained.

The boundary of a slab may have a variety of shapes: instead of covering a rectangle it may cover a skew, a polygonal, or a circular area. The behavior of a circular slab simply supported at the boundary does not differ substantially from that of the circumscribed simply supported square slab [Fig. 10.22(a)], since the corners of the square slab are rigid and only its central portion presents sizable deflections. The behavior of a circular slab fixed at the boundary is similar to that of the inscribed square slab [Fig. 10.22(b)].

Ring slabs may be built to span the area limited by concentric outer and inner circular supports. As soon as the radial span of the slab is small in comparison to its average radius, two-way plate action under uniform load is considerably reduced, and the slab exhibits stresses of the same order of magnitude as those of beams spanning the radial distance between the two circular boundaries.

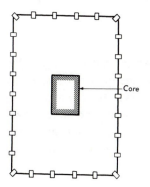

10.21 Floor slab of building with inner core.

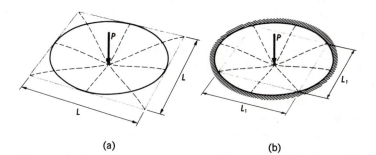

| (a) | (b) |

10.22 Circular plates.

Slabs may also be "point-supported" on columns, either hinged or fixed to the slab. The connection between the columns and the slab must be designed to absorb the so-called "punching shear" from the columns, and may require the use of capitals or of intermediate distributing plates called **drop-panels** (Fig. 10.23). In order to avoid capitals, **shear connectors** of steel are used sometimes in reinforced-concrete design to guarantee the transmission of load from the column to the slab (Fig. 10.24).

Slabs used as floors, or **flat slabs,** present the constructional advantage of smooth underside surfaces which permit the unimpeded running of pipes, ducts, and other parts of the various mechanical systems required in a modern building. The savings achieved by the avoidance of pipe and duct bends around beams often justify the selection of a flat-slab system for floors and roofs. Flat-slab and column systems of reinforced concrete are among the most economical structures for buildings with limited spans and are commonly used in high-rise apartment buildings all over the world.

Reinforced concrete slabs supported by steel or concrete columns are easily poured on plane forms. An additional saving in formwork is achieved by pouring the slabs on the ground, one on top of the other, and lifting them to the top of the columns by means of hydraulic jacks. Buildings with a large number of floors have been built by this lift-slab technique.

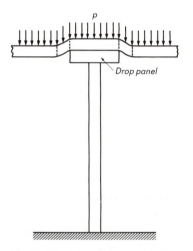

10.23 Punching shear in column-supported slab.

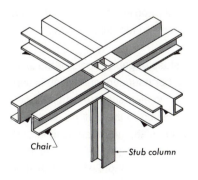

10.24 Shear connector.

An important application of reinforced-concrete slabs as both vertical walls and horizontal floors occurs in **prefabricated panel construction.** The slabs are fabricated and cured in a factory, and erected and joined on the site, with savings in manpower and construction time, particularly when the electrical and plumbing systems are incorporated in the panels. The various panel systems invented and patented so far differ mostly in the method adopted for joining the plates. In **box construction,** boxes made out of panels are built integrally at the factory and erected at the site. Box construction has been used in the USSR since the nineteen-fifties, and was applied by Safdi to the construction of the apartment cluster called "Habitat" in Montreal in 1966.

Inclined slabs are used in roof design as the sides of gabled roofs or the sloping sides of "north-light roofs," in which the higher boundary of the slab is supported on a truss (Fig. 10.25). The vertical trussed elements are light, and permit the use of large glass surfaces, usually exposed to the uniform north light required in factories and artists' studios. Inclined slabs are often used in storage bins and other components of industrial buildings (Fig. 10.26). Such inclined slabs carry some of the load by tension or compression down their slope, and some by plate action in a direction perpendicular to the plate.

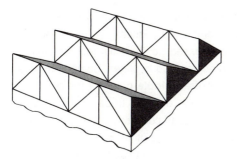

10.25 Plates in north-light roofs.

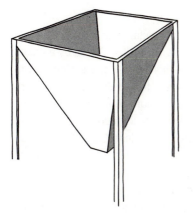

10.26 Inclined slabs in storage bins.

10.6 Ribbed Plates

The structural efficiency of plates is reduced by the linear stress distribution across their thickness. Only the top and bottom plate fibers at the most stressed **point,** in the most stressed **direction** develop allowable stresses. In the case of beams this inefficiency is remedied by locating as much material as possible at a distance from the unstressed neutral axis, thus obtaining I and T sections; the same remedy can be adapted to plates. Some of the material may be located away from the **neutral middle plane** of the plate and used to create ribs, which run in one, two, or even three directions (Fig. 10.27). A ribbed slab presents the advantages of continuity due to plate action and the advantages of depth due to its ribs. On the other hand, the underside of a ribbed plate is not smooth, and a soffit may have to be hung from it. Pipes and ducts are not bent around the ribs but, usually, hung from them. In **composite action** floors a concrete slab is poured and rigidly connected to the top of steel beams; the beams stiffen the slab, which in turn acts as an upper compression flange for the beams.

An economical solution of the slab problem for rectangular floors with relatively small spans is commonly obtained outside the United States by a mixed structure of reinforced concrete and tiles. The hollow tiles are set on a horizontal scaffolding of planks to create the formwork for parallel reinforced concrete ribs; steel bars are set between the tiles to reinforce the ribs and above the tiles to reinforce the slab (Fig. 10.28); concrete is then poured in between the tiles and above them. Once the concrete has hardened, the floor acts as a reinforced concrete slab, ribbed in one or two directions, but with a smooth underside due to the tiles. For fairly large spans the portion of the tiles in the compressed area of the cross section is included in the evaluation of the ribbed slab strength. Cinder blocks or other insulating material may be used instead of tiles as formwork for the ribbed concrete slab.

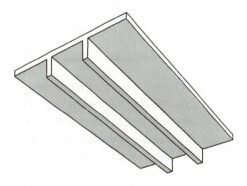

10.27 Ribbed slab.

10.28 Concrete and tile floor.

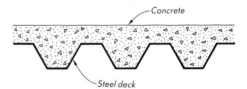

10.29 Steel deck concrete floor.

In the United States the floors of steel buildings are often built by pouring a concrete slab on a **steel deck,** which is supported on steel beams and acts as both the formwork for and the tensile reinforcement of the concrete slab (Fig. 10.29). The steel deck is made of thin galvanized plate and, through its wavy cross-section, introduces one-way ribs in the concrete slab.

A concrete slab ribbed in two perpendicular directions is called a **waffle slab** and is used to cover a rectangular area. When the sides of the rectangular area are substantially different, deeper ribs may be used in one direction, or, in the case of reinforced concrete, the two sets of ribs may have the same depth and be reinforced differently (Fig. 10.30). Waffle slabs are obtained by laying steel or plastic "domes" on a horizontal scaffold in a grid pattern, laying reinforcing bars between and above the domes and pouring concrete between the domes to create the ribs, and above the domes to create the slab. The domes can be reused a large number of times.

The appearance of a ribbed concrete slab may be enhanced by the suggestion of the Italian engineer Arcangeli to have curved ribs along the isostatic lines of the plate (see Section 10.4). The pattern depends on the support conditions at the plate boundary, and on the loads to be carried. For simply supported plates under uniform load the isostatic pattern is often similar to that shown in Fig. 10.13, and was actually used by Nervi in floor design (Fig. 10.31). Such curved ribs require expensive forms, and are economically acceptable only if the forms can be reused a number of times.

270

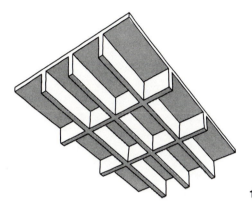

10.30 Waffle slab.

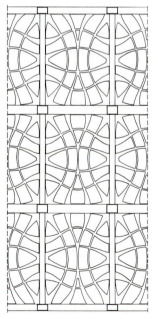

10.31 Slab ribbed along isostatics.

Two-layered concrete slab structures, analogous to I beams, are obtained by pouring a concrete slab on a flat scaffold and then pouring on it a waffle slab. In this case the disposable boxes, used instead of the domes to create the ribs or webs, are lost in the process. Similar **sandwich plates,** with high strength-to-weight ratios, are obtained by inserting between two thin plates of plywood, gypsum, steel, aluminum, or plastic materials a plastic foam with good shear resistance. The plastic foam constitutes a lightweight two-dimensional web, while the two plates develop the bending resistance of the sandwich. Such plates have, in addition, good thermal and acoustical insulating properties. Sandwich plates of cardboard with honeycomb paper webs are used in many applications where a reduced dead load is essential, as in aircraft structures and packaging.

Steel plates constitute the webs of **plate-girders,** deep beams used in bridges or other large structures. Their buckling resistance is highly increased by vertical and longitudinal stiffeners, which essentially reduce the length of the plate strips that tend to buckle (see Section 7.1). Thus, steel and aluminum webs are often ribbed, not only to increase their direct load-carrying capacity, but to reduce their weakness in buckling (see Fig. 7.25).

10.7 Strength Reserve in Plates

Plates are called **two-dimensional resisting structures** because two numbers are needed to define the location of one of their points. In the case of rectangular plates, these numbers are the distances of the point from each of the two sides, measured parallel to the other side.

One of the essential characteristics of two-dimensional structures is their high reserve of strength, which stems from two separate sources: **stress redistribution** and **membrane action** (see also Section 11.2).

It was shown in Section 9.3 that a simply supported rectangular beam can only redistribute stresses across its depth at the most stressed section, but that a fixed-end beam, after redistributing stresses first across the depth of the most stressed sections at the supports, proceeds to redistribute stresses across the depth of another less stressed section. In a plate, peak stresses, that is, maximum **principal** stresses, occur only at one or at a few sections, and most sections are understressed. As the load increases, the most stressed sections redistribute stresses across their depth, while stresses increase at other sections. As soon as one of the sections yields and flows, the stresses at other sections increase progressively up to the yield point and then flow until entire **lines of sections** may flow, thus creating **hinge lines** (Fig. 10.32). When the plate has developed enough hinge lines to become a moving mechanism, it cannot carry additional loads. Whereas redistribution of stress in a beam can take place at only one or a few sections before failure occurs, in a plate redistribution takes place along an entire line of sections. Hence, the reserve of strength is generally greater in a two-dimensional element like a plate than in a one-dimensional structure. The reserve of strength in a simply supported square plate under uniform load is 80 per cent as against 50 per cent in a simply supported beam.

In the discussion of stress redistribution in beams (see Section 9.3) it was emphasized that the end sections of both simply supported and fixed beams are assumed free to move **longitudinally** relative to each other, so that the neutral beam axis **does not change length** [Fig. 10.33(a)]. When the end sections are restrained from moving longitudinally, the deflection of the beam under load requires a lengthening of the middle axis of the beam, and introduces tension in the beam [Fig. 10.33 (b)]. Thus, in a beam made of tensile material the longitudinal restraint of the end sections develops a certain amount of **cable action,** due to the tension along the beam axis curved by the loads. A beam with ends free to move carries loads exclusively by bending and shear, that is, by **beam action;** a longitudinally restrained beam carries loads partly by beam, and partly by cable action. An additional reserve of strength thus appears in the restrained beam; as the beam yields at some sections, and finally becomes a mechanism incapable of carrying additional load in bending, the sag of the middle axis increases and additional load is carried by cable action. Such cable action cannot take place in longitudinally unrestrained beams, because, due to the movable hinge, they can deflect **without** stretching their middle axis.

A rectangular plate, simply supported along **two opposite** sides and free along the other two, behaves very much like a series of parallel beams; if its simply supported sides are free to move relative to each other, the plate can-

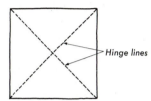

10.32 Hinge lines of simply supported square plate.

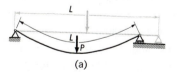

(a)

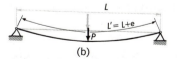

(b)

10.33 Cable action due to longitudinal restraint of beam ends.

not develop cable stresses. Cable stresses will be developed only if the two opposite sides are restrained from moving.

A square plate, simply supported on **all four** sides, deflects under a uniform load into a shape which **stretches** its middle surface **even** if its sides are free to move (see Fig. 10.14). Such shapes are called **nondevelopable,** because they cannot be "developed" or flattened into a plane without stretching them or introducing appropriate cuts. A sphere is a nondevelopable surface; it can be flattened without being stretched only if it is cut radially at an infinite number of sections (see Fig. 12.4); a cylinder, on the other hand, is a developable surface because it can be flattened without stretching or cutting (see also Section 12.2). The rectangular plate with two opposite sides simply supported and two sides free cannot develop cable stresses because it deflects under load into a cylindrical surface.

The deflection surfaces of plates under loads are in almost all cases non-developable. Hence, the middle plane of the plate must stretch to acquire such deflections, and stresses are developed in the **middle plane** of the plate capable of carrying some load by **membrane action.** Membrane action is the two-dimensional equivalent of one-dimensional cable action; it is the action developed under load by a very thin sheet of flexible material, such as cloth (see also Section 11.2). Membrane action develops even when the plate sides are free to move, but is substantially greater when the sides are restrained.

In general, whatever its support conditions, a plate develops membrane action as soon as it deflects under load; its load-carrying capacity is due to both plate action and membrane action. Under growing loads, a plate first redistributes bending stresses at various sections until it becomes incapable of carrying any additional load by plate action. But, at the same time, the plate develops membrane action, and does not fail until the tensile membrane stresses reach the yield point. It is thus seen that, inasmuch as the plate deflects into a non-developable surface because of its "two-dimensionality," the continuity of the plate material in two directions gives the plate an inherently greater reserve of strength.

10.8 Folded Plates

The structural efficiency of plates can be increased by stiffening them with ribs, thus removing some of the material from the neighborhood of the "middle plane" of the plate and increasing its moment of inertia. The same result may also be achieved by folding the plate. A sheet of paper, held along one side, cannot support its own weight, because its minute thickness does not give a sufficient lever arm to the bending stresses [Fig. 10.34(a)]. Folding the paper sheet brings the material of the cross section away from its middle plane, and increases the lever arm of the bending stresses, which becomes comparable to the depth of the folded strips [Fig. 10.34(b)]. In fact, the moment of inertia of two plates at an angle is equivalent to that of a rectangular cross-section beam with a depth equal to the depth of the plates, and a width equal to the combined **horizontal** widths of the two plates (Fig. 10.35).

Folded plates spanning 100 feet or more may be made of wood, steel, aluminum, or reinforced concrete. Reinforced-concrete folded plates are particularly economical because their formwork may be built of straight planks, or the concrete slabs may be prefabricated on the ground, lifted into place, and connected by welding the transverse bars at the folds and concreting the joints, thus eliminating most of the formwork altogether.

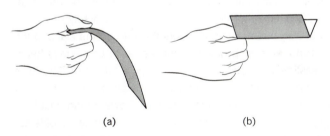

(a)   (b)

10.34 Folded plate.

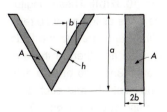

10.35 Rectangular beam equivalent to folded plate.

Folded-plate action is a combination of transverse and longitudinal beam action. Since the length of the slabs is many times their width [Fig. 10.36(a)], the single slabs behave like plates with large aspect ratio and develop only one-way beam action in the direction of their width, that is, transversely (see Section 10.4). This transverse beam action transfers the load on the slabs to the folds so that each **transverse** strip of slab behaves like a continuous beam with equal spans, elastically supported at the folds [Fig. 10.37(a)]. The folds are actually rigidly supported in the neighborhood of the plate ends, where the folded plate rests on rigid end frames [Fig. 10.36(a)]. Towards the middle of the span, instead, the fold supports are actually flexible; but since all folds deflect practically by the same amount, the transverse slab strip moves down by the same amount at each fold and the fold supports act everywhere **as if** they were rigid, as far as transverse bending is concerned. The reactions of the transverse strips at the folds may be split into components (as in a triangular truss), which load the slabs in their own planes [Fig. 10.37(b)]. These longitudinal reactions are carried to the end frames by the slabs acting as deep rectangular beams [Fig. 10.36(b)]. Thus, the load is first transferred to the folds by beam action of the slabs in the transverse direction and then to the end frames by longitudinal beam action of the slabs: each unit strip of slab acts transversely as a fixed-end beam of unit width and depth h, and each slab acts longitudinally as a rectangular beam of width b and depth a (Figs. 10.35, 10.36, and 10.37).

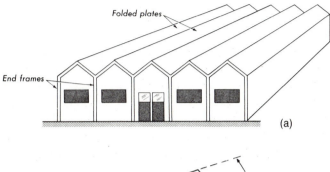

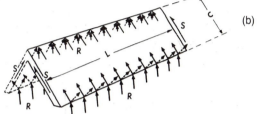

10.36 Longitudinal beam action in folded plate.

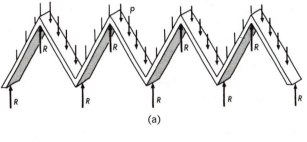

10.37 Transverse continuous-beam action in folded plates.

A uniformly loaded roof, consisting of a large number of folded plates, develops the same deflections in all the slabs, except those near its external longitudinal boundaries. It was seen that the transverse strips of interior slabs move down by the same amount at each fold, and behave as continuous beams on **rigid** supports, since equal displacements of all the supports do not stress a continuous beam. The exterior slabs, instead, have differential displacements between the external and the internal fold supports, and carry more load by transverse bending than the interior slabs. To avoid overstressing, the exterior slabs may be stiffened by additional vertical deep beams at the boundary; the one-sided lack of support of the exterior slabs is thus compensated for by the supporting action of the boundary beams (Fig. 10.38).

Folded plates may be given a variety of cross-sectional shapes. Some of the commonly used arrangements are shown in Fig. 10.38.

The increase in stiffness due to folding may be extended to other than longitudinal folds. Polygonal and circular folded plates may be used to cover circular areas; in this case the plates are given a rise at the center, where the depth of the slabs peters out [Fig. 10.39(a)]. Each radial element of the folded plate behaves like a truss or arch; it develops a thrust, usually absorbed by a circumferential tie-rod, and may be considered hinged at the crown, since the small depth available there makes impossible the development of bending stresses [Fig. 10.39(b)].

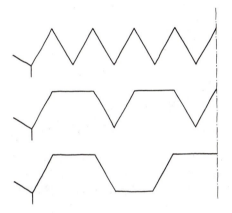

10.38 Folded-plate cross sections.

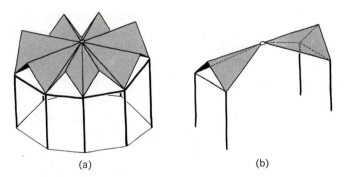

    (a)   (b)

10.39 Polygonal folded plates.

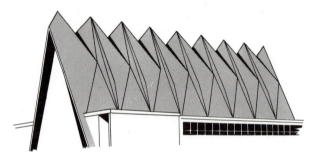

10.40 Folded-plate construction.

Folded plates are used mainly as roof structures, but their application to floors may become practical when their depth can be used to house mechanical systems. Folded plates may also be used as vertical walls to resist both vertical and horizontal loads. Combinations of folded-plates have been used to enclose large spaces (Fig. 10.40). The reader may wish to experiment with this type of construction by folding a sheet of paper along the lines indicated in Fig. 10.41 and taping it to a piece of cardboard. The barrel-type structure thus obtained is capable of supporting 300 or more times its dead load, although the paper may be only one hundredth of an inch thick (Fig. 10.42). The creased-paper structure collapses if its boundary is allowed to move. The collapse is due mostly to buckling of the thin slabs in those areas where compression is developed.

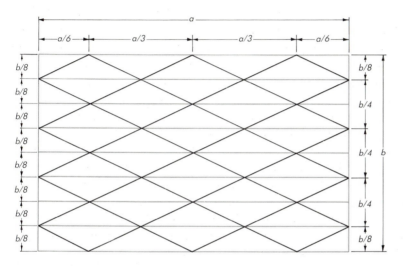

10.41 Creased-paper barrel folds (up along thin lines, down along thick lines).

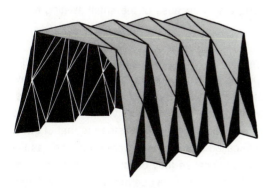

10.42 Creased-paper barrel.

10.9 Space-Frames

The two-way action of a rectangular or a skew grid system can be used to span large areas by substituting trusses for beams. The rectangular, or skew, roofs thus obtained (Fig. 10.43) exhibit a minor amount of load carrying capacity through twisting action because of the small twisting resistance of the trusses.

A substantial increase in the twisting action of such roofs can be obtained if panel points of parallel and perpendicular trusses are connected by **skew bars**, as first suggested by Alexander Graham Bell (Fig. 10.44). The truss systems thus become triangulated in space and their behavior is analogous to that of thick plates made out of a spongy material rather than to that of grids. Such triangulated space trusses, called **space-frames,** are often used as flat roof structures to cover large areas because they consist of a large number of identical bars of a few different lengths and may be built in a variety of patterns whose laced appearance has high aesthetic content.

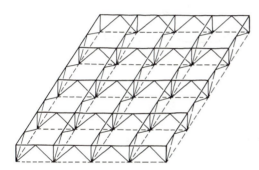

10.43 Rectangular space truss.

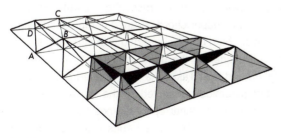

10.44 Space-frame.

(a)

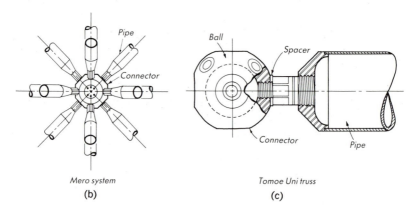

Mero system
(b)

Tomoe Uni truss
(c)

10.45 Slotted and screwed connectors.

Although entire space-frames have been assembled on the ground (by welding, bolting, or screwing their steel bar ends to joint **connectors**), and then jacked up in place, most of them consist of prefabricated sections built by the use of standard connectors (Fig. 10.45) and erected in place without requiring costly scaffolds. The highly efficient Takenaka truss (Fig. 10.46) has compressed bars on a square grid in its upper chord, inclined compressed diagonals, and tensile bars in its lower chord on a square grid with sides the square root of 2, that is, 1.41 times the sides of the upper chord grid, skew to this grid. du Château has designed and built Takenaka-type space-frames by the use of identical prefabricated pyramids connected at the corners by high-strength bolts (Fig. 10.47). Lightweight planar space-frames have also been built by means of steel pipe elements with crimped ends inserted in slotted connectors [Fig. 10.45(a)].

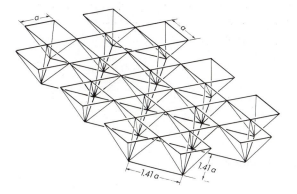

10.46 Takenaka truss.

10.47 du Château space-frame element.

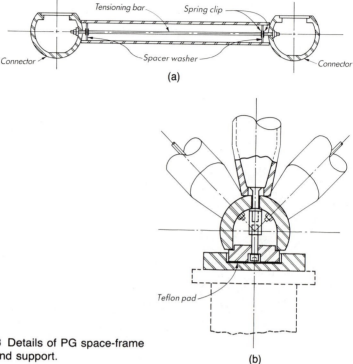

Tensioning bar — Spring clip —

Connector —

Spacer washer —

Connector

(a)

Teflon pad —

(b)

10.48 Details of PG space-frame
bar and support.

In the PG system, developed by Gugliotta, the bars of steel pipe are connected to hollow spherical connectors by tensioning against the connectors'
steel rods running inside the bars (Fig. 10.48). The precompressed units of a
PG frame can thus be assembled on the ground as a tinker toy and lifted in
place (Fig. 10.49). The PG system was used to build the 570,000 square foot
space-frame for the roof of the Jacob K. Javits Convention Center in New
York City, engineered by Weidlinger Associates, the largest in the world to
date (1986), which consists of square units supported on concrete pilons 90
feet on center (Fig. 10.49). It can be shown that a simply supported Takenaka
truss under uniform load is statically determinate (see Sections 4.2 and 9.3)
and hence is not redundant, while other types of space-frames are statically
indeterminate and may be designed with various degrees of redundancy (see
Section 13.3). The research of Makowski shows that because of their twisting
capacity space-frames can be built with span-to-depth ratios as high as 60.

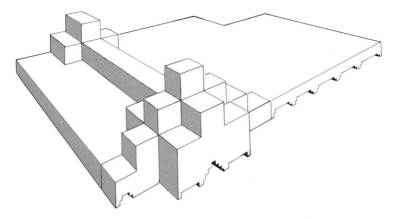

10.49 (a) Isometric of the Jacob K. Javits Convention Center in New York City.

10.49 (b) Space-frame of the Jacob K. Javits Convention Center in New York City. Courtesy I. M. Pei and Partners.

Chapter Eleven

Membranes

11.1 Membrane Action

A membrane is a sheet of material so thin that, for all practical purposes, it can only develop tension. A piece of cloth or a sheet of rubber is a good example of a membrane. Soap films are among the thinnest membranes we can build: they are only a few thousandths of an inch thick, can span plane or skew closed boundaries and have the remarkable property of being surfaces of minimim area among all those with a given boundary (Fig. 11.1). By the same token, a soap film is also the smoothest surface connecting the points of the given boundary.

Although a membrane is a two-dimensional resisting structure, it cannot develop appreciable plate stresses (bending and shear) because its depth is very small in comparison with its span (see Section 10.4), neither can it stand compression without buckling. Therefore, the load-carrying capacity of membranes is due exclusively to their tensile strength.

It was noted in Section 6.1 that a cable can support loads in tension because it sags, and that it is structurally efficient because its tensile stresses are distributed uniformly across its sections. A membrane supports loads by a similar two-way mechanism and presents the same kind of structural efficiency. But just as a plate develops, in addition to beam actions, a twisting action which is due to its two-dimensional character, a membrane, due to its two-dimensionality, develops, in addition to cable actions, an in-plane "shear action" which increases its load-carrying capacity.

294

11.1 Minimum surface membrane.

Figure 11.2 shows an element cut out of a curved membrane and acted upon by a load **normal** to it, i.e., a pressure. Since the sag of the element produces in the membrane **curvatures** in two directions, the membrane may be considered as the intersection of two cables; each cable carries a share of the load, and the total load carried by the membrane is the sum of the two "cable supported" loads. Thus, a membrane is seen to be capable of "cable action in two directions" due to its curved shape, that is, to the geometrical characteristic of its shape called **curvature**. It will now be shown that the two-dimensional resisting character of a membrane makes it also capable of a second load-carrying mechanism through the development of in-plane or **tangential shears** acting **within** the membrane surface.

One may prove that a thin piece of material can develop such shears by holding a **vertical** sheet of paper along one of its edges and by pulling down **vertically** along its opposite edge. The paper sheet carries the load **acting in its own plane by tangential** shears (Fig. 11.3). But, just as the tension in a horizontal cable cannot carry vertical loads, the shears in the plane of the paper sheet cannot, by themselves, carry loads perpendicular to it. The load-carrying action of a membrane due to tangential shears is essentially connected with another geometrical characteristic of its shape.

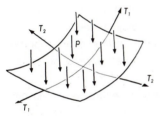

11.2 Cable actions in membrane.

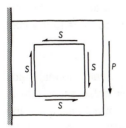

11.3 Shear development in plane of membrane.

Figure 11.4 shows a rectangular element cut out of a curved membrane, and indicates that, in general, its four sides are not parallel, but askew in space; this means that one of its sides slopes more than the opposite side, and that a **difference** in slope occurs between these two sides. The figure also shows that a difference in slope between two opposite sides necessarily requires a difference in slope between the **other** two opposite sides, since the two more inclined sides must meet at a point. The difference in slope between two opposite sides one unit apart, that is, the unit change in slope **at right angles to the direction of the slope,** is called the **geometrical twist** of the membrane surface. Since, in addition, the slope of a membrane surface usually changes from point to point in the direction of the slope, membranes, in general, also have what we call **curvatures**. The curvatures and the twist characterize the geometrical behavior of the membrane surface at a given point (see Section 11.2).

The two pairs of equal shears on the opposite sides of any membrane element have directions that guarantee equilibrium in rotation (see Section 5.3), as shown in Fig. 11.3; but in a twisted membrane the difference in slope between two equal shears on opposite sides produces an **excess** of upward forces (Fig. 11.5). It is this excess that balances part of the load and gives the membrane its load-carrying capacity **by shearing action** within its own surface.

Inasmuch as shear is equivalent to tension and compression, this additional load-carrying capacity can be developed by the membrane if and only if the equivalent compression due to shear is smaller than the tension due to cable action. Otherwise, the excess of compression would tend to buckle the thin membrane. If this happens, the membrane changes shape to carry the load by tension only.

Membranes that do not tend to buckle are thus seen to carry normal loads without changing shape by three separate mechanisms: cable action due to curvature in one direction; cable action due to curvature at right angles to the first; and shear action due to twist. Any one of these actions vanishes if the corresponding curvature, or the twist, vanishes.

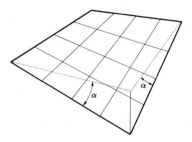

11.4 Geometrical twist.

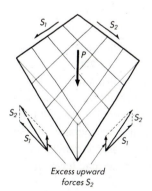

11.5 Portion of normal load carried
by membrane shears.

11.2 Principal Curvatures and Principal Membrane Stresses

The results obtained in the preceding section indicate the two essential characteristics of membrane action: (a) **Membrane stresses,** both tensile and shearing, are always developed within the membrane surface and never at right angles to it; (b) Membrane action depends essentially on the geometrical characteristics of the membrane shape, that is, on its curvatures and its twist.

In order to visualize the curvatures of a surface, one must cut the surface with a plane perpendicular to it. For example, Fig. 11.6 shows that, in a cylinder, a perpendicular plane parallel to the axis cuts the cylinder along a straight line, indicating a lack of curvature in this direction. A cut at right angles to the axis has, instead, a large curvature, while cuts in any other direction show **smaller** curvatures. It is thus seen that as the cutting plane rotates around the normal to the cylinder, the sections acquire curvatures that vary from zero in one direction to a maximum value at right angles to it. The two perpendicular directions in which the curvatures become respectively maximum and minimum (in the present example the minimum is zero) are called the **principal directions of curvature** of the membrane surface. For an element of the cylinder with sides parallel to these directions, it is seen that the element has **no twist:** the horizontal slope remains horizontal as one moves at right angles to it [Fig. 11.7(a)]. But an element cut out of the cylinder with sides not parallel to the principal directions has twist [Fig. 11.7(b)]. Thus a surface may have twist in certain directions and no twist in others. (The only surface without twist in any direction is the sphere, since an element cut by any two pairs of parallel sides is identical to an element cut by any other two pairs of sides.)

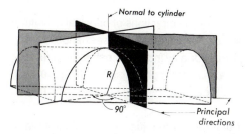

11.6 Cylinder curvatures.

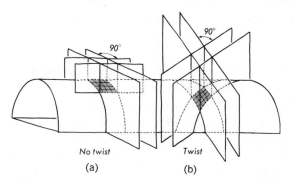

11.7 Cylinder twist.

The properties exhibited by the cylinder in relation to curvature and twist are not peculiar to this surface, but completely general. **Any surface** cut by planes passing through its normal at a point exhibits two directions at right angles to each other for which the curvature becomes, respectively, maximum and minimum; for these two perpendicular directions the surface has no twist. It is often convenient to spot principal curvature directions by the lack of twist—that is, of slope change—in these directions.

One may mark by means of small crosses the directions of principal curvature on a surface, as was done for the case of principal stresses, and obtain a pattern of **lines of principal curvature**. For a cylinder this pattern is a rectangular mesh with sides parallel to the axis and at right angles to it. Figure 11.8 indicates the principal curvature lines for a more general surface.

The tensile direct stress at a point of a membrane, just like the stresses in a plate, has different values in different directions. As the orientation of the tensile stress rotates around a point, the stress becomes maximum and minimum in two directions at right angles to each other, the **directions of principal stress**. Elements oriented in these directions do **not** develop shear; shear instead becomes greatest at 45 degrees to the directions of principal stress. The perpendicular directions of principal stress are those in which the membrane acts as two sets of cables at right angles; one set develops the maximum stress, the other set the minimum stress at each point. Shear stress develops between the cables in any other direction.

Indicating by small crosses the directions of principal stress at a number of points, one may obtain a pattern of **principal stress lines** for the membrane. Whereas the lines of principal curvature are a **geometrical** characteristic of the membrane surface, the lines of principal stress depend on the shape of the surface but also on the character of the load and the conditions of support [Fig. 11.9(a),(b)]. In certain cases of symmetry, the two patterns may exceptionally coincide, as for a sphere or a cylinder under internal pressure [Fig. 11.9(b)].

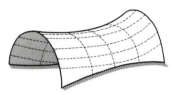

11.8 Principal curvature lines.

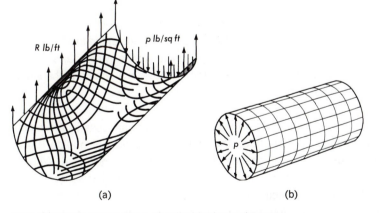

(a)   (b)

11.9 Principal stress lines of cylindrical membranes
(a) under dead load, (b) under internal pressure.

303

The analysis of cable action showed that the stresses developed in a cable are related to its span-to-sag ratio (see Section 6.1). Conversely, **for a given allowable stress,** the greater the sag, the greater the load the cable can safely carry. Considering the cable action of a membrane along its principal stress directions, it is thus found that the direction with greater sag ratio—that is, greater curvature—carries more load than the direction with smaller sag ratio, smaller curvature. In the case of a sphere, the curvature is the same in all directions, and a spherical membrane under uniform pressure carries half of it by cable action in one direction and half of it by cable action at right angles to it. In the case of a cylinder under uniform normal pressure, the straight lines carry no load, since they have no curvature, and the entire load is carried by stresses along the curvature lines at right angles to the cylinder axis. These so-called **hoop stresses** are twice as large as those in a sphere of the same radius under the same pressure.

When the load distribution on a membrane changes, stresses in the membrane also change, but, **provided the new stresses do not buckle it,** the membrane does not have to change shape to support the new load. While a cable is funicular for only one set of loads, a membrane is funicular for a variety of load distributions because it can distribute the load between its two-dimensional tensile and shear mechanisms in a variety of ways. Thus, a membrane is inherently more stable than a cable, although it is unstable under

304

loads that tend to buckle it. Under such loads the membrane changes shape so as to support them by purely membrane stresses.

In general, membranes must be stabilized, mostly because their funicular shape for horizontal loads differs from that for vertical loads. Stabilization is obtained either by means of an inner skeleton or by prestressing produced by external forces or by internal pressure. Prestressing allows a loaded membrane to develop compressive stresses up to values capable of wiping out the tensile stresses locked in the membrane by the prestressing; it adds to the advantage of greater aerodynamic stability that of an increased carrying capacity through the shear mechanism.

It must be noted that the tensile stresses in a membrane are uniformly distributed across its thickness; the utilization of the material in membranes is optimal. Moreover, tensile strains are always small compared to bending strains, so that the membrane deflections due to loads are usually small. (These deflections should not be confused with the **displacements** of the membrane due to load **variations,** which require changes in its shape.) Thus, by the nature of their load-carrying action, membranes are light and stiff under steady loads. As noted above, their use in permanent structures must take into account their mobility, which can be greatly reduced, but not totally eliminated, by prestressing.

11.3 Tents and Balloons

Notwithstanding their instability, from time immemorial human ingenuity has found ways and means of using membranes for structural purposes, mainly because of their lightness. The nomad's tent is a membrane capable of spanning tens of feet, provided its skins are properly supported by compressive struts and stabilized by tensioned guy ropes. The circus tent spans hundreds of feet using the same technology (Fig. 11.10). The tent withstands the pressure of the wind, but even under ideal circumstances presents the drawback of moving under variable loads. Moreover, because of its light weight, the tent vibrates or "flutters" under the action of a variable, or even a steady, wind. Tents are useful as temporary covers, and acceptable as permanent roofs only if highly prestressed.

Large tents supported by complicated cable nets on vertical or inclined compression masts have been used by Frei Otto to build temporary or permanent pavillions for fairs and other uses. One of the largest to date (1986) covers 808,000 square feet at the site of the 1972 Olympics in Munich, Germany (Fig. 11.11). It is supported by nine masts up to 260 feet tall, and has prestressing cables of up to 5000 tons capacity, which give the roof the appearance of a series of interconnected saddle surfaces. The cables support translucent Plexiglass slabs, lightly tinted a neutral gray-brown.

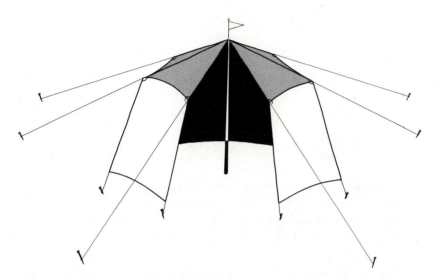

11.10 Circus tent.

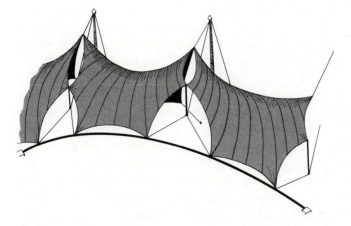

11.11 Cable-supported tent of the Olympic Stadium in Munich, West Germany.

The largest tent built to date (1986) is the prestressed tent for the Haj terminal of the Jiddah Airport in Saudi Arabia, engineered by Geiger-Berger for the pilgrims to Mecca. It consists of 210 square modules, 151 feet by 151 feet, covering an area of 23 acres (Fig. 11.12).

The tent of the Franklin Zoo in Boston, Massachusetts, engineered by Weidlinger Associates, consists of three cable-reinforced panels of plastic fabric, supported by a tripod of three inclined steel arches resting on a reinforced-concrete ring that is compressed by the tension in the cables (Fig. 11.13). It covers a circular area of 7 acres with a radius of 176 feet. Its membrane is partly stabilized by a minor internal suction. Although designed to support a snow load of 30 pounds per square foot, under normal conditions it will not carry such load because the snow will be melted by the warm air of the air-conditioned interior.

The structural action of a membrane is greatly improved by tensioning it before it is loaded. Firemen use a round sheet of cloth, tensioned on an outer ring, to catch people jumping from great heights. The tension in the sheet and the compression in the ring are produced by the radial pull of the rope connecting the sheet to the ring. The thin sheet takes the impact of the falling person, deflects elastically, and saves the jumper by its flexibility and strength. The combination of sheet and ring, even though unloaded, has "locked-in" stresses of the type described in Section 2.5. Firemen's membranes are typical prestressed elements.

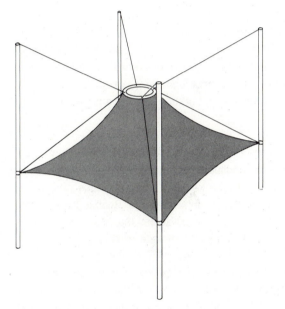

11.12 Jiddah tent module.

11.13 Franklin Zoo tent, Boston, MA.

The umbrella is another example of a prestressed membrane with locked-in stresses. The steel ribs, pushed out and supported by the compressive struts connected to the stick, tension the cloth, and give it a curved shape suited to resisting loads. Within limits, the membrane of an umbrella can take pressures from above and from below: the supporting steel skeleton reverses its stresses with the reversal of wind action, but the membrane is under tension in both cases (Fig. 11.14).

The Eskimo kayak is built by means of a membrane of seal skins tensioned by a skeleton of compressed longitudinal bars and circumferential rings pushed into it. A modern version of the kayak is built by means of a membrane of rubberized cloth, stretched by an internal frame. Such is the strength of these little boats that they have been sailed across the Atlantic by solitary navigators, although only 17 feet long and 3 feet wide.

The interesting roof shapes of membranes prestressed by external forces are always **saddle shapes**. Figure 11.15 shows a tent in the form of a saddle, designed by Frei Otto, in which the tension of the ropes anchored to the ground stabilizes the tent suspended from two poles (see also Section 6.2). Figure 11.16 illustrates a circular tent roof, designed by Horacio Caminos, in which a circular cloth attached to a compression ring is tensioned by the action of compressive struts. Prestressed membranes are stiffer and more stable than unstressed membranes: they do not flutter or move as easily under variable loads.

The stabilization of the hull of the Zeppelin dirigibles was obtained by two separate methods; an internal skeleton supported the membrane, which was stressed by the pressure of hydrogen. The rigidity obtained by this combination allowed the hull to take the severe dynamic loads imposed by air pockets and turbulence.

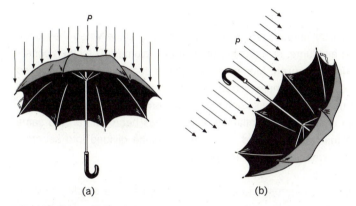

(a)   (b)

11.14 Prestressed membrane of an umbrella.

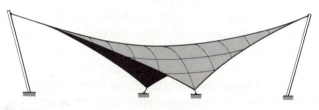

11.15 Prestressed membrane tent.

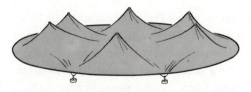

11.16 Prestressed circular membrane tent.

Membranes can be prestressed by internal pressure alone when they completely enclose a volume, or a number of separate volumes. They then constitute **pneumatic structures**. Membrane structures consisting of an enclosed volume are used, for example, in rubber rafts: the outer inflated ring is stiff enough to be used as a compression ring for the unstressed membrane forming the bottom of the raft. An inflatable airplane has been built on the same principle, with inflated wings and an inflated fuselage divided into separate compartments; it was flown by a light engine.

The long plastic balloons used at children's parties become so stiff when inflated that they can develop compression and bending action. The internal pressure locks into the cylindrical balloons tensile stresses in the circumferential and in the longitudinal directions. (The circumferential stress is often referred to as the "hoop stress" by analogy with the tensile stresses locked into the hoops of a barrel.) The inflated cylinder supports compressive loads, as a column, up to the point where the compression due to the load equals the longitudinal tension due to the internal pressure. When the compression nears this value, the membrane buckles.

Similarly, a balloon used as a horizontal simply supported beam carries vertical loads up to the point where the compressive stresses in the upper fibers of the beam equal the tensile stresses produced by the internal pressure. The reader may easily prove that when the compressive stress nears this value, the beam buckles at the top.

Based on this principle, the Fuji pavilion at the Osaka World's Fair of 1970, designed by Murata, had a curved roof spanning 164 feet obtained by means of inflated curved tubes of plastic material, in which the internal pressure could be varied to increase the stability of the structure with increasing wind velocities (Fig. 11.17). Enclosures for athletic fields, warehouses, and meeting halls have been built on the same principle.

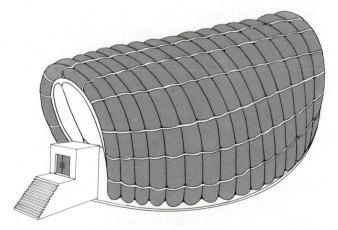

11.17 Fuji pavilion at Osaka World's Fair.

Figure 11.18 illustrates the balloon roof of a summer theater in Boston designed by Koch and engineered by Weidlinger. The balloon, in the form of a lens, spanned 150 feet and was inflated by a pump to an overpressure of 10 pounds per square foot. The balloon had a circular opening at the top, and new air was continuously pumped into it to reduce overheating and the consequent changes in shape of the balloon due to thermal variations in air pressure. The roof could be lifted to the top of its supporting steel ring and inflated in less than 20 minutes. Its shape was insensitive to steady winds; the balloon did not tend to fly away. The inflated balloon was to be used, for the last time, as formwork for a concrete dome to be sprayed over it.

Inflated plastic "mattresses," similar to those used to lie on the beach or to float on water, have been used structurally as horizontal roofs, vertical walls, and inclined floors, e.g., for theatre floors.

All the pneumatic structures mentioned so far are inflated, **closed** membranes. Some of the most interesting and impressive example of pneumatic structures belong, instead, in the category of air-supported roofs, the so-called **balloon roofs** or **bubbles**.

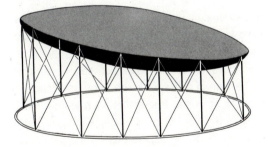

11.18 Boston balloon roof.

Plastic fabric balloons covering swimming pools, tennis courts, and other temporary installations may be blown up by a small pressure to create stable barrels (Fig. 11.19). An overpressure of only one to two tenths of a pound per square inch is sufficient to hold up such structures, which can be entered through revolving doors, since the loss of pressure in the large enclosed volume is negligible even when doors are used frequently; such losses as do occur are replaced intermittently under control of a pressure gauge. Large spherical domes over radar installations (radomes) are built on the same principle by means of extremely thin plastic membranes, which do not interfere with the reception and transmission of electromagnetic beams. Radomes are built up to diameters of 150 feet, using high-strength membranes capable of developing allowable tensions of 300 to 800 pounds per inch.

Balloon forms for concrete were used in the construction of the so-called "igloo houses," invented by Neff and designed by Noyes and Salvadori (Fig. 11.20). The inflated balloon supports a reinforcing steel mesh, over which a layer of a few inches of Gunite concrete is sprayed by a concrete gun. Once the concrete has hardened, the form is deflated and pulled out of the house through the door opening.

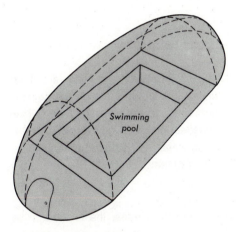

11.19 Pneumatic roof.

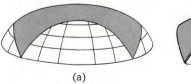

(a)   (b)

11.20 Igloo (balloon) houses.

The technique invented by Bini to build his "Binishells" is an improvement on the Neff idea. A special type of sliding reinforcement is set on the deflated balloon, on which is also poured very fluid concrete; the inflation of the balloon lifts both the reinforcement and the concrete, which is kept in place by the helical steel springs sheathing the reinforcement and vibrated after inflation. Over 1,000 Binishells with spans of up to 120 feet have been built and larger spans are technically feasible.

As the span of the air-supported balloon roof increases, the tension in the membrane exceeds its strength and the membrane must be reinforced, usually by steel cables. In such systems, the membrane spans only between cables and can be thinner, lighter, and more economical. In the Birdair domes, which can span up to one thousand feet, the cables are laid on a triangular mesh about 10 feet by the side (Fig. 11.21). In the U.S. Pavillion at the Osaka World's Fair of 1970, engineered by Geiger, the cables were laid on a skew grid 20 feet by the side and anchored to a funicular compression ring of concrete in the shape of a rectangle with rounded corners 460 by 262 feet (Fig. 11.22). The internal overpressure was only 4.3 pounds per square foot (three hundredths of a pound per square inch) because the low rise of the roof (23 feet) and the earth berm surrounding it induced wind suction over almost the

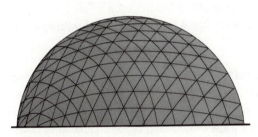

11.21 Birdair pneumatic dome.

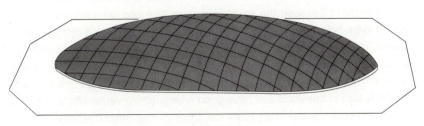

11.22 Pavilion at Osaka World's Fair of 1970.

entire roof. Air-supported roofs based on this scheme have been built to date covering stadiums with areas of over 300 thousand square feet and seating over 80,000 spectators, like the Silver Dome stadium in Pontiac, Michigan, engineered by Geiger.

Studies by Weidlinger Associates and others show that air-supported, cable-reinforced roofs, spanning over 6000 feet and covering over 600 acres, are feasible with present-day technology. The recent development of stronger and longer lasting membrane fabrics allow the building of roofs capable of covering entire towns.

The cost per square foot of air-supported bubbles is among the lowest for large span roofs. Their behavior in case of fire is safer than originally predicted because their membranes do not support flames, and superior to that of other large structures because the membranes are light and deflation takes hours even if large holes open in them. Transparent, translucent, and opaque membranes, glass-reinforced and vinyl-, hypalon-, or teflon-coated, permit a variety of natural lighting, different temperature distributions, and various degrees of privacy. They create artificial environments adaptable to human use in practically any part of the world and have good energy conservation characteristics. Since, moreover, under such roofs the architect has great freedom in "landscaping" the space with structures which are independent of the outer environment, their use is bound to increase in popularity. Air-supported, cable-reinforced bubbles are one of the modern breakthroughs in large-span roof construction.

Membrane roofs have been built not only of cloth and plastics, but of steel, aluminum, and reinforced concrete. Metal membranes, well adapted to carrying loads by tensile stresses, have been used to build stiff, permanent, circular roofs in Austria and the USSR. Reinforced concrete may be so reinforced, or prestressed, as to make it suitable to the development of tensile stresses: the Viera circular roof may be considered a concrete prestressed membrane (see Fig. 6.14). The cable-supported roof of the Nowicki arena may be considered a cable-supported membrane made up of metal sheet elements (see Fig. 6.13). It was indicated in Section 6.2 that light metal structures have a tendency to flutter, while the heavier concrete membranes do not. Thus, the thickness of a structural membrane may be increased for reasons other than strength, and the membrane may acquire some of the characteristics of a plate. Just as plates are bound to develop some membrane action in deflecting under applied loads (see Section 10.7), membranes are bound to develop some plate action due to their finite thickness. In view of the greater efficiency of membrane action (see Section 11.1), the thickness of a membrane should be kept minimal, provided its shape and displacements are functionally acceptable.

Chapter Twelve

Thin Shells
and
Reticulated Domes

12.1 Form-Resistant Structures

A sheet of paper held in the hand bends limply and cannot support its own weight. The same sheet of paper, if pinched and given a slight upward curvature, is capable of supporting its own weight and some additional load (Fig. 12.1). The new carrying capacity is obtained not by increasing the amount of material used, but by giving it proper form. The upward curvature increases the stiffness and the load-carrying capacity of the cantilevered paper sheet because it locates some material away from the "neutral axis," so that the bending rigidity of the sheet, acting as a cantilevered beam, is substantially increased. The same result is achieved by creasing the paper, that is, by giving it sudden changes in slope or **concentrated curvatures** (see Section 10.8).

Structures in which strength is obtained by shaping the material according to the loads they must carry are called **form-resistant structures**. Membranes (see Chapter 11) depend on curvature and twist to carry loads; they belong to the category of form-resistant, purely tensile structures. A membrane turned upside down, frozen and carrying the same loads for which it was originally shaped is the **two-dimensional antifunicular** for those loads (see Section 6.1): it is a form-resistant structure developing only compression.

Their mobility and their incapacity to resist compressive stresses restricts the use of membranes (see Section 11.1). All the disadvantages of membrane action are avoided, and most advantages maintained, in **thin shells**. Thin shells are form-resistant structures thin enough not to develop appreciable bending stresses, but thick enough to carry loads by compression, tension, and shear. Although thin shells have been built of wood, steel, and plastics, they are ideally suited to reinforced concrete construction. Thin shells allow the construction of domes and other curved roofs of varied form and exceptional strength. They are among the most sophisticated expression of modern structural design.

Thin shells, like membranes, owe their efficiency to curvature and twist. In order to understand their structural action one must first become familiar with their purely geometrical characteristics.

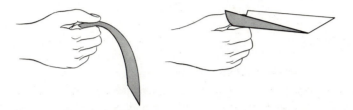

12.1 Form-resistant structure.

12.2 Curvatures

It was seen in Section 11.2 that the curvatures of a surface **at a point** are exhibited by cutting it with a plane pivoted around the normal to the surface at that point. The curvature varies as the plane rotates; it may be up or down in all directions, or up in some and down in others. Moreover, a surface has, in general, a twist, since its slope changes as one moves at right angles to the direction of the slope.

All the intersections of a dome with a plane passing through its normal have **downward** curvatures. For spherical domes the curvatures are all identical (Fig. 12.2); for any other type of dome, they change from a maximum to a minimum as the plane rotates (Fig. 12.3). On the other hand, the curvatures of a dish are all up. Surfaces like domes or dishes, in which the curvature changes value around a point but is always up or down, are called **synclastic** (from the Greek words **syn** = with, and **klastein** = to cut). It is convenient to call downward curvatures positive, and upward curvatures negative; with this convention, at any point on their surface domes have positive curvatures and dishes negative curvatures in all directions. Surfaces with positive or negative curvature at all points in all directions are said to be **nondevelopable,** because they cannot be flattened without stretching them, unless they are cut at a number (usually infinite) of sections (Fig. 12.4). Their stiffness and strength stems, in large part, from their resistance to those deformations which tend to flatten them, that is, to reduce their curvatures.

As the curvature of a synclastic surface becomes smaller in a given direction, the surface approaches the shape of a cylinder. The curvature in the direction of the cylinder axis, one of the principal curvatures, is zero (see Fig. 11.7). Surfaces, like those of barrel roofs or gutter channels, with curvatures always positive or always negative but vanishing in one direction, are called **developable** surfaces; they can be flattened without stretching them or introducing cuts. Developable surfaces are obviously less stiff and strong than synclastic surfaces.

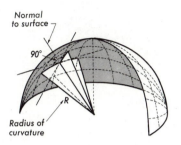

12.2 Curvatures of spherical dome.

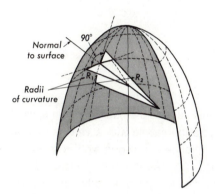

12.3 Curvatures of parabolic dome.

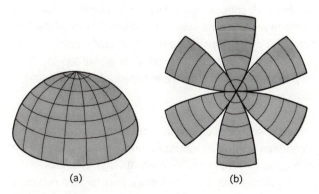

(a)   (b)

12.4 Development of synclastic surface.

A horse saddle has a downward curvature "across the horse" and an upward curvature "along the horse": as one cuts the saddle with a vertical rotating plane its curvature changes not only in value, but also in sign; a mountain pass presents the same behavior (Fig. 12.5). As the cutting plane rotates around its axis, the curvature of the saddle changes **gradually** from positive to negative values, and back to positive values again; therefore, the curvature must become equal to zero, i.e., **vanish,** in two directions. Saddle or **anticlastic** surfaces have, in general, two directions of zero curvature, that is, two directions along which straight lines lie **on** the surface (Fig. 12.5); they are also nondevelopable. The lines of principal curvature of a saddle surface are shown in Fig. 12.6. One may talk of the "top of the dome," or even the "top of the cylinder," which is a ridge of tops, but one cannot really define the top of a saddle surface. The "top of the mountain pass" is a real top for those coming from the valley, but is a "bottom" for those coming down the ridges of the adjoining mountains.

Surfaces exhibiting zero curvatures at a point in **more** than two directions are easily constructed. A surface with no curvature in three directions is called a **monkey saddle,** since a monkey can straddle it with its legs and have its tail down on it (Fig. 12.7). A surface with more than three lines of zero curvature has a scalloped shape.

12.5 Saddle surface.

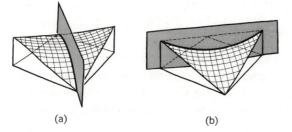

(a)   (b)

12.6 Principal curvature lines of saddle surface.

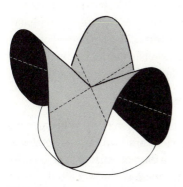

12.7 The monkey saddle.

12.3 Rotational Surfaces

Shell surfaces were classified in Section 12.2 according to their curvatures **at a point**. A different classification, depending on their general shape, is also of great significance in thin shell design, and will be used in later sections to analyze the overall behavior of the most commonly encountered thin shell roofs.

Rotational surfaces are described by the rotation of a plane curve around a vertical axis (Fig. 12.8). The plane or **meridional curve** may have a variety of shapes, thus giving rise to a variety of dome forms, well suited to the roofing of a circular area. The most commonly used dome is **spherical**: its surface is obtained by rotating an arc of circle around a vertical axis. The vertical sections through the axis of a rotational shell are called its **meridians** and its horizontal sections, which are all circles, its **parallels;** the largest parallel is called the **equator**.

Complete spheres, supported on a ring of stilts, are often used as metal tanks for liquid chemicals (Fig. 12.9). Liquid containers are also built as rotational surfaces in the shape of a drop of water. Since a drop of water is kept together by the constant capillary tension of its surface, these containers are designed to develop a constant tension, and are most efficient in storing liquids.

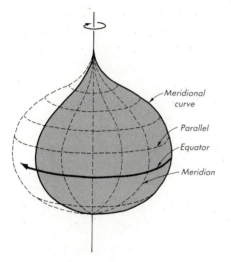

12.8 Rotational surface.

12.9 Shell tank for liquids.

Elliptical domes are described by half an ellipse rotating around its vertical axis [Fig. 12.10(a)]; their action is not as efficient as the action of a spherical dome because the top of the shell is flatter, and the reduction in curvature introduces a tendency to buckle. On the other hand, the parabolic dome [Fig. 12.10(b)] has a sharper curvature at its top and presents structural advantages even in comparison with the sphere.

The surface described by rotating a straight line around a vertical axis it intersects is a **cone**. Conical surfaces are commonly used as umbrella roofs when supported at a point, and as domes when supported on their circular boundary (Fig. 12.11). The lack of curvature in the radial direction of the cone makes the forming of cones in reinforced concrete somewhat simpler than the forming of curved domes.

Circular barrels are obtained by rotating around a vertical axis the upper half of a circle or any other curve **not intersecting the axis;** such doughnut-like surfaces, called **toroidal,** are well suited to roof ring areas (Fig. 12.12).

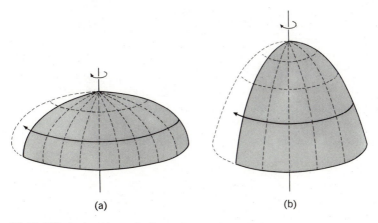

(a)   (b)

12.10 Elliptical and parabolic surfaces of revolution.

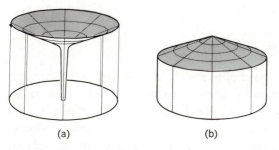

(a)   (b)

12.11 Conical surfaces.

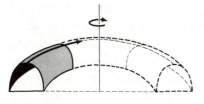

12.12 Toroidal surface.

12.4 Translational Surfaces

The surface of a **translational shell** is obtained by "translating," that is, sliding a plane curve on another plane curve, usually at right angles to the first, while maintaining it vertical. A cylinder is obtained by translating a horizontal straight line along a vertical curve or translating a vertical curve along a horizontal straight line, perpendicular to it; depending on the curve, the cylinder may be circular, parabolic, or elliptic (Fig. 12.13). When the straight line is inclined, the cylinder also becomes inclined and is well suited to roof a staircase by means of a barrel-like vault.

The translation of a vertical parabola with downward curvature on a perpendicular parabola also with downward curvature generates a surface called an **elliptic paraboloid,** which covers a rectangular area; its horizontal sections are ellipses, its vertical sections are parabolas (Fig. 12.14). When the two parabolas are identical, the paraboloid covers a square area, and its horizontal sections become circles. The elliptic paraboloid was the first shape ever used to build a thin concrete shell (in 1907).

334

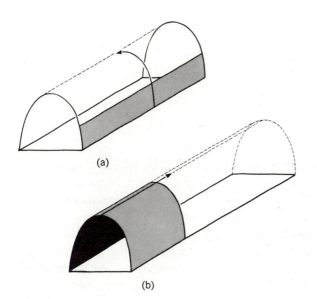

(a)

(b)

12.13 Cylindrical surfaces.

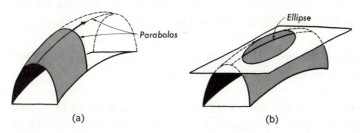

Parabolas

Ellipse

(a)   (b)

12.14 Elliptic paraboloid.

A **hyperbolic paraboloid** (**hypar** for short, in Great Britain) is obtained by translating a parabola with downward curvature on a parabola with upward curvature [Fig. 12.15(a)]. This surface has the shape of a saddle; its horizontal sections are two separate branches of a curve called a hyperbola, while its vertical principal sections are parabolas [Fig. 12.15(b)]. As for all other saddle surfaces, the curvature of the hyperbolic paraboloid vanishes in two directions; but for a hyperbolic paraboloid these two directions are **the same at all points**. This means that the vertical sections parallel to these two directions are **all straight lines,** called **generatrices,** and that the hyperbolic paraboloid has a **double** set of straight lines **lying on its surface**. Hence, this surface may also be generated by a straight-line segment sliding with its two ends on two straight line segments **askew** in space (Fig. 12.16). The forming of such a surface in reinforced concrete is relatively simple, since it involves the use of straight planks in the direction of one set of lines of zero curvature.

When the two curves used in translation are not at right angles to each other, the translational surface may cover a skewed rectangle.

A great variety of surfaces can be obtained by translation, since **any** curve may be translated on **any other** curve for this purpose, but not all translational surfaces are well suited to carry loads.

336

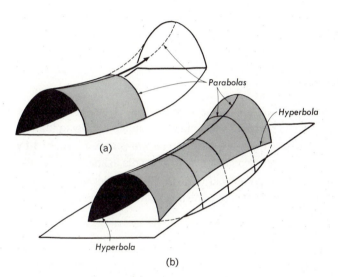

12.15 Hyperbolic paraboloid.

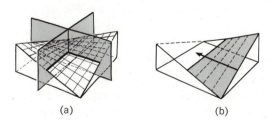

12.16 Straight-line generatrices of hyperbolic paraboloid.

12.5 Ruled Surfaces

The hyperbolic paraboloid was shown in Section 12.4 to have two sets of straight lines lying on its surface. Any surface generated by sliding the two ends of a straight-line segment on two separate curves is called a **ruled surface**. When the two curves are two straight line segments askew in space, the ruled surface is a hyperbolic paraboloid (Fig. 12.16). The cylinder is a ruled surface generated by sliding a horizontal line segment on two identical vertical curves [see Fig. 12.13(a)].

A different family of ruled surfaces called **conoidal surfaces,** is obtained by sliding a straight-line segment on two **different** curves lying in **parallel** planes. Conoidal roofs cover a rectangular area and allow light to enter from a given direction, usually from the north (Fig. 12.17).

Conoids are conoidal surfaces obtained by sliding a straight-line segment with one of its ends on a **curve** and the other on a **straight line** (Fig. 12.18). The conoid is called circular, parabolic, or elliptic depending on whether its end curve is an arc of a circle, a parabola, or an ellipse. The conoid is a saddle surface; its principal-curvature lines show that the curvature in the direction of the two lines connecting the top of the curve to the ends of the straight line segments is upward, while the other principal curvature is downward (Fig. 12.18). Conoids may be used as cantilevered shells with their curved end at the root of the cantilever; in this case their transverse curvature is directed upward (Fig. 12.19).

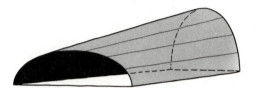

12.17 Conoidal surface.

12.18 Conoid.

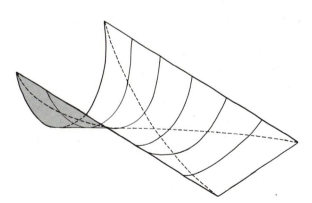

12.19 Cantilevered conoid.

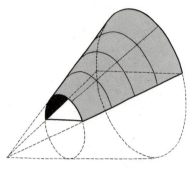

12.20 Conical sector.

Cones are ruled surfaces in which one end of the segment rotates about a point and the other slides on a curve. **Conical sectors** are conoidal surfaces and may be used to cover trapezoidal areas or, as cantilevered roofs, much as conoids are (Fig. 12.20).

An inclined segment, sliding on two horizontal circles lying one above the other, describes a surface called a **hyperboloid of one sheet,** whose vertical sections are the two branches of a hyperbola (Fig. 12.21). These easily formed surfaces are extensively used to build cooling towers in cement factories and other industrial plants.

When the sliding line segment is vertical, the hyperboloid becomes a vertical cylinder; when it connects diametrically opposite points of the two circles, the hyperboloid becomes two inverted half-cones. It is thus seen that the same surfaces, say the cone, may be generated in a variety of ways and be considered rotational, translational, conoidal, or ruled.

12.6 Complex Surfaces

The elementary, mathematically defined surfaces of the previous section may be combined in any number of ways to obtain more complex surfaces. Two cylindrical shells intersecting at right angles cover a square or a rectangular area with a so-called **groined vault** (Fig. 12.22). Parallel cylinders with curvatures alternately upward and downward create an undulated roof similar to a folded plate (Fig. 12.23).

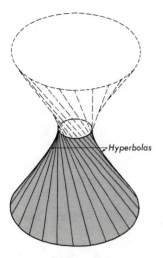

12.21 Hyperboloid of one sheet.

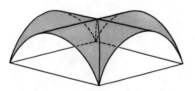

12.22 Groined vault.

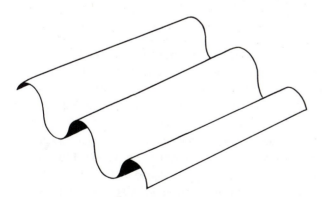

12.23 Undulated cylindrical surface.

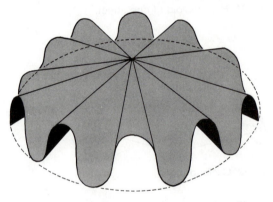

12.24 Undulated conical surface.

Scalloped roofs over curved boundaries may be obtained by joining sectors of cones with curvatures alternately upward and downward (Fig. 12.24). Moreover, any of the elementary forms may be scalloped to obtain more playful and, at times, more efficient structural thin shells. An ellipsoid may be scalloped to give it transverse curvatures towards the supported edge (Fig. 12.25). Spherical domes may be undulated for the same purpose (Fig. 12.26). A parabolic cylinder may be undulated to transform it into a surface with curvatures in two directions rather than in one, thus stiffening it (Fig. 12.27). The largest concrete spherical dome built to date (1986), designed by Christiansen, covers the King County Stadium in Seattle, Washington, spans 661 feet, and is scalloped.

12.25 Scalloped ellipsoid.

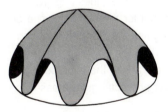

12.26 Scalloped spherical dome.

12.27 Undulated parabolic cylinder.

12.28 Hyperbolic paraboloidal roof.

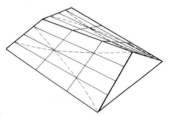

12.29 Hyperbolic paraboloidal conoid.

Hyperbolic paraboloids may be used in a variety of combinations. Four identical paraboloidal segments form a corner-supported roof covering a rectangular area, one of the most commonly used combinations of this surface (Fig. 12.28). Two hyperbolic paraboloidal segments may be combined to form a northlight conoidal roof (Fig. 12.29) or a cantilevered conoid shell (Fig. 12.30). A series of such shells was used by Nervi as a roof for the stands of one of his stadiums in Rome, Italy. Four paraboloidal segments supported on a central column form an umbrella roof (Fig. 12.31). When the angle between the planes of the two translating parabolas is not a right angle, the hyperbolic paraboloid is called **skew,** and may be used to cover nonrectangular areas (Fig. 12.32).

There is no reason to limit the shape of a thin shell to forms definable by geometrical formulas. Structurally sound, "free" shapes may be invented. But the imagination of the designer becomes mere fancy unless he is familiar with the structural behavior of the basic geometric forms. Thin shells are extraordinarily efficient **structural** elements, and their shapes should be dictated primarily by structural considerations. The behavior under load of the most commonly used thin-shell forms must be considered first in terms of their **membrane action,** following the basic ideas presented in Chapter 11. More refined considerations of stress, as well as additional practical requirements, will be taken up in some detail in later sections.

344

12.30 Cantilevered hyperbolic paraboloidal conoid.

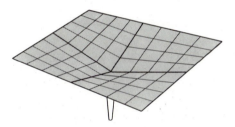

12.31 Hyperbolic paraboloidal umbrella.

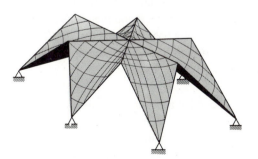

12.32 Skew hyperbolic paraboloidal combination.

12.7 Membrane Action in Circular Domes

The structural action of a rotational and, in particular, of a circular dome, supported around its entire boundary and acted upon by vertical loads **symmetrical** with respect to its axis (as the dead load), is a simple consequence of its geometrical characteristics. In these **axi-symmetrical shells** the meridional sections and the sections at right angles to the meridians are both principal curvature and principal stress sections (see Section 11.2). The stresses on these sections are simple tension or simple compression evenly distributed across their small thicknesses.

Figure 12.33 shows the stresses developed at a parallel of an axi-symmetrical shell; they are **compressive** stresses in the direction of the meridian and constant **along** the parallel because the shell and the loads are symmetrical about the axis. Each meridian behaves as if it were a funicular arch for the applied loads, that is, it carries the loads without developing bending stresses.

12.33 Meridional stresses at a parallel of a spherical dome.

Arches were shown in Section 6.4 to be funicular for **only one set** of loads. The meridians of a dome, instead, are funicular for **any set** of symmetrical loads. This essential difference in structural behavior is due to the fact that while isolated arches have no lateral support, the meridians of the dome are **supported by the parallels,** which restrain their lateral displacement by developing hoop stresses. As a consequence of its funicular behavior under **any** set of **symmetrical** loads, a dome does not change shape to adapt itself to a change in such loads; therefore, it is a stable structure for such loads. (It will be seen later in this section that a dome is stable under **any** set of loads, symmetrical or unsymmetrical.)

The contribution of the parallels to the funicular behavior of the dome is indicated by the deformations of the meridians under load. In a shallow or small-rise dome the meridians, shortening in compression, move down under load, and in so doing move **inward,** that is, towards the dome axis (Fig. 12.34). In the two-dimensional structural dome this motion is accompanied by a **shortening** of the parallels, because of their radii decrease. Hence, the parallels are compressed, and their compressive stiffness reduces substantially the freedom of the meridians to move inward. In other words, an axisymmetric **shallow** dome may be considered to act as a series of meridional funicular arches elastically supported by the parallels. It develops compressive stresses along both the meridians and the parallels and could be built of materials incapable of developing tensile stresses, such as masonry or bricks.

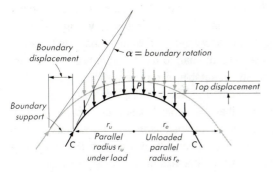

12.34 Deformation of shallow spherical dome under load.

When the dome has a high rise, it flattens at the top and opens up at the bottom; the points of its top portion move inward under the action of the loads, but the points of its lower portion move outward, that is, **away** from the axis (Fig. 12.35). The parallels of the upper portion shorten, but those of the lower portion lengthen and develop tensile stresses, again restraining the motion of the meridians. Depending upon the type of load, one specific parallel remains unchanged in length, while all those above develop compression and all those below develop tension. In a spherical dome under dead load the parallel at an angle of 52 degrees from the axis does not change length (Fig. 12.35). Under a snow load, uniformly distributed on the horizontal projection of the dome, the unstressed parallel is at 45 degrees to the axis.

Since the stresses developed by a dome are purely compressive and tensile, and the corresponding strains are very small (see Sections 5.1 and 5.2), the stiffness of circular domes is exceptionally high. The top of a concrete dome in the shape of a half sphere, 100 feet in diameter and only 3 inches thick, acted upon by a very heavy load of snow and its own dead load, deflects less than one tenth of an inch. The ratio of span to deflection is twelve thousand and should be compared with an acceptable ratio of between 300 and 800 for a bending structure such as a beam. The outward displacement of the dome at its boundary is even smaller than its vertical deflection: only three one-hundredths of an inch; the rotation of the meridians at the boundary, that is, their change in direction, is only one hundredth of a degree (Fig. 12.35). A similar behavior is exhibited by rotational shells having other meridional sections.

350

12.35 Deformation of high-rise spherical dome under load.

The stiffness of circular domes explains why the thickness of reinforced-concrete domes may by reduced to such small values; ratios of span-to-thickness of the order of 300 or more are customary. For example, a reinforced-concrete dome spanning 100 feet with a thickness of 3 inches has a ratio of span-to-thickness of 400. The steel domes used as containment spheres in nuclear reactors have ratios of the order of one thousand. Such ratios may be compared with the ratio of span-to-thickness in an eggshell, which is only 30, or in bending structures, which is of the order of 20. A shell thickness is limited mostly by the requirements of buckling resistance.

It was shown in Section 11.2 that membranes may change shape under varying loads in order not to develop compressive stresses. In a thin-shell dome, instead, compression can be developed, and, moreover, even if direct stresses along the meridians and the parallels cannot carry the entire load, a third mechanism is always available to equilibrate the unbalanced difference: the shear mechanism considered in Section 11.1. Provided safe stresses are not exceeded, direct stresses (compression and tension) on one hand, and shear within the shell surface on the other, will always share and equilibrate the total load on a spherical dome element without requiring a change in its shape. Taking into account the shear mechanism, a dome may be said to be funicular for **all** (smooth) loads and, hence, to be a **stable structure** under practically any circumstance. For example, a dome resists lateral loads, such as wind pressures and suctions, by developing all three types of membrane stresses (Fig. 12.36). The shear stresses due to wind are also of modest intensity: a 100 mile-an-hour wind on a spherical concrete dome 3 inches thick spanning 100 feet produces membrane shear stresses of only 14 pounds per square inch, while the allowable shear stress in concrete is at least 75 pounds per square inch.

352

12.36 Shear mechanism in dome under wind load.

12.8 Bending Stresses in Domes

A dome was shown to carry loads essentially by **membrane stresses** (compression, tension, and shear), because the development of shear makes it funicular for **all** loads. On the other hand, because a dome is usually very thin, if there were a tendency to develop bending stresses anywhere in the dome, these could easily exceed allowable values. It is therefore necessary to investigate the possibility of such a tendency.

In the analysis of the carrying capacity of thin domes it was tacitly assumed that domes are free to develop the minute displacements required by their membrane state of stress. Thus, the dome considered in Section 12.7 develops membrane stresses under load, and the corresponding strains give its top a small vertical displacement. Since this top deflection is not prevented, a pure state of membrane stress exists in its neighborhood. An entirely different situation may develop, instead, at the boundary of the shell.

A hemi-spherical dome under load opens up at the equator; its boundary displaces outward, even though by a very small amount (see Figs. 12.34 and 12.35). Moreover, the reactions supporting the dome must be in the direction of the slightly rotating meridians, since the meridional arches are funiculars of the load; reactions in any other direction would produce bending in the dome. In other words, in order to have a pure state of membrane stress in the shell, the boundary should be free to move outward, and the reactions should rotate in the direction of the meridians at the boundary. **In practice this is impossible**. A moving boundary presents practical difficulties and disadvantages and it is impossible to allow the reactions to rotate in order to remain tangent to the deformed meridians when the boundary rotates because of the deformation of the shell under load (see Figs. 12.34 and 12.35). In common practice, instead, the equator of the shell is reinforced by a stiff ring, which prevents almost entirely the outward motion of the boundary and its rotation, and hence introduces an additional inward radial thrust and bending at the equator. The shell, which would open up and rotate at the equator under the load-induced membrane stresses, develops a kink or sudden change in curvature and, hence, bending stresses around the boundary [Fig. 12.37(a)].

354

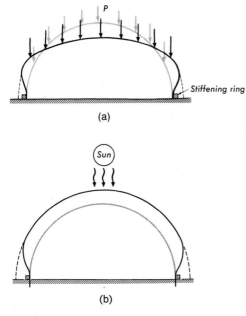

12.37 Bending deformations at ring-stiffened dome boundary.

The **bending disturbance** thus introduced at the boundary does not penetrate deeply into the shell, but is limited to a narrow band in the neighborhood of the boundary. This "damping out" of boundary disturbances, another useful characteristic of thin shells, occurs because the bending displacements of the meridians, which could be large in view of the small bending rigidity of the shell, are restrained by the parallels. Large meridional bending displacements imply large changes in the radius of the parallels, and, hence, large tensile or compressive strains in the parallels. The parallels, instead, are stiff in tension and compression, and do not allow such large displacements; they permit a small amount of bulging, in and out, of the meridian and, hence, a small amount of bending, which peters out as one moves away from the shell boundary (Fig. 12.38). This petering-out of bending stresses is analogous to the phenomenon occurring in continuous beams (see Section 7.3), where bending vanishes rapidly away from the loaded span due to continuity over the supports. In the shell the meridians are continuous over the "supports" of the parallels and bending vanishes away from the boundary with the same wavy displacement typical of continuous beams [see Fig. 7.35(a)].

The width of the area affected by the bending boundary disturbance is proportional to the square root of the ratio of thickness to radius of the dome; in order to reduce the width of the disturbed zone the shell must be made thinner. For a thickness equal to one four-hundredth of the radius, the arc of the disturbed zone is only one tenth of the radius (Fig. 12.38). Thus most of the shell is actually in a state of undisturbed membrane stress.

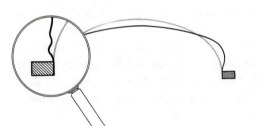

12.38 Bending disturbance at dome boundary.

Bending disturbances, usually more severe than those due to the loads, are produced by thermal conditions. When exposure to the sun increases the shell temperature, the entire dome changes shape, uniformly increasing its radius [see Fig. 12.37(b)]. If an underground ring prevents the boundary displacement, the shell once again presents a sudden change in curvature and develops high bending stresses of the same nature as those discussed above. Since boundary displacements due to thermal changes are usually larger than those due to the loads, the bending stresses due to thermal changes are also usually larger than those due to the loads. If the temperature of a dome spanning 100 feet increases uniformly by 30 degrees Fahrenheit with respect to the foundation ring, the dome boundary displaces radially by one tenth of an inch. This displacement is three times larger than that produced by the dead load and a heavy snow load; hence the thermal bending stresses at the boundary, when the thermal displacement is prevented, are three times as large as those due to the loads.

Whenever the reactions are not tangent to the meridians all along the boundary, bending stresses occur in the neighborhood of the boundary. Thus, if a dome is supported on evenly spaced columns rather than all around its boundary, not only does the membrane stress pattern change (Fig. 12.39), but, moreover, the columns introduce horizontal reactions at the dome boundary, and bending stresses develop there in the dome. Similarly, if portions of the dome are cut out by vertical or inclined planes and the dome rests on a few points, the support conditions differ substantially from those ideally required by membrane action, and bending stresses are to be expected. Finally, any load capable of producing a kink or sudden change of curvature in a thin shell is bound to produce bending stresses: thus, concentrated loads cannot be carried by membrane stresses (Fig. 12.40). The thickness of the shell is often dictated by bending disturbances rather than by the membrane stresses due to the loads.

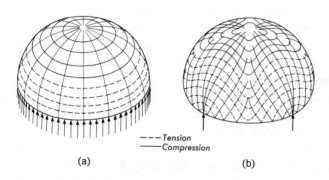

- - - Tension
——— Compression

(a)   (b)

12.39 Principal stress lines of dome under load.

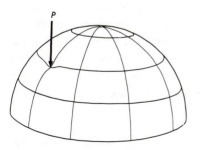

12.40 Concentrated load on thin shell.

Two additional conditions may call for a thickening of shells above the modest requirements of membrane stresses. One concerns reinforced-concrete shells and is of a purely practical character: enough thickness must be provided to cover the reinforcing bars on both the outside and the inside of the shell. The exact location of the bars in the shell thickness is a delicate and expensive matter; in countries with high labor costs it is often found less expensive to increase the shell thickness than to locate the steel carefully. Shells thinner than 2 or 3 inches are seldom economical in the U.S.; shells as thin as half an inch have been built in other countries.

Shells must often be thickened to prevent buckling. Any thin structural element subjected to compressive stresses may buckle, and thin shells are no exception. The buckling load for a thin-shell dome is proportional to the modulus of elasticity of the material and to the **square** of the thickness-to-radius ratio. With ratios often as small as one three-hundredth or one four-hundredth, the buckling load may be exceptionally low. The buckling load for a spherical dome 3 inches thick, spanning 100 feet is about 150 pounds per square foot; with a factor of safety of 2 1/2, the maximum uniform load on the shell cannot exceed 60 pounds per square foot. This is equivalent to the dead load of the shell, including the roofing or insulating materials, and a small snow load. A shell of this sort could be built in the tropics, but not in the northern part of the United States.

The buckling resistance of a dome may be substantially increased, without increasing its thickness uniformly, by using meridional and parallel ribs. This practice is well suited to the stiffening of steel domes, in which the thickness required by membrane stresses may be quite small in view of the tensile and compressive strength of the material. Concrete domes are seldom stiffened by ribs because of the cost of forms, except in the case of very large spans. In order to ensure buckling resistance the largest concrete thin-shell roof built to date, the C.N.I.T. dome in Paris, spanning 760 feet, consists of two separate shells connected by vertical diaphragms.

A shell acts "properly" if it develops membrane stresses almost everywhere; it is then said to carry loads by thin-shell action. It was shown above that the following three conditions must be satisfied for a dome to develop thin-shell action:

1. The dome must be thin; it will thus be incapable of developing substantial bending action.
2. It must be properly curved; it will thus be strong and stiff because of its form resistance.
3. It must be properly supported; it will thus develop a small amount of bending in a limited portion of the shell.

These three conditions are essential to thin-shell action, whatever the shape of the shell and the loads on it. Whenever these conditions are not met because of construction difficulties, aesthetic considerations or architectural requirements, bending action becomes important and the structural efficiency of the shell is reduced.

12.9 Membrane Action in Cylinders

Cylindrical or **barrel** shells are used to cover rectangular areas and are commonly supported on end frames, stiff in their own vertical plane and flexible at right angles to it (Fig. 12.41). Their action may be considered a combination of beam action in the longitudinal direction and a particular funicular-arch action in the transverse direction.

The longitudinal membrane stresses in a "long barrel"—a barrel in which the length is at least three times the width—are similar to those developed in a beam. The thin shell obtains its strength from its curved shape, and one may think of the barrel as a beam with a curved cross section. The longitudinal membrane stresses are linearly distributed across the depth of the barrel; the upper fibers are compressed, the lower fibers are tensed (Fig. 12.42).

Beam action carries the load to the frames. These, because of their horizontal flexibility, cannot react longitudinally; the longitudinal stresses vanish at the end of the shell, just as they vanish at the end of a simply supported beam. The load is transferred to the end frames or **stiffeners** by shear action; tangential shear reactions develop on the cylinder end sections, and their **vertical** components add up to the value of the load (Fig. 12.43). On the other hand, the action of the barrel differs slightly from beam action because the cross section of a beam is solid and not deformable, whereas the thin cross section of a shell deforms under load. If a thin, curved piece of material (paper or plastic) is supported on two grooved stiffeners, and loaded, the longitudinal boundaries of the cylinder will be seen to move **inward,** indicating the absence of the outward thrust typical of arch action, and showing the deformability of the cross section.

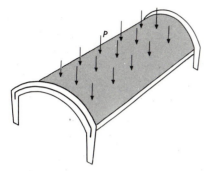

12.41 Barrel shell on end stiffeners.

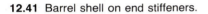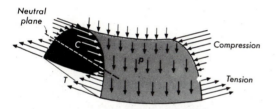

12.42 Beam (membrane) stresses in long barrels.

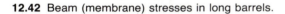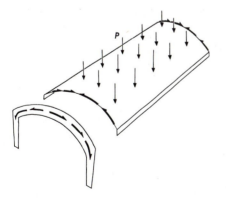

12.43 Shear reactions on barrel ends.

As the barrel becomes shorter, the influence of the deformability of its cross section is more felt and the longitudinal stresses deviate from the straight-line beam distribution. There comes a point where the stresses acquire the curved distribution of Fig. 12.44(a), in which both the top and bottom shell fibers are in tension, while the intermediate fibers are in compression. If the cross section of the barrel is prevented from deforming, either by intermediate stiffeners or by the continuity with adjacent barrels, the stress distribution becomes linear once again, indicating a return to the beam behavior of long barrels [Fig. 12.44(b)].

12.10 Bending Stresses in Cylinders

As the barrel becomes shorter, arch action and eventually longitudinal plate action become preponderant. One may visualize the behavior of short barrels as due to the action of arches supported by longitudinal beams consisting of barrel strips near the boundaries (Fig. 12.45). Transverse, compressive arch stresses develop in the upper part of the barrel, petering out towards its longitudinal edges.

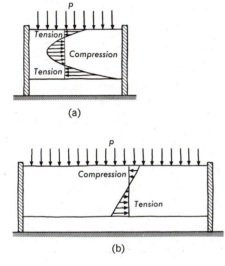

(a)

(b)

12.44 Longitudinal stresses in short and in long barrels.

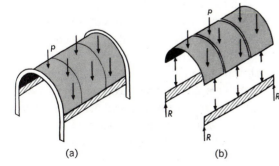

(a)

(b)

12.45 Short-barrel action.

The compressive arch stresses introduce bending in the neighborhood of the barrel stiffeners. The arch compression produces a shortening of the transverse fibers of the barrel, and an inward displacement of the barrel section (Fig. 12.46). This displacement takes place freely at midspan, but at the barrel ends it is prevented by the stiffeners, which are rigid in their own plane. In order to restrain the inward displacement at the stiffener while allowing it at midspan, the shell must bend; thus it develops some bending stresses at the stiffeners (Fig. 12.46). This bending disturbance is of the same kind as that encountered at the boundary of a circular dome when its outward displacement is prevented by a stiff ring. The bending disturbance at the stiffeners peters out rapidly and is felt only in a short portion of the barrel. The width of the longitudinal band affected by the bending disturbance depends again on the square root of the thickness-to-radius ratio; the bending displacements bulge in and out and are rapidly "damped." In concrete barrels the bending stresses at the stiffeners' edges are often absorbed by a local reinforcement in the shell thickness.

In any thin barrel the disturbed area at the end stiffeners is narrow **in comparison with the shell radius**. When the barrel is long—that is, when its length is substantially greater than its radius—only a small fraction of its **length** is under bending stresses [Fig. 12.47(a)]. But when the barrel is very short—that is, when the barrel length is **less** than twice the radius—the width of the bending stress band, even if small compared to the radius, may become comparable to the length of the barrel [Fig. 12.47(b)]. Thus, in short barrels the bending disturbance may affect a large portion of the total shell area. This result could be foreseen intuitively: in short barrels the load is carried directly to the stiffeners by the bending action of longitudinal shell strips, because the thickness of the shell even if small relative to the radius is large compared to the short span. Actually, since the short barrel is a two-dimensional resisting structure, it acts very much like a plate in carrying the load directly to the two stiffeners, and necessarily develops bending stresses over most of its surface.

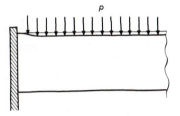

12.46 Bending at barrel stiffener.

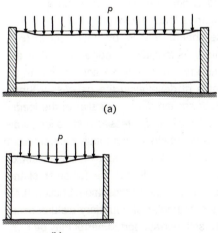

(a)

(b)

12.47 Bending in long and short barrels.

Thermal displacements and shrinkage of the concrete during setting may produce bending disturbances at the stiffeners substantially greater than those produced by the loads. They often require an increase in thickness and reinforcement at the stiffeners' edges.

How essential it is for a shell to be "properly supported" in order to develop almost exclusively membrane stresses is clearly seen in barrel shells. A long barrel, supported on end stiffeners, carries loads by longitudinal tensile and compressive stresses and transverse shears, that is, by beam action (Fig. 12.42). The same barrel, supported along its longitudinal edges, develops essentially arch action, since each transverse strip may be considered as an arch supported at its ends and capable of developing the necessary thrust (Fig. 12.48). If the shape of the cylinder section is the funicular of the loads, each strip will develop only compressive transverse stresses and no longitudinal stresses. This is also a membrane state of stress, but totally different from that developed by the stiffener-supported barrel, which consists essentially of longitudinal stresses. If the barrel cross section is not the funicular of the loads, bending stresses will develop in the arched strips (see Section 6.4); these bending stresses do not have the character of boundary disturbances, but pervade the entire shell. Although a stiffener-supported barrel may be relatively thin, a barrel supported on its longitudinal edges and acting as a vault must be fairly thick to resist the bending stresses in the arched strips.

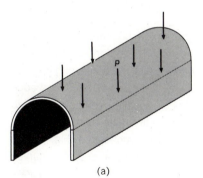

(a)

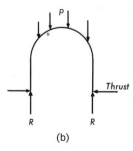

(b)

12.48 Barrel acting as vault.

The stiffener-supported barrel also develops some boundary disturbances along its longitudinal, free edges. These are minor disturbances, but have a tendency to penetrate **more** into the shell than the disturbances along the stiffener boundaries. It is not difficult to realize why. If a moment bends the edge of a thin flat plate, one must apply an equal and opposite bending moment to the opposite edge in order to equilibrate it. The entire plate bends and transfers the bending action from one edge to the other, unchanged (Fig. 12.49). If the thin plate is curved into a cylinder, bending applied at one of its curved boundaries is not transmitted to the opposite boundary, but dies out quickly [Fig. 12.50(a)]. It is thus seen that the curvature acquired by the plate "damps out" bending **in a direction at right angles to the curvature**. The bending disturbance at the stiffener ends of the barrel is damped out rapidly by the cylinder curvature at right angles to it. A curvature **in the direction of the bending disturbance** produces a lesser amount of damping, so that a longitudinal-edge disturbance dies out slowly, although usually it is not transmitted all the way to the other longitudinal edge [Fig. 12.50(b)]. The longitudinal-edge disturbance in the barrel is dampened less rapidly than in a shell curved at right angles to the disturbances; for most shells the width of the disturbed band along the longitudinal edges is about twice as large as that along the curved boundary.

12.49 Bending of flat plate.

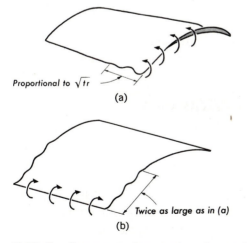

Proportional to $\sqrt{tr}$

(a)

Twice as large as in (a)

(b)

12.50 Bending penetration at edge of curved plate.

Barrel shells are not as stiff as domes, since their single curvature makes them behave very much like beams. Whenever it is necessary to increase their stiffness, it is customary to add longitudinal beams along their edges. This adds area on the tensile side of the cross section, so that a larger part of the barrel shell is under compression and the tensile stresses are absorbed mostly by the edge beams, acting as flanges. The edge beams, moreover, are used to absorb longitudinal shears developing at the edge of the shell, which introduce tension in the edge beams (Fig. 12.51).

Just as the upper flange of an I beam may buckle in compression, the upper fibers of a long barrel shell may buckle under longitudinal compression. The resistance of a long barrel shell to buckling is higher than that of domes, since compressive stresses are developed only in a portion of the shell and only in the longitudinal direction.

Notwithstanding the greater buckling strength of a long barrel shell, the danger of buckling may often demand an increase in the barrel thickness above the value required by a state of membrane stress.

Whenever the thickness required to avoid buckling makes the bending resistance of the shell so large as to reduce its membrane action, it becomes more economical to rib the shell transversely (Fig. 12.52). Stiffeners are commonly used in steel shells; they are used less often in concrete shells because they increase the cost of the forms.

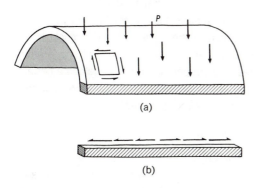

(a)

(b)

12.51 Shears on longitudinal edge beams.

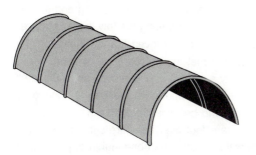

12.52 Ribbed barrel.

12.11   Stresses in Synclastic Translation Shells

A variety of curves may be used to generate translational shells with double positive curvature; arcs of circles and arcs of parabolas are the most common among them. Translational shells are supported by shears on boundary arches, just as barrels are supported by shears on end stiffeners (Fig. 12.53). The supporting arches are rigid in their own plane and flexible at right angles to it, so that compression or tension perpendicular to the arches is not developed at the shell boundary. The action of translational shells may be considered as barrel action in two directions, since the shells have curvature in two directions, but the central portion of the shells acts very much like a shallow dome, and develops compressive stresses along both generating curves. The portion of the shell near the supporting arches develops a certain amount of bending disturbances, and although these peter out rapidly into the shell in view of the curvature at right angles to it, a thickening of the shell is often required at the boundary.

A particular type of translational shell, engineered by Salvadori, is commonly used in Europe. These elliptic paraboloidal shells are built of hollow tile and concrete, with a minimal amount of reinforcing steel (0.6 pound per square foot), on a movable form a few feet wide, shaped as one of the two generating curves and sliding on wooden arches having the shape of the other generating curve (Fig. 12.54). The shell is built in slices, which act as separate arches and require tie-rods until they are made monolithic by the pouring and setting of concrete over the entire surface. These are among the few thin shells ever tested under total and partial loads. The tests proved that all the basic assumptions made about their action are met in practice. The bending disturbance at the boundary penetrates only a short distance into the shell; the shell does not thrust out along its sides and is supported exclusively by boundary shears. The rigidity of the shell proved to be exceptionally high: under a uniform live load of 30 pounds per square foot over its entire surface, a 60-by-90 foot shell presented a top deflection of less than one eighth of an inch, or a span-to-deflection ratio of 9000.

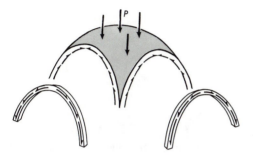

12.53 Boundary shears in translational shell.

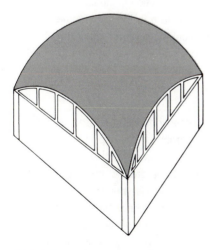

12.54 Tile and concrete elliptic paraboloid.

12.12 Saddle-Shell Action

The behavior of the most common saddle shell, the hyperbolic paraboloid, shows the dependence of its structural action on support conditions.
This surface was shown in Section 12.4 to be generated either by a vertical
parabola with downward curvature sliding on a vertical parabola with upward
curvature, or by a straight-line segment the ends of which slide on two straight
line segments askew in space (see Figs. 12.15 and 12.16).

When the shell is supported on two parabolic arches or stiffeners, it transfers
the load to the support by shears (Fig. 12.55). Its action is similar to that of a
stiffener-supported barrel, but the upward curvature in the longitudinal direction gives the shell additional strength, particularly **against buckling**. If the
shell tends to buckle, the parabolas with downward curvature tend to buckle
downward and flatten; this deformation is resisted by the parabolas with upward curvature, since their tension stabilizes the compressed parabolas.

If the paraboloid reaches the ground, its intersections with the ground consist
of two outward-curved boundaries (the two branches of a hyperbola), so that
the area covered by the shell has two straight sides and two curved sides (see
Fig. 12.15). When the paraboloid does not reach the ground, the shell may be
supported at its four corners, but the end stiffeners must then carry the vertical
and horizontal loads on the shell as arches. Bending disturbances, similar to
those at the curved boundaries of barrels, are encountered at the intersection
of the paraboloid with the stiffeners. Their values and the width of the disturbed band are of the same magnitude as those in cylindrical shells.

12.55 Hyperbolic paraboloid supported on end stiffeners.

It is easy to see that even when the hyperbolic paraboloid is supported on its straight-line generatrices, the directions of principal stress coincide with those of principal curvature, that is, the parabolas (see Fig. 12.6). Since the straight lines have no curvature, no cable or arch stresses can be developed along these lines by the shell, that can only react in shear. Hence, tension along the upward parabolas must combine with compression along the downward parabolas to create a state of pure shear along the straight lines (Fig. 12.56). The load is thus carried to the supporting boundaries by pure shear directed along the straight lines, and these shears accumulate along the boundary supports. The supporting elements are usually "beams," but these elements, rather than by vertical loads, are loaded by the shears accumulating along their lengths, so that they behave like compressive struts (Fig. 12.57) or tensile bars (Fig. 12.58), except for the action of their own dead load.

When the hyperbolic paraboloid is shallow, not only the **principal** membrane stresses are **identical** tensions and compressions producing shears of the same intensity (Fig. 12.56), but all three membrane stresses have the same value **all over the shell**. Inasmuch as membrane stresses are uniformly distributed across the depth of the shell, the hyperbolic paraboloid may be said to have a 100 per cent overall efficiency; the material of the shell is equally stressed **at any point of any cross section.** The membrane stresses in the paraboloid are proportional to the total uniform load on it, and inversely proportional to the shell rise and shell thickness. The shell rise should not be less than one-sixth to one-tenth the span in order to avoid high compressive stresses, which may buckle the shell.

It may be proved that the membrane stresses considered above arise in the hyperbolic paraboloid **only if** its straight-line boundary stiffeners are very rigid vertically and very flexible horizontally. Such conditions are seldom encountered in practice. If, for example, the boundary stiffeners are cantilevered from the two low points of the shell (Fig. 12.56), the boundary of the shell is not rigidly supported vertically, as required by the theoretical assumptions. Actually, some of the stiffeners' weight hangs from the shell, and the two halves of the paraboloid behave very much like cantilevered beams with the variable, curved cross section of the downward parabolas.

378

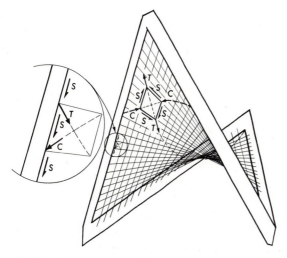

12.56 Hyperbolic paraboloid supported on straight generatrices.

Boundary disturbances are always present at the intersection with the boundary stiffeners; they penetrate into the shell more than the disturbances at the curved boundary of a cylinder, but less than those encountered along a cylindrical straight boundary.

Roofs are often built by combinations of hyperbolic paraboloid segments. One of the most commonly used involves four identical segments, the outer corners of which are supported on columns (Fig. 12.57). In this case, the inclined outer stiffeners and the horizontal inner stiffeners are all compressed by the accumulation of boundary shears (Fig. 12.57). The thrust of the compressed outer stiffeners is absorbed by tie-rods, while the inner beams are in horizontal equilibrium under the equal and opposite compressions of each pair of paraboloidal segments (Fig. 12.57). The roof has the appearance of a regular gabled roof, and its reactions at the corners are purely vertical, once the tie-rods are tensioned.

The same combination of four segments may be used as an umbrella supported on a central column (Fig. 12.58). In this case, the outer horizontal stiffeners are tensioned by the accumulation of shears, and the tension in one of them balances the tension in the stiffener of the adjoining segment. The roof is innerly equilibrated and its boundary stiffeners are its tie-rods (Fig. 12.58). In either combination, the weight of the horizontal stiffeners (the boundary stiffeners for the umbrella, and the inner cross for the gabled roof) is carried in part by the shell itself; the shell, therefore, develops some bending stresses. The roof supported at the corners may also buckle in the central region where it is flat, that is, where no appreciable curvature increases the buckling resistance of the thin shell.

12.57 Shears on boundary beams of hyperbolic paraboloidal roof supported on outer columns.

12.58 Shears on boundary beams of hyperbolic paraboloidal umbrella.

A variety of other combinations of hyperbolic paraboloids may be used to cover areas of varied shape. Each one of these combinations must be carefully analyzed to determine whether it is innerly balanced. A typically unbalanced combination, consisting of two segments, is used as a northlight roof (see Fig. 12.29). The thrust of the inclined boundary struts is equilibrated by a tie-rod, but the two compressive forces accumulating along the inclined strut common to the two segments are not equilibrated (Fig. 12.59). Hence, the horizontal boundary beam is acted upon by a concentrated load at midspan and is subject to bending. The shell behavior, in this case, is a bending action in horizontal projection, with compression at the upper boundary segments and tension at the lower horizontal boundary, due to a load concentrated at midspan; the two tensile forces at the outer lateral boundaries of the shell equilibrate the concentrated load, just like beam reactions (Fig. 12.59).

Hyperbolic paraboloids with a very high rise have also been used as roof elements; others as almost vertical elements. In such cases their behavior is totally different from that of the shallow paraboloids considered above, and similar to the behavior of a thin plate loaded in its own plane. It may be often approximated by the behavior of deep beams (see Section 7.1).

The different mechanisms by which the hyperbolic paraboloid carries loads are one more example of the dependence of shell behavior on support conditions.

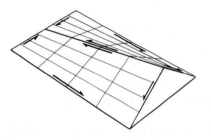

12.59 Shears on boundary beams of hyperbolic paraboloidal conoid.

12.13 Stresses in Scalloped and Other Types of Shells

Interesting shell shapes may be obtained by adding local curvatures to a simple surface, according to structural needs or aesthetic requirements.

An ellipsoid intersected by a horizontal plane is a smooth surface covering an elliptic area. In order to enhance its appearance and stiffen its boundary, it may be scalloped, thus creating local curvatures that peter out toward the interior of the shell (see Fig. 12.25). The introduction of such curvatures substantially changes the shell behavior. The smooth ellipsoid carries load by stresses similar to those encountered in a rotational shell: compression along the meridians, and compression or tension along the elliptical parallels. The introduction of local curvatures destroys the parallels' stiffness typical of membrane behavior. Under the action of loads the shell tends to open up, since its undulated parallels cannot develop the hoop stresses that play such an important role in stiffening rotational shells. The action of the shell is similar to that of a series of arches with variable cross section, hinged at the supports and at the crown, where the lack of curvature reduces the bending resistance of the shell (see Section 8.5). Circular domes of large diameter have also been built by scalloping a spherical surface with the purpose of increasing its buckling resistance (see Fig. 12.27). The waving of the parallels very much reduces their stiffening action; such shells behave as a series of arches crossing at the top of the dome and hinged there.

The membrane stresses of conoidal shells also depend on support conditions. If the straight boundaries are supported vertically and connected by tie-rods, each slice of the shell acts as a tied arch, and substantial bending stresses are to be expected for all loads for which the cross section of the shell is not a funicular curve. When the longitudinal boundaries are not supported, the conoid behaves as a cylinder with a variable rise and develops bending stresses in the neighborhood of the end arches only. If such a shell is scalloped, the transverse arch action is destroyed, since the conoid tends to open up; in order to restore its rigidity, the undulations must be stiffened by transvers stiffeners at regular intervals.

12.60 Cross section of north-light barrel shell.

North-light roofs for industrial buildings are often built by means of thin shells. Their structural behavior is similar to that of a beam with a shallow, curved cross section, whose neutral axis is not horizontal, but inclined towards the upper shell boundary (Fig. 12.60). The shell fibers above the inclined neutral axis are compressed and those below are tensed. When the beam stiffening the shell at its upper boundary is large, the neutral axis may cross it, and most shell fibers may be in tension.

Some of the largest thin shells in the world have been built to resist horizontal rather than vertical loads. Retaining walls loaded by the thrust of the earth may be built as vertical cylinders or conoids (Fig. 12.61). Cylindrical tanks containing water, oil, or other liquids are built as thin steel or prestressed concrete shells to resist the outward pressure of the liquid. Dams, with heights of over 1000 feet, have been built with curvatures both in the vertical and the horizontal sections and a thickness of only a few feet (Fig. 12.62). The ratio of radius of curvature to thickness in these dams is of the order of 400 or more, so that such shells are to be considered thin even though they may be several feet thick at their foot.

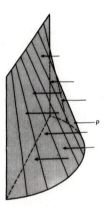

12.61 Conoidal retaining wall.

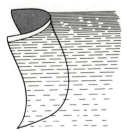

12.62 Thin-shell dam.

12.14 Thin Shell Formwork

The aesthetic, architectural, and structural possibilities of thin shell construction are practically unlimited; only their cost may, at times, hamper their diffusion. The problem of building expensive curved forms on which to pour reinforced-concrete shells has made their use uneconomical in countries with high labor costs. The solution of the forming problem has been attacked in a variety of ways. Roofs consisting of identical shell elements are built by pouring an element on a movable form, which is then lowered, shifted and reused again to pour the next. Prefabrication of shell elements and their erection on a light scaffold has become a standard procedure which eliminates expensive forms. The joining of the prefabricated elements must be carried out with great care, and often requires welding the reinforcing bars sticking out of the elements and pouring the joints at a later date. Some of the exceptional thin-shell structures designed by Nervi were built by this procedure.

Prefabrication of shells by elements is often used in conjunction with post-tensioning. It was observed in previous sections that certain types of shells develop tensile stresses over large portions of their area. These tensile stresses may be eliminated by introducing in the thickness of the shell steel cables or **tendons** which are tensioned after the concrete has hardened; they compress the shell so as to eliminate altogether the tensile stresses due to the loads (see Section 3.3). The thin shells of cylindrical tanks are usually post-tensioned by spirals of steel cables, thus guaranteeing the waterproofness of the tanks under all conditions. North-light shells with large spans may also be post-tensioned by curved tendons so as to eliminate tensile stresses in the shell portions below the inclined neutral axis (see Fig. 12.60).

The use of a concrete gun allows the spraying of layers of concrete (Shotcrete or Gunite) on the reinforcing bars with a minor amount of formwork. The bars are supported on simple scaffolding, in which the insulation panels constitute the actual form surface against which the concrete is shot. Finally, balloons have been used as inflated forms to support the steel and against which to spray the concrete or, as in the Bini process, as inflatable forms to lift both the reinforcing steel and the concrete (see Section 11.3).

12.15 Reticulated Domes

Space-frames (see Section 10.9) behave like structures in which the distributed material of a plate, and hence the stresses in it, are lumped in the frame bars. Their load carrying mechanisms can be understood by analogy with those of plates. Similarly, the behavior of **reticulated** or **ribbed domes** may be grasped readily, by analogy, with that of thin-shell domes.

For example, if the material in a spherical dome is lumped in bars lying along the two families of curves created by the meridians and the parallels (Fig. 12.63), the meridional bars will absorb the compressive membrane stresses from the top to the boundary of the dome, and the parallel bars will be in tension or in compression depending on the value of the opening angle (see Section 12.7). The continuous thin shell has been transformed into a **discrete structure** of the same shape. In order to use bars which do not differ too much in area, the meridional bars often branch off from the top of the dome down. The steel structures of some of the largest domes in the United States, like those of the 642-foot-diameter Astrodome in Houston, Texas (Fig. 12.64), and of the 680-foot-diameter Louisiana Superdome in New Orleans, Louisiana, follow this scheme (Fig. 12.65).

12.63 Ribbed spherical dome.

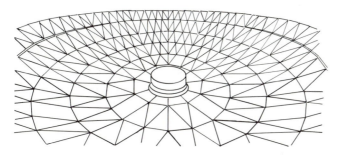

12.64 Houston Astrodome.

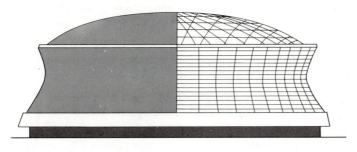

12.65 Louisiana Superdome.

The meridional-parallel lattice presents the disadvantage of using bars of different lengths. Other schemes have been invented to avoid this difficulty and simplify the connections between the bars, but since the surface of a sphere cannot be entirely covered by a lattice of regular polygons, the bars of a spherical dome cannot all be identical. In the **geodesic domes,** designed by Fuller, triangles and pentagons are used to obtain a subdivision in terms of bars of equal length (Fig. 12.66). An irregular triangular lattice of ribs is used instead in the classical **Schwedler dome** (Fig. 12.67), that presents the design advantages of being statically determinate (see Section 4.2), and in the **Zeiss-Dywidag dome** (Fig. 12.68).

12.66 Geodesic dome.

12.67 Schwedler dome.

12.68 Zeiss-Dywidag dome.

Ribbed domes spanning up to three or four hundred feet have been built in Europe with standard connectors, using bars made out of steel pipes on a triangular grid. These structures require only 4 to 5 pounds of steel per square foot, as against 10 to 20 pounds per square foot for domes built of rolled sections, but are very sensitive to local buckling. Their behavior in this context is analogous to that of a thin shell in which the steel of the bars, uniformly distributed over the dome surface, has a much smaller apparent modulus of elasticity and a smaller apparent density. In other words, these domes behave like a thin shell made out of a thicker, spongy material, just as space-frames do in relation to plates. As the buckling load is proportional to the elastic modulus of the material, the lower apparent modulus lowers the buckling capacity of these latticed domes. The analogy between latticed roofs and thin-shells subsists for roofs of other than spherical shape. Latticed barrel roofs can be built with bars parallel and perpendicular to the barrel axis (Fig. 12.69) and can be supported on end diaphragms; the forces in their discrete bars are, to a good approximation, the resultants of the stresses in the barrel shell areas "contributory" to the bars, and can be obtained by considering the barrel as a beam (see Section 12.9). When the barrel roof springs from the ground and, hence, behaves like a series of parallel arches, a skew grid of discrete arches leads to a so-called **Lamella roof** (see Fig. 12.70), which is used to span hundreds of feet in wood, concrete or steel (see Section 8.5). Zeman has built domed Lamella roofs spanning up to 300 feet, by erecting prefabricated steel-pipe sections with standard bolted connections. The structure of these roofs, also, weighs not more than 5 pounds per square foot.

Saddle roofs, in the shape of hyperbolic paraboloids, made out of steel pipes oriented along the straight line generatrices of these surfaces, have been used by Candela as units to plug the openings between the reinforced concrete arches of the Olympic Stadium in Mexico City (Fig. 12.71).

12.69 Latticed barrel roof.

12.70 Lamella roof.

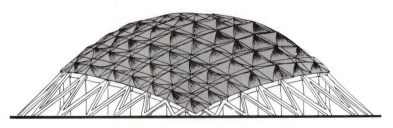

12.71 Roof with hyperbolic paraboloids of steel pipe.

The bending disturbances at the shell boundary (see Section 12.8) correspond to local bending of the bars of the latticed roof near its supports. All other bars are only stressed by the axial forces corresponding to the membrane shell stresses (compressive or tensile) and hence use the material to great efficiency. As is the case for the thickness of thin shells, limitations in the bar sizes may be due to the requirements of buckling.

The erection of latticed domes is facilitated by the Binistar system patented by Bini and first designed in 1985 for a triangulated dome on an hexagonal base of 131-foot diameter in Bari, Italy. The "telescopic" steel bars of a Binistar dome consist of outer pipes and two inner rods sliding in each pipe (Fig. 12.72). Short lugs, set into the inner rods in correspondence with holes in the outer pipes, can be pushed out radially by springs. The inner rods are attached to spherical connectors that allow their ends to rotate freely. To erect the dome the pipe-rods bars are mounted, over a deflated plastic balloon, into a flat triangular lattice, anchored to a base ring of reinforced concrete. As the balloon is inflated to the required dome shape, the inner rods slide inside the pipes until the lugs are shot into the pipe holes by the springs: the lugs, thus engaged into the pipes, transform the telescopic bars into rigid bars and freeze the shape of the triangulated dome (Fig. 12.73). The ballon is then attached to the external latticed dome and becomes its permanent surface. As Geiger's tensile domes (see Section 6.2), Binistars may be considered membrane balloons supported by reticulated domes rather than by air pressure.

In countries with high material costs and low labor costs, thin shells of poured, prefabricated or prestressed concrete are usually economical in comparison to similar latticed steel domes. The opposite is usually true in countries with high labor costs and low material costs. The same considerations of relative materials and labor costs explain the favor encountered by the latticed pipe domes outside the United States. While rolled-section domes can be built in sectors, using a single center support for their erection, lightweight pipe domes require more complicated scaffolds and greater amounts of labor. Since moreover, in the United States steel pipe is, pound per pound, more expensive than rolled steel sections, the fabrication and erection costs of pipe domes do not, in general, make these structures competitive.

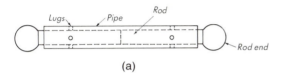

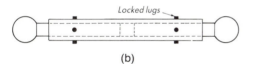

12.72 Bar of Binistar dome:
(a) unextended, (b) extended and locked.

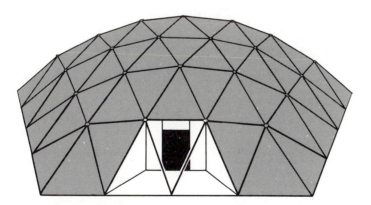

12.73 Binistar dome.

Chapter Thirteen

Structural Failures

13.1 Historical Failures

The moment man started erecting structures, structures began to fail. In prehistoric times corbelled domed houses of stone were built all along a band running uninterruptedly through Asia Minor, Greece, Crete, Sardinia, southern France, and England, but only a few survive intact after 2,000 to 5,000 years. The pyramids of Egypt stand lonely among the Seven Wonders of the Ancient World: the Colossus of Rhodes, an over-100-foot-high bronze statue to the sun god Helios, vanished, and an earthquake destroyed the second longest lived, the lighthouse of Pharos at Alexandria (Egypt), said by some historians to be 200 feet, by others 600 feet tall.

Collapses and failures plagued some of the greatest monuments of history. The dome of Saint Sophia in Constantinople began showing signs of weakness during construction and tradition has it that it was saved by the intervention of the emperor Justinian, who urged the architect Anthemius to complete one of its main arches that was falling, because "when it rests upon itself it will no longer need the uprights under it." Yet, after two earthquakes, the eastern arch collapsed in 557, the western in 989, and the eastern for the second time in 1346; the dome was made stable only in 1847 by placing iron chains around the base. The masterpiece of Gothic architecture, the Cathedral of Saint Pierre at Beauvais, had the main vaults of the choir collapse in 1284 only 12 years after it was completed, and its 502-foot tower collapse 13 days after its erection in 1573. The great domes of Renaissance Italy, those of Santa Maria degli Angeli in Florence and of Saint Peter's in Rome, cracked, and few if any of the monuments of the past still extant do not show signs of weakness today.

400

We accept such failures because of the lack of sound structural knowledge by the men of the times, but we are shocked and puzzled by the rash of collapses of some of our large buildings and bridges. How does our scientific age explain and countenance such disasters? If we are interested in learning why most of our buildings stand up, we also want to know why some fall down.

In the following sections the main causes of contemporary failures are discussed using the intuitive approach of this book, but it must be pointed out at the outset that such failures occur in a small percentage of our increasingly large, tall, and complex structures. As should be expected, our record is far superior to that of our predecessors, although the number of exceptional structures being erected grows yearly all over the world.

13.2 Main Causes of Structural Failure

In the last analysis all structural failures are caused by human error, that is, are due to lack of knowledge or judgment, but for purposes of classification they may be attributed to deficiencies in design, in fabrication and erection, or in materials. One could put failures due to unexpected events, natural or man-made, in a separate category, but even these are due, most of the time, to our incomplete knowledge or lack of caution. Different causes often conspire and result in collapses. **Technical investigations** should try to explain them so that their repeated occurrence might be avoided, but should waste no time assigning blame, since this is the province of the law. Yet, it might interest the reader to learn the professional and legal consequences of engineering and architectural failures, which is the subject of Section 13.6.

13.3 Faults in Structural Design

Design deficiencies may occur for a number of reasons: pure and simple mistakes in calculations, undetected errors in computer inputs, incomplete or mistaken interpretation of building codes, unfamiliarity with dynamic or "hidden loads," defective detailing, lack of redundancy, lack of coordination between the members of the construction team, and many more.

As shown in Section 2.3, good design can only result from experience, since design cannot be taught. Hence, the young practitioner should not be expected to assess the relative importance of the many facets of design and should not be given responsibility for the design of essential structural components. The organization of a professional office requires clear assignment of tasks and careful supervision at all levels. Before drawings are signed (see Section 4.6), an experienced professional must carefully examine them and be satisfied that they faithfully interpret the design concept for the other members of the construction team. Unfortunately, under the time and economic pressures of our culture, such supervision and coordination are not always given the consideration they deserve and often become causes of failure.

Contrary to what the layman may believe, **errors in calculations** seldom cause deficient design: if flagrant, they are easily caught; if minor, they may be unimportant. The advent of the computer has immensely refined structural calculations (see Section 4.4) at the cost of drowning the designer in a sea of numbers: the experienced professional, aware of the common occurrence of input errors, will never accept a computer result without checking it long hand with a simplified formula or against personal experience and past records.

It must not be construed from the above that errors in calculations are never responsible for failures. In certain cases the mistakes in design are so flagrant that their most probable cause may be shown or inferred to be an uncaught numerical mistake. According to the investigation by the National Bureau of Standards of the failure of the pedestrian bridges at the Hyatt Regency Hotel in Kansas City, Missouri, in 1982, in which 112 people died and almost 200 were wounded, the collapse was due to an obvious error in design (Figure 13.1). The reader of the NBS report may justifiedly surmise that a numerical mistake, accompanied by a lack of judgment on the part of an inexperienced designer, may be the source of such an error.

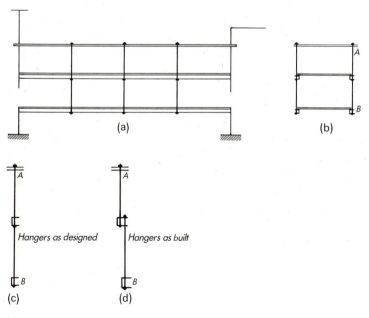

(a)

(b)

Hangers as designed   *Hangers as built*

(c)   (d)

13.1 Hyatt Regency Hotel's walkways.

A thorough knowledge of **building codes** requires years of patient study, careful interpretation, and frequent updating. Codes are modified every few years to take into account the accumulation of new knowledge and to clarify the meaning of their requirements. The American professional is confronted not only with a variety of codes applicable to different types of structures and materials, but with the proliferation of codes by states, counties, and cities. Most of the structural requirements in local codes are derived from or refer to a few widely accepted national codes, but still vary sufficiently from one another to demand careful scrutiny, particularly because of their legal implications (see Section 13.6). The situation differs from that existing in other countries, where unique national codes govern. In any case, it must be remembered that the building codes make minimum recommendations and that adherence to their requirements does *not* exempt the designer from technical responsibilities.

Fields in rapid evolution, like those of **dynamic design** for wind and earthquake loads, have requirements seldom timely updated in building codes because they demand time-consuming debates before being approved. Moreover, the practice of dealing with dynamic conditions is not common in architectural engineering because most of our buildings are usually subjected to static loads only (see Chapter 2). Hence, the design practitioner must not only be aware of the possibility of dynamic loads, but must keep abreast of the current literature so as to make safe and economic use of the latest information on these dangerous conditions. For example, the design of the Toronto City Hall building for wind forces, wisely determined by wind tunnel tests, indicated an unexpected wind load due to the channeling of the wind through the gap between its two buildings (Figure 13.2). Similarly, the heavy steel gates of one of our first missile silos were torn off their hinges and collapsed when first used for lack of consideration on the part of the designers of the dynamic forces due to their accelerated motion.

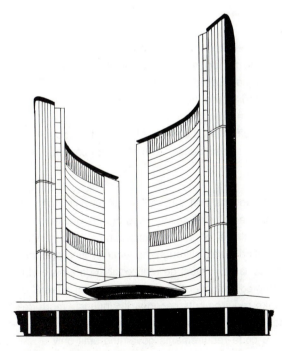

13.2 City Hall, Toronto, Canada.

The wind-bracing system of a building must not only meet conditions of strength but those of stiffness to minimize discomfort to its occupants and avoid damage to its curtain wall (see Section 2.4). In a high-rise steel building of a metropolitan city in the United States the excessive flexibility of the frame was one of the main causes of the dislodgement of a high percentage of the curtain wall glass panes, and required the damping of its wind-induced motion by means of two dynamic dampers (see Section 2.6) at a high cost and with long construction delays.

The knowledge of earthquake motions and their influence on buildings has rapidly improved during the last decades. Detailed maps of earthquake intensities in the United States are available to the designer and must be consulted by all members of the construction team, although the technicalities of earthquake design are left to the specialist. It must be realized that data on earthquakes are gathered uninterruptedly all over the world and that as a result of these investigations earthquake requirements become continuously more demanding. Some of the recent California earthquakes surpassed in intensity those forming the base of the code requirements governing until only a few years ago and areas of the United States, thought until recently to be free of higher-intensity earthquakes, have been proved to be subjected to them. Even in areas of minor earthquake activity the codes now take them into account, for example, in the detail requirements of reinforced-concrete frames. On the other hand, it is comforting to realize that our improved techniques of earthquake design allow high-rise buildings, like the Torre Latino-Americana in Mexico City, to survive undamaged earthquakes that caused the failure of low buildings of older vintage.

The same caution must be used in dealing with thermal differences, the main source of locked-in stresses (see Section 2.5). Because of their dependence on a large number of parameters, the investigation of thermal stresses is advised by most codes without specific recommendations on temperature differences or methods of analysis. As a consequence structural failures may often be attributed to neglected thermal conditions. In a concrete dome for one of the first nuclear reactors built in the United States the stresses due to a "thermal explosion" (a sudden, large temperature rise on the interior of the reactor), originally ignored, required a modification of the design. Most of the cracks in the brick masonry veneers of air-conditioned buildings, particularly in veneers of prefabricated panels, are due to the rigid connections between the exposed masonry and the interior structure that do not allow the thermal expansions and contractions of the masonry due to daily and seasonal temperature variations of the outdoor air [Figure 13.3(a)]. Similarly, cracking in the partitions of high-rise buildings occurs when the climate produces large differences in temperature between southern and northern facades. The thermal bending of such buildings [Fig. 13.3(b)] is the source of high shears in the partitions, acting as webs of vertical cantilevered beams, and of cracks due to the tensile component of these shears (see Sections 5.3 and 7.1).

The mechanics of soils has become a reputable field of science through the investigations of the last one hundred years: it is one of the most sensitive facets of foundation design. No structural engineer will assume the responsibility of such design without a soil investigation performed by specialized laboratories that specify the bearing capacity of the soil, the maximum differential settlements to be expected, and the type of foundation most appropriate for a chosen location (see Section 4.3). Settlement differentials are of particular interest to the designer since they may cause large cracks in curtain walls and partitions and weaken the structure (Fig. 13.4). A substantial number of failures in slabs on grade and curtain walls are due to foundation deficiencies related to changes in underground water levels and new construction. The National Theatre in Mexico City, founded on a soil consisting of a mixture of sand and water, subsided many feet at first when its weight squeezed the water out of the sand, but then was pushed integrally above its original level when a number of high-rise buildings were erected around it. In this case the evenness of the displacements and the monolithic reinforced-concrete structure prevented damage to the building.

408

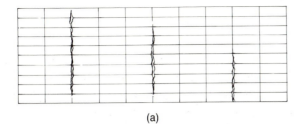

(a)

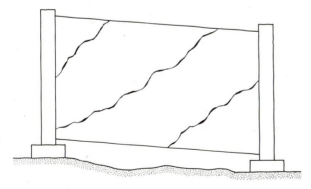

Cracked
panel

(b)

13.3 Thermal cracks in building facades.

13.4 Settlement cracks in curtain wall or partition.

Some of the most spectacular failures take place in structures lacking **redundancy.** Statical indeterminacy is a necessary but not a sufficient condition of redundance (see Section 4.2). For example, if a uniformly loaded **fixed** beam were to fail at one of its support sections, indeterminacy might theoretically allow it to carry the load as a cantilever [Fig. 13.5(b)]. But if it was originally designed to resist the largest bending moments in a fixed beam, which usually occur at its ends (see Section 7.3), the stresses at the cantilever root would increase by a factor of 6 and collapse the beam. If the midspan section of the same beam failed and it carried the load as two cantilevers half its length [Fig. 13.5(c)], the stresses at the roots of these cantilevers would be 50 per cent above the maximum original stresses and dangerously near collapse since, on an average, safety factors take into consideration a load increase of the order of 67 per cent.

Redundancy thus requires providing additional structural resistance in case of failure, particularly when the loads on a structure are supported by a large number of identical elements, as in space-frames (see Section 10.9). The roof of the Kansas City (Missouri) Arena was hung by means of 48 steel hangers from three external pipe frames (Fig. 13.6). When one of the hanger connections failed during an exceptional rainstorm the load supported by that hanger was transferred to adjoining hangers that presumably were unable to carry the additional load: a chain reaction developed that collapsed a large section of the roof, luckily without loss of life because the arena was unoccupied at the time. A similar chain reaction of failing hangers was said to cause the collapse of a suspended ceiling at the Jersey City terminal of the PATH railroad, causing two deaths. It must be noted that tensile hangers work in simple tension, distributing the load uniformly over their cross section (see Section 5.1): hence they do not have the reserve of strength derived from stress redistribution at a section, typical of bending action (see Section 9.3).

410

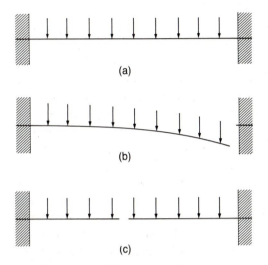

(a)

(b)

(c)

13.5 Redundancy in fixed beams.

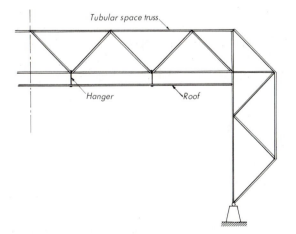

Tubular space truss

Hanger

Roof

13.6 Hanging roof of Kansas City Arena.

Redundancy is particularly needed whenever a chain reaction may be started by buckling. It was noted in Section 5.2 that buckling is a sudden phenomenon that occurs without warning and is usually followed by failure. The particular case of buckling involving torsion, called **lateral buckling,** presents the same dangerous characteristics. According to the published results of the structural investigations on the collapse of the space frame roof of the Hartford Civic Center in Hartford, Connecticut, spanning 300 by 270 feet and supported on four pilons (Fig. 13.7), the collapse of the roof during a heavy snowstorm was started by the buckling failures of an unbraced compression bar near the boundary of the frame. When the load supported by this bar was transferred to the adjoining bars, these in turn failed in buckling, precipitating a chain-reaction collapse that dropped to the floor of the empty hockey rink, in a matter of minutes, the 1,500 tons of steel of the entire roof. It is not clear whether axial or torsional buckling was responsible for this chain reaction collapse.

As shown in Sections 9.1 and 9.2, the states of stress in the **connections** of structural elements are particularly complex. Hence it will come as no surprise to the reader that they are often the source of failures. Codes and manuals give criteria for the design of connections based not only on refined mathematical stress analyses but on series of tests on models or full-size connections. Since, because of their complexity, failures of connections occur more frequently than those of structural members, connections are designed with high coefficients of safety. This is particularly true of space-frames whose connectors may have complex shapes and stress distributions (see Fig. 10.45).

412

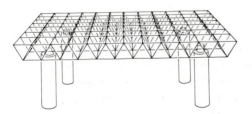

13.7 Space-frame of Hartford Civic Center.

Failures have often been attributed to **unexpected natural** or **man-made phenomena,** such as hurricanes, snowstorms, tsunamis, and fires or explosions. These do indeed bring havoc to all kinds of small and large structures, but only when the structures were not designed to resist them, when forces reach new highs (a common occurrence), or when engineers forgot the lessons of the past. The collapse of the Tacoma Narrows Bridge in 1940 (see Section 2.6) was identical with that of the Wheeling suspension bridge over the Ohio River in 1854, but the memory of this disaster, vividly described in the local press, had vanished. Descriptions of similar collapses of wooden suspension bridges had appeared in the British press early in the nineteenth century, but had also been forgotten, allowing the repetition of past disasters.

In most recent collapses of large structures the loads due to natural forces did not reach the design values recommended by the codes and must be attributed to faulty design. For example, the collapse of large flat roofs subjected to rainstorms is often due to a chain reaction phenomenon called "ponding." The flat roof caves under the weight of the rain, acquiring a convex shape that does not allow the water to reach the level of the drains. The increasing weight of rain increases the caving of the roof, which is transformed into a pond containing an increasing load of water that eventually collapses the roof (Fig. 13.8). Appropriate distribution of drains at correct levels prevents ponding.

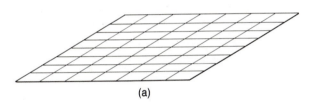

(a)

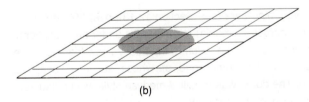

(b)

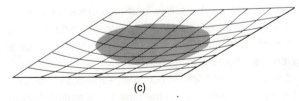

(c)

13.8 Ponding of flat roof.

A reticulated dome of light pipe bars (see Section 12.13), over 300 feet in diameter, collapsed in Bucharest (Romania) in the 1960's under an exceptional snowfall. The collapse was not due so much to the heavy snow load as to the weak buckling capacity of the dome, one of whose sections "snapped through," i.e., caved in. The dome was rebuilt, American style, with rolled section bars, giving it greater buckling capacity.

The man-made causes of failures, such as fires and explosions, can be as damaging as those due to natural phenomena. A high-rise industrial building in New York City had two of its facades blown out from top to bottom by a bizarre sequence of events attributable to human error. A cylindrical, steel, compressed air tank, 10 feet high and 2 feet in diameter, exploded in the middle of the night, probably due to a deficiency in the tank or the malfunctioning of a pressure gage. The tank explosion shot up its domed top against an overhead gas pipe that sprang a leak under the impact. The gas would have been confined to the floor where the tank was located were it not for the alternate motion of the elevators in the building that sucked the gas up to the high floors and pushed it down to the low floors in a pumping action, thus spreading gas throughout the building. When in the early morning an occupant of the building put a match to his cigarette, the mixture of gas and air exploded, destroying the two facades, whose debris damaged buildings across the adjoining streets and hurt a number of their occupants.

This brief review of some of the most common causes of structural failures illustrates their great variety and suggests the responsibility of the structural engineer in the design of important structures. It will be shown in the following sections that the involvement of the other members of the construction team, and particularly of the architect, is as great as that of the engineer.

13.4 Faults in Coordination and Supervision

The construction team of a large modern structure consists of a large number of specialists: the architect in charge and his team of design architects, coordination architect, landscape architect, and interior designers; the structural engineer and his team; the mechanical engineer and his team; the electrical engineer and his team; the plumbing engineer and his team; the soils engineer; the environmental designer; the contractor and his team; the owners' representatives; and a variety of other experts on curtain walls, roofing, costing, scheduling, and materials. Last but not least is the **construction manager,** who takes responsibility for the feasibility of the design and the coordination of all trades, acts as the owner's agent, and directs the execution of the job with the help of the scheduling experts, responsible for the sequence of operations and the delivery of materials. At the frequent general meetings on the progress of construction it is not unusual to have thirty or more experts around the table, fighting their personal battles in the interest of the expeditious erection of the building.

The smooth **coordination** between all the facets of construction requires cooperative communication between the members of the team and implies a knowledge of the basic requirements of the other trades on the part of the representatives of each trade. The architect, as team leader, must be conversant with the needs of **all** the trades and capable of settling the disputes arising from the mutually conflicting requirements of the consultants. In this he is helped by the construction manager, whose job demands practical experience and a capability for conciliation and compromise within narrow limits of acceptability. The **construction documents** (drawings, specifications, and contracts) are of the utmost importance in avoiding misunderstandings and mistaken interpretations that only too often lead to delays and failures. Whether a contractor is chosen at the start of the design or by bids on contract documents, he must be given documents that leave little doubt as to the meaning of what he is to deliver. The time and effort spent on these documents avoids failures and costly litigation (see Section 13.6).

In spite of the interest and goodwill of the members of the team, unavoidable conflicts will arise during construction and clarifications or **change orders will be issued.** In this phase of construction competent **supervision** becomes essential on the part of the job's **superintendent,** the commander of the contractor's crews, and of the architect's and/or owner's representative. It is their duty to ensure that the building is erected in strict accordance with the construction documents, since even a minor deviation from the design may be the cause of catastrophic failures. Besides any tendency on the part of the contractor to cut corners in order to maintain the schedule or to enhance profit, involuntary human error may be responsible for such mistakes. In this context it suffices to mention the consequences of the misplacement of the reinforcement in concrete structures, the deviation from a prescribed sequence of operations in welding of steel connections, the tightening of connections that should allow thermal movements, or the improper curing of poured concrete. These are a few among the many operations that must be carefully monitored to eliminate possible failures.

Many of the structural elements, such as steel beams and columns or prefabricated beams, columns, and slabs of concrete (often prestressed), come to the site from a **fabrication shop.** A check of these elements for dimensional compliance with the design is necessary to make sure that any discrepancies are within prescribed **tolerances,** lest the erectors be compelled to force the elements together, inducing in them dangerous locked-in stresses (see Section 2.5).

The architect and the engineers must realize that there is a wide gap between a theoretical conception and its execution in the field, and that the job of the contractor may appear less creative than theirs but is certainly as complex and demanding. A harmonious collaboration between the "legislative" and "executive" branches of the construction team is a necessity if failures are to be avoided.

13.5 Faults in Materials

The most essential properties of structural steel are **strength** and **ductility,** i.e., the capacity of plastic flow, which guarantees elimination of stress concentrations and a reserve of strength (see Section 9.3). These properties depend on the chemical composition, the thermal treatment, and the rolling of steel shapes during manufacture, and should be checked for each batch of steel used by obtaining the corresponding data from the manufacturer: they are essential not only for beams and columns, but for nuts, bolts, and other connection components. Since the 1960's engineers have been alerted to the dangerous phenomenon of **delamination** due to the welding of thick steel sections: unless their steel is adequately treated thermally any parts of sections thicker than 2 or 3 inches have a tendency to separate into thin laminae, greatly reducing their strength. Research stemming from these disasters emphasized the importance of checking the treatment of steel used in large structures.

No operation involves greater risks in steel construction than the welding of connections: the welding materials, the type of flame, the temperature, and the speed used in this operation influence dramatically the strength of the connections. Since a number of failures of steel structures is attributable to welds, most codes require **welders** to be duly trained and **certified.**

Concrete properties depend on its composition, i.e., the ratios of cement, sand, stone, and water used in the mixture. Besides the type of cement and the strength of the stone, one must establish the granulometry of sand and stone i.e., the size distribution, so as to guarantee that the voids between stones are filled by the sand grains and those between the sand grains by the cement. Both stone and sand must be carefully washed to eliminate impuri-

420

ties. The **water-cement** ratio is the most important factor in determining the concrete strength: a low ratio increases the strength but makes more difficult the pouring and vibrating of the concrete; a high ratio weakens the concrete. In all projects of any importance the concrete mixture is designed by a **concrete laboratory** and its compressive strength is checked after 7 and 28 days by testing cylinders of concrete taken from daily concrete batches. The following unusual episode illustrates the need of vigilance in concrete supervision. During the construction of one of the most famous air-terminals in the United States it was noticed that concrete batches gave acceptable strength results at all times except those reaching the site in the early afternoon. When all investigations failed to discover the reason for this anomaly, the design engineer decided to follow the trucks leaving the concrete plant at lunch time, which usually reached the site an hour later. He thus discovered that the truck drivers, before stopping for lunch, poured water into the revolving drums of the trucks so as to prevent the setting of the concrete during their leisurely meal. The concrete reaching the site had the right consistency but a reduced strength due to the higher water-cement ratio, as revealed by the tests at 7 days.

Particular care must be exerted in locating the steel reinforcing bars in the concrete, but moreover, the steel bars must be covered with zinc or epoxy whenever highly corrosive salts may percolate through the concrete, as often happens in the slabs of garages when snow-melting salts are used on roads. The architect should be aware of the dangers due to faults in the two most commonly used structural materials, but only the metallurgist and the concrete specialist can assist him in the determination of their properties and thus prevent the corresponding failures.

13.6 Consequences of Structural Failures

Structural failures result at times in bodily damage and loss of life and are **always** the cause of financial losses, damaged professional standing, and even more dire consequences for one or more members of the construction team. Unless amicably settled among the parties involved, major collapses as well as minor failures lead to litigation through the courts or arbitration proceedings and, since the architect's technical consultants are often his subcontractors, the architect becomes legally and financially involved in litigation. The architect is then compelled to sue his consultants **and** the contractor, and the contractor, in turn, to sue the entire architectural team. The owner, who certainly has no responsibility for the failure, is usually the originator of these complex, prolonged, and costly maneuvers, in which each party is supported by a group of experts. It is not unusual for these legal proceedings to last long periods of time (sometimes years) and for the requests of damages to reach large amounts of money even when punitive damages, attributable to bad faith or fraud, are not involved. In few human endeavors is an ounce of prevention worth so many pounds of cure.

It may seem strange to read in a book on structures the recommendation that the architect should use, besides the services of competent technical consultants, those of a legal advisor. But the realities of the construction world prove that an attorney's advice on the writing of contracts, the preparation of construction documents, the approval of consultants' drawings, and, in general, on all written communications, is particularly important for the professional architect. The recommendation may even be illuminating for the layman who reads in the daily press stories about the human, financial, and professional consequences of structural failures. It should be no wonder to him that **forensic engineering,** the art and science of expert testimony in court, has become a recognized specialty of the engineering profession, when he learns that plaintiffs' demanded damages in the collapse of the walkways of the Hyatt Regency Hotel in Kansas City, Missouri, (see Section 13.3) amounted to $3 billion and that the designing engineers of this project have been tried for disbarment.

Is there any remedy for the occurrence of structural failures in our technological era? A measure suggested to alleviate the situation and so far taken by only a few states, consists in requiring the construction engineers to update their knowledge by successful attendance at courses in their specialty before having their professional licenses renewed. Professional engineering societies and schools of engineering offer such courses and engineering companies and offices offer them in-house or require their engineers to attend the courses given at universities and professional societies.

The continuous and rapid evolution of the field of structures has noticeably increased the use by design offices of outside consultants and advised, in particular circumstances, the use of so-called **peer reviews.** These consist in requesting a reputable design firm to analyze in depth a structural design **before** it is submitted for execution, and to point out deficiencies and suggest alternative solutions to the structural problems of the design. This valuable practice, beginning to be adopted by the best design firms in the United States, is **required by law** for designs of exceptional importance **in France,** where companies specializing in peer reviews are licensed by the state.

A number of other suggestions have been made which would require apprenticeship periods for engineering graduates and a strengthening of the state license examinations. Whatever procedure or combination of procedures may eventually be adopted, there is little doubt about the importance of updating the knowledge of the professionals in a field evolving as rapidly as that of structures, and influencing so deeply the lives of all citizens.

Chapter Fourteen

Structural Aesthetics

14.1 Aesthetics and Structures

There is no architecture without an aesthetic component, but is there an aesthetics of structure? And if there is, does it influence architecture deeply enough for architects to take an interest in it?

In answering these questions one may ignore the many definitions of "the beautiful" and notice instead that aesthetic tenets change with time: a piece of architecture considered a masterpiece at a given time is demoted to a second-rate achievement in another, and vice versa. The tenets of aesthetics vary but the satisfaction of aesthetic needs is one of the permanent aspirations of humanity.

Aesthetically satisfying buildings can be built that partially disregard structural laws: the example of the Parthenon was mentioned in this context in the very first section of this book. On the other hand, great structuralists have preached that one should not bother with aesthetics because if a building is correctly designed, beauty is bound to fall out from its structural correctness. Innumerable ugly buildings, correctly engineered, prove this theory to be baseless. Even if unconcerned with aesthetics, engineering geniuses like Maillart and Nervi designed wonderful structures because of their innate feeling for beauty (Fig. 14.1).

In considering the influence of structure on architectural aesthetics one must distinguish those buildings in which structure is relatively unimportant, and hence not uniquely determined, from those in which structure is essential. The appearance of a one-family house rarely depends on its structure, which may be of steel, concrete, wood, or stone, but that of a large suspension bridge is inherent in its structural requirements. Buildings between these two extremes have structures that by influencing in varying degree their appearance, influence the aesthetic response of their users. By the same token, the constraints of architectural aesthetics influence in varying degrees the structural solutions adopted by the engineer. Totally satisfying aesthetic solutions can only be achieved through the interplay of architecture and engineering.

14.1 Maillart bridge.

14.2 Semiotic Messages

Since the early twentieth century the concept of the **semiotic message** of a completed building has become widely accepted by architects, architectural historians, and other specialists in the field of construction. Semiotics, a branch of philosophy developed over the last ninety years, considers any and all human activities and products from the particular viewpoint of **nonverbal** or **sign communication**. Communication consists of messages: verbal communication is concerned with communication of meaning and to this purpose uses the words of a given language; a verbal communication is totally dependent on the culture in which the language is understood. Nonverbal communication may also consist of a meaningful message that could be expressed as well verbally. The semiotic message of a road sign may stand for the English message: "No parking" (Fig. 14.2), but, in contrast with the verbal message, it is understood internationally. On the other hand, a semiotic message may also be the by-product of an object or artifact whose main purpose is **not** to communicate but to perform a function. Clothing, for example, is made to protect the human body, but semiotically it communicates status, as in the case of military uniforms or church garments.

Both kinds of semiotic messages are found in architecture: the pushbuttons in an elevator perform a specific function but also express semiotic messages related to their function of moving the elevator to specific floors. The message of a window, instead, communicates something beyond its intrinsic function of transmitting light and air; the barred windows of a jail say clearly: "This building is a jail," while the ornamented windows of a Renaissance palace state unequivocally the status of its owner (Fig. 14.3).

It is obvious from these elementary examples that the semiotic message is as deeply embedded in a culture as the verbal message. A savage entering the lobby of a high-rise building would not understand the "meaning" of the eleva-

14.2 Semiotic message of a road sign.

14.3 Renaissance palace.

tor buttons; neither would he grasp the social significance of the windows of the Renaissance palace.

Finally, the meaning of a semiotic message, as much as that of a verbal one, changes with time: the pyramids communicated a religious message at the time of the Pharaohs, an incitement to glory to Napoleon and his troops, and a mixture of artistic, sociological, and structural meanings to the modern visitor.

Structure introduces in architecture two kinds of semiotic messages. When it is not visible, the structural component of the architectural message may not be apparent to the lay person, even if the building may depend essentially on it for its architectural message. On the other hand, buildings structured uniquely by the requirements of statics express a semiotic message that, while not independent of its architecture, is strictly related to structural action and acquires a meaning **of its own**.

14.3 Origins of the Structural Message

Purely structural messages originate in an intuitive understanding of structural action stemming both from physical experience and the perception of structural forms in nature. To exemplify the first kind of source, one may mention the lifting of weights by means of a rope, like the lifting of water from a well. This action goes back to the beginning of civilization and gives us an intuitive grasp of the properties of all tensile structures. Similarly, the primordial act of breaking tree branches against our knee gives us an intuition of bending action.

The visual perception of natural forms has been basic in extending our intuitions about man-made structures. The branches of a tree, acted upon by their own weight and that of snow, suggest the behavior and correct shape for cantilevers, with larger dimensions at their root than at their tip. The trunks of trees bent by the wind confirm this behavior, while the shape of straight trunks introduces us to the accumulation of vertical loads. Due to these intuitions we are puzzled by the sight of a Mycenaean column (Fig. 14.4(a)), larger at the top than at the bottom, but accept as instinctively correct the tapered-up shape of a Doric column, [Fig. 14.4(b)]. Similarly, we consider "ugly" a cantilever tapering toward its root [Fig. 14.5(a)] because it contradicts a structural behavior we have seen in nature since the beginning of the race [Fig. 14.5(b)].

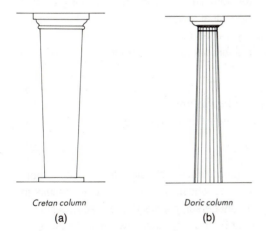

Cretan column   Doric column
(a)   (b)

14.4 Mycenaean and Doric columns.

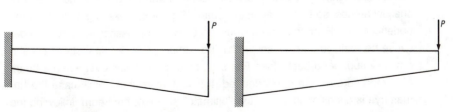

14.5 Incorrect and correct cantilever beams.

A similar reaction of shock occurs when we are confronted with a large mass in the shape of an inverted pyramid. Due to the action of gravity, mountains are shaped as right-side-up pyramids and the Egyptian pyramids have an idealized geometrical shape identical to that of the mountains. A modern building progressively cantilevered upward (Fig. 14.6) does not "say" to the lay person how it stands up: it suggests that some "trick" was used to achieve an "unnatural" result, arousing in us a sense of uneasy surprise rather than the feeling of balance expressed by an "honest" static behavior.

Natural arches have taught us that stone spanning a gap must acquire a downward curvature because this material, strong enough in compression to support a mountain, is weak in tension. This intuitive understanding of arch action can be extended to two-dimensional structures, like domes, by referring to our experience of living in caves. Caves do not explain the required thickness of domes, but this cannot be appreciated either from their inside or from their outside, anyway.

Similarly, the vine catenaries linking tree to tree show us the need of upward curvatures in tensile structures, a feature that even modern engineering must use in suspension bridges.

It is thus seen that for those of us who are not structuralists the structural message derives from atavistic experiences whose accumulation often results in aesthetic reactions. This is why the lay person considers a correctly designed cantilever [see Fig. 14.5(b)] "elegant" and "dynamic," while a simply supported beam (Fig. 14.7), correctly designed with a larger depth at midspan, is hard to understand and may be considered "ugly" by the lay person, who has seldom if ever seen such a beam in nature. On the contrary, most natural beams are rigidly connected to their supports and have the visual profile of shallow arches, so that a haunched beam (Fig. 14.8) looks "right" to the inexperienced eye. Even the expert would agree with this instinctive evaluation because he realizes that, as shown by the compressive principal stress lines in a simply supported beam (see Fig. 9.9), arch action takes over when a beam of reinforced concrete is overloaded. It would seem that in this case the human eye is conditioned to see the "ultimate" shape of the beam, following the basic principle that a structure will not collapse until it really cannot help it.

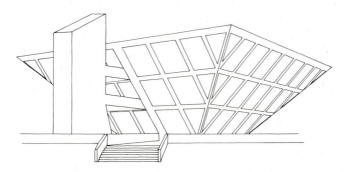

14.6 Cantilevered building.

14.7 Simply supported beam.

14.8 Haunched beam.

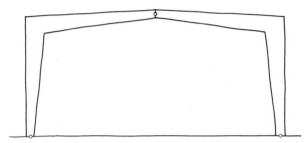

14.9 Hinged steel beam.

With the production of strong, inexpensive steels, frames hinged at their foot (Fig. 14.9) made their appearance on the structural scene in the nineteenth century, but because their structural behavior is complex, their message is still equivocal to the lay person. While the curved shape of the arch has a strong aesthetic charge, a frame appears neither ugly nor beautiful and is outside the universe of aesthetics.

Similar reactions are elicited by those **correct** structural forms that have their justification in subtle physical phenomena. For example, a compressed member with a shape dictated to avoid buckling (Fig. 14.10) is looked upon as a component of a machine and is hardly viewed as beautiful or ugly. In fact, for a long time machines were considered ugly because, while their shapes are correct functionally and structurally, they could not be accepted as elements of the universe of aesthetics. Some revolutionary painters, like Picabia, did introduce machines in their oeuvre, but were careful to disassociate their images from the reality of the factory: by painting machines that did not work (Fig. 14.11), Picabia made them symbols of a new order rather than real objects whose visual content was related to their role in the outside world.

The same kind of consideration applies to the three-dimensional world of structures. In nature concave spatial elements are quite common: seashells are not only symbols of protection but have a strong aesthetic content whenever ribbed in one of the ways nature strengthens them. The analogy of the large dome to the mysterious sky might fall in the same category.

14.10 Compression strut.

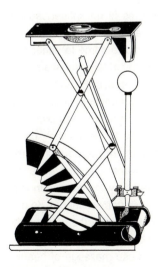

14.11 Picabia machine.

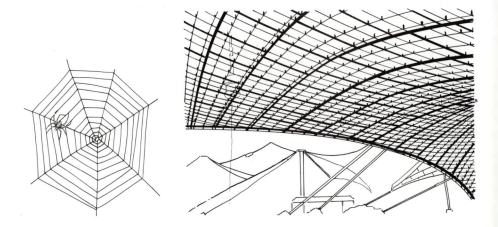

14.12 Tensile structures.

14.4 Scale and the Structural Message

The semiotic message of man-made structures is not influenced by **scale** because the message refers to common experiences of the race that have to do with form and not size. The comparison of the dome to either the seashell or the sky is significant in this context, as is that of large tensile structures to a spider web, which always elicits feelings of surprise. Because of the extreme efficiency of tension fields, tensile structures, whatever their geometry and size, are also light in appearance and considered intriguing and beautiful [Fig. 14.12(a)]. Besides, they have shapes dictated by the loads they carry and imply to the reader of their message a correctness not obvious in compression or bending structures. If, following Gaudí's example, one uses an antifunicular (upside down) compressive shape dictated by the corresponding tensile funicular shape (Fig. 14.13), one finds that these correct shapes do not always communicate a message of beauty. On the other hand, the particularly beautiful shape of the shallow cables of a suspension bridge becomes by inversion that of a shallow arch shape (Fig. 14.14), whose message of beauty is obvious because it is often seen in nature.

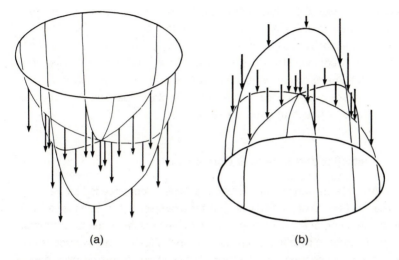

(a)   (b)

14.13 Gaudí tensile model and its antifunicular dome model.

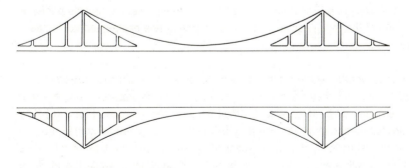

14.14 Arch bridge and suspension bridge.

One may object that no domed structure is lighter than a cable-reinforced, pneumatic roof (see Fig. 11.19) and should look elegant even to the inexperienced eye. Instead, balloon structures are so far considered unattractive because they spell heaviness: a comparison with the traditional message of the stone dome in compression does not allow us to "understand" as yet their structural action and confuses us structurally and aesthetically. Such a confusion never arises in tents because these tensile structures have their counterparts in nature, although at a reduced scale.

14.5 Aesthetics and Structural Correctness

An understanding of structural behavior is seldom needed for aesthetic appreciation (see Section 14.1). A striking example of this unimportance is given by the general admiration for a roof shape seldom understood structurally. The hyperbolic paraboloid, one of the most efficient structural roof forms when correctly supported (see Section 12.12), is characterized by a saddle shape often encountered in nature and in art: whether used correctly horizontally or incorrectly vertically (Fig. 14.15), the message of the hyperbolic paraboloid is always one of beauty. The reaction of a 12-year-old when first seeing this form indicates the associations dictated by its message: after comparing it to a horse saddle, he felt that it also looked like a bird in flight.

In some cases an unconscious understanding of structural behavior may enhance aesthetic appreciation. The ribs of a slab oriented along the lines of the principal bending moments (see Fig. 10.31) become a source of aesthetic satisfaction even to those who have no idea of plate theory. Similarly, the compressive lines of principal stress in a beam (see Fig. 9.9) express its behavior in terms of the much "easier" behavior of arches and cables and constitute a pleasing pattern.

One may wonder whether the puzzling message of certain structures will ever lead to their aesthetic acceptance. The shape of prestressed concrete elements governed by the tension in their invisible tendons (see Fig. 3.10) may contradict human intuition. One may ask how future generations may react to masses magnetically floated in space (Fig. 14.16) that, for lack of reference in nature, will seem to defy some of nature's basic laws, while the airplane looks elegant by comparison with the planing bird.

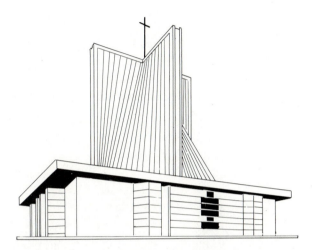

14.15 Hyperbolic paraboloid roof of San Francisco's Cathedral

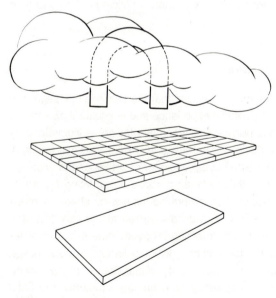

14.16 Magnetically supported roof.

It is the harmony between the visual needs of beauty and the respect of natural laws that dictated in the past and dictates today the exhibition of a building structure. Our admiration for the vaults of the Gothic cathedrals (see Fig. 8.30) is the same as that for the John Hancock Company building in Chicago (see Fig. 8.20).

14.6 The Message of Structure

It was shown in the previous sections that the semiotic message of a structure is influenced by our personal experience and the cultural experience of our society. The relative importance of these two factors is illuminated by the classic example of the Eiffel Tower in Paris (Fig. 14.17). This extraordinary iron structure, designed and erected by an engineer of genius on the occasion of the exposition of 1889, had the utilitarian purpose of attracting visitors to the exposition and the patriotic goal of celebrating the one-hundredth anniversary of the French revolution. It was to be dismantled at the closing of the exposition. The campaign against its erection involved some of the most respected representatives of French culture, including famous writers, poets, painters, and politicians who were incensed by the "ugliness" of the Tower. But, as is often the case with supposedly demountable structures, the Eiffel Tower was not demounted and, only 23 years after its erection, became the

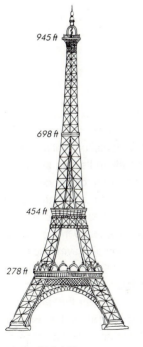

945 ft

698 ft

454 ft

278 ft

14.17 Eiffel Tower.

theme of a famous series of paintings by Delaunay, showing its acceptance from a purely aesthetic viewpoint. It did not take much longer for the tower to become not just one of the sights of that center of world culture called Paris, but its very symbol. And a few years later the tower, all on its own structural steam, became the semiotic symbol of France. In this extraordinary case, the semiotic message stems directly and uniquely from a structure: the Eiffel Tower is a masterpiece in which nothing was conceded to decoration and nothing was used to hide its necessary sinews. Its acceptance indicates the amazing fact that a pure structure can communicate a complex symbolic message. A similar interaction between structural and aesthetic messages led to the nakedness of the towers of the George Washington Bridge, against the opposition of a large part of the New York intelligentsia and of the designing engineer himself, who wanted them clad in stone (Fig. 14.18), and is another indication of the rapid change in cultural meaning of the semiotic message of structure.

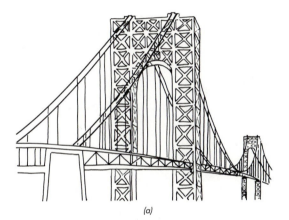

(a)

(b)

14.18 Unclad and clad George Washington Bridge.

The Beauborg Museum (Fig. 14.19) was inaugurated in Paris a few years ago. The dismay of the art world at the erection of an art shelter whose aesthetic message is based not only on its structure, but on its mechanical systems, must be accepted in the light of our recent past. One cannot forecast that the Beauborg will become the new symbol of Paris or of modern art, but one should not be surprised if the incorporation of mechanical elements into its aesthetic message were to lead to a widening of the vocabulary of architecture and become accepted as a matter of course a few generations or even a few years hence. Art and technology are thus seen to be two facets of a culture and not two incompatible aspects of human activity.

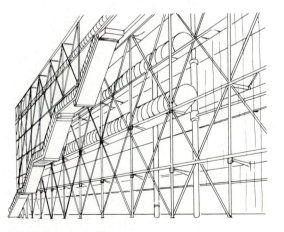

14.19 Beauborg Museum.

Chapter Fifteen

Conclusion

15.1 Intuition and Knowledge

The preceding chapters have attempted a **qualitative** presentation of structural principles on the basis of general experience with forces, materials, and deformations. A casual reading of the foregoing pages may illuminate the structural actions most commonly encountered in architecture; a careful reading may clarify, in addition, more sophisticated types of structural behavior seldom considered by the layperson. In any case, the purely intuitive approach used to introduce these principles cannot be expected to lead to **quantitative** knowledge in a field as complex as structures. For this, an analytical, mathematical presentation is needed, of the kind required for an understanding of any branch of physics.

Intuition is an essentially synthetic process which brings about the sudden, direct understanding of ideas more or less consciously considered over a period of time. It becomes a satisfactory road to knowledge on two conditions: it should be based on a large amount of prior experience, and it should be carefully verified. Pure, that is, unchecked intuition is misleading most of the time.

Intuition may be greatly refined by experience. One of the best tools for refining structural intuition is the use of models demonstrating the diversified actions considered in this book. Since all structural actions involve displacements, and displacements are the visual result of these actions, models are ideally suited for the intuitive presentation of structural concepts. This is why, at times, the reader has been invited to build elementary models which demonstrate the structural behavior of simple elements more convincingly than any drawing ever will; and why films have been developed for the same purpose.

On the other hand, it cannot be overemphasized that intuition without experience is a dangerous tool, since it leads to unchecked assumptions. The reader should be wary of what he "seems to feel should happen" in a given physical situation, and, in particular, of the suggestions from the purely geometrical aspects of a structure. It is hard to believe, at first, that the straight sides of a stiffener-supported cylindrical barrel move inwards under load, because the curved section of the cylinder suggests arch action, and arches are "known" to push outwards.

15.2 Qualitative and Quantitative Knowledge

Qualitative knowledge should often be a prerequisite to quantitative analysis, since interest in a field is seldom aroused without some prior understanding. It is hoped that the reader interested in structures may obtain from the preceding chapters that minimum understanding of structural behavior required to arouse his interest, and be led by it to a serious study of the subject.

Structures are best presented in the language proper to the quantitative analysis of measurable phenomena: mathematics; not the complex mathematics required for an understanding of the more advanced aspects of science, but the simple mathematics of arithmetic and algebra, and, sometimes, elementary calculus. In this context one cannot overemphasize the importance of numerical computations, and the fact that the calculator and the computer have made them fast, reliable, and painless for all. No thorough **knowledge** of structures may be acquired **without** the use of these **mathematical tools**. Mathematics does not explain physical behavior; it just describes it. But mathematical descriptions are so efficient that a short formula may clearly and simply express ideas that in verbal form would require pages of complex statements.

The availability of structural knowledge, made possible by the use of mathematics, has produced impressive results. Structures that in the past could have been conceived and built only by architectural geniuses, are designed, at present, by modest engineers in the routine of their office work. This democratization of structural knowledge, while putting advanced structures within the reach of the average architect, introduces the danger of architectural misuse by the practitioner who lacks a solid structural foundation.

There is little doubt in the minds of both engineers and architects that modern structural concepts are used properly only when the architect has a thorough understanding of structures. This does not imply that all architects should become mathematicians; it simply suggests that those practitioners who wish to express themselves through structural forms should first learn to use the tools of quantitative analysis. They will be amazed to find, later on, that their cultivated intuition will often reach "correct" structural solutions without too many mathematical manipulations.

The field of structures is evolving rapidly under the pressure of the growing needs of society. The structuralist and the architect must strive, by all means at their disposal, toward mutual understanding and fruiful collaboration. May the technician and the designer work together to the greater glory of architecture and in the greater service to mankind.

Index

upperchord of, 128
  buckling of, 130
verticals of, 128
Vierendel, 190
windbracing:
  in bridges, 20
  in buildings, 132
T sections, 144
Tubular frames, 194
  bundled, 194
Tubular high-rise buildings, 194
Tuned dynamic dampers, 38
Twist:
  geometrical, of surfaces, 298
  of surfaces, 300
Twisting action:
  in plates, 252
  in welded grids, 246
Twisting, in lateral buckling, 156
Two-dimensional antifunicular, 324
Two-dimensional resisting structures,
  grids and plates, 238
Two-way action:
  of plates, 250
    beam, 250
    cable, 276
    torsional, 252
Two-way load dispersal, 240

Ultimate load, 51
Ultimate load capacity:
  in beams, 230–232
  in plates, 273–277
Ultimate strength, 51
  of concrete, 51
  of steel, 51
Ultimate strength design, 51
Umbrella:
  hyperbolic paraboloid, 344
  prestressed membrane of, 310
Umbrella roofs, hyperbolic paraboloid, 380
Undulated cylinnder, 340
U. S. Pavilion, at Osaka World's Fair, 318
Utica, NY, auditorium roof, 122

Variable cross-section beams, 146
Vaults, barrel, 368
  groined, 340
Verrazano Narrows Bridge, 112

Viera, Leonel, 118
Vierendel trusses, 190

W sections, 142
Waffle slabs, 270
  domes for, 270
Walls:
  curtain, 198
  shear, 196
Water–cement ratio, 421
Water Tower Building (Chicago), 196
Web:
  buckling of, in beams, 146
  of W sections, 142
Weidlinger Associates, 290, 320
Weidlinger, Paul, 314
Welders, certified, 420
Welding, certification of, 420
Wheeling, Ohio, suspension bridge, failure of,
  414
Wide-flange sections, 142
Wind:
  gusts, 33
  live load of, 20
  on multistory frame, 192
  on single-bay frame, 184
  stresses, in thin-shell domes, 352
Windbracing:
  in bridges, by horizontal trusses, 20
  in buildings, 20–22, 132
Wind drift, 198
Wood:
  anisotropic behavior of, 46
  unit load of, 18
World Trade Center Towers, New York City,
  194
  wind drift in, 198

Yale University skating rink, 118
Yamasaki, M. 210
Yield, 44
Yield load, 42
Yield point, 42
Yield stress:
  of aluminum, 50
  of steel, 50

Zeman, Jo, 395
Zeppelin dirigibles, 310
Zetlin, Lev, 122